XENOPHON'S RETREAT

XENOPHON'S RETREAT

Greece, Persia, and the End of the Golden Age

ROBIN WATERFIELD

The Belknap Press of
Harvard University Press
Cambridge, Massachusetts
2006

First published in 2006 by Faber and Faber Limited
3 Queen Square London WCIN 3AU

Library of Congress Cataloging-in-Publication Data

Waterfield, Robin, 1952–
Xenophon's retreat : Greece, Persia, and the end of the
Golden Age / Robin Waterfield
p. cm.
Includes bibliographical references and index
ISBN-13: 978-0-674-02356-7 (alk. paper)
ISBN-10: 0-674-02356-0 (alk. paper)
1. Cyrus, the Younger, d. 401 B.C.
2. Xenophon
3. Xenophon. Anabasis
4. Greece—History—Expedition of Cyrus, 401 B.C.
I. Title

DF231.32 .W37 2006   2006049504

This book is an offering to the spirits of my Greek home:
may they keep the peace

This book is an offering to the spirits of my Greek home:
may they keep the peace

Contents

List of Illustrations and Maps

Preface and Acknowledgements

The backbone of this book is a summary of Xenophon's *The Expedition of Cyrus*, the western world's first eyewitness account of a military campaign. Xenophon told how a band of unruly Greek professional soldiers travelled east to fight for the Persian prince Cyrus the Younger in his attempt to wrest the throne of the mighty Persian empire from his brother. Though the Greeks performed well in the battle of Cunaxa (in the desert somewhere to the west of modern Baghdad), Cyrus lost his life and so the battle was lost. The Greeks then had to return home – a journey of hundreds of kilometres north from modern Iraq into the mountains of Kurdistan and north-eastern Turkey and down to the coast of the Black Sea. In terms of gripping adventure, human interest, strong characters, drama and pathos, the story is a survival epic: the 2,750-kilometre journey *to* Babylonia was long but only occasionally arduous, but the journey *back* took weeks of hard travel across some of the roughest terrain in the world, under frightful conditions of almost constant life-threatening danger from hostile forces, treachery, unravelling loyalties and extreme weather.

Xenophon's book is a masterpiece of western military history, the account of a remarkable campaign written by a soldier who took part in it and who was sufficiently senior to understand the problems of command. There would be little point in my retelling the entire story, when 2,350 years ago Xenophon himself brought the thrilling, appalling expedition alive with incontestable skill. The summary of Xenophon's original that I provide, then, is incomplete and forms no more than the backbone of this book.

In any case, I wanted to explore aspects of the expedition that Xenophon did *not* mention, such as the gruesome nature of ancient battle (which Xenophon took for granted and of course could expect his immediate audience to be familiar with) and logistics. I also wanted to contextualize the expedition with information about Greek and Persian interaction both before and after Cyrus's march. I hazard more guesses than Xenophon did about people's motivations and agendas, and otherwise fill gaps in his account and delve, often speculatively, deeper than he allowed himself to. My first concern in this respect has been to present a rounded version of the story of the expedition. I have also given as much reliable information about Xenophon's life and personality as can be recovered or inferred; I am more sympathetic towards him than many scholars, but I see him very much as a product of his times. He did not have the largeness of spirit, or whatever it takes to transcend one's times and even to change them.

In addition, my subtitle promises something on 'the end of the golden age'. *The Expedition of Cyrus*, written thirty or more years after the events, is not straightforward history. Xenophon had time to reflect and the book is nuanced and enriched by a number of themes, one of them being a record of his own and the army's gradual disillusionment. When he came to write his account, he could look back on thirty years in which the mainland Greek states had been battered into disillusionment themselves, and so the two years of his and his men's suffering came in his mind to encapsulate and adumbrate what followed. (I should say straight away that I do not take this to be a flaw in his work: all history-writing is biased or angled in some way or another.) By sheer coincidence, the expedition also fell on the exact cusp between what we now call the fifth and fourth centuries BCE – it took place between 401 and 399 – and so in shorthand I could speak (though the numbers would of course have meant nothing to Xenophon and his contemporaries) of a contrast between the optimism, adventurousness and high values of the fifth century, the 'golden age', giving way to the more pragmatic, materialistic and cynical realism of the fourth.

In many history books, there is a real danger of bewildering readers with a plethora of exotic names. In a history book covering the times and places I have covered here, the danger is exacerbated by the various versions available for many proper names. Although the matter has some intrinsic interest, how many readers really need to know that a certain Median king was called 'Arshtivaiga', the 'javelin thrower', in his own language, 'Ishtumegu' in Babylonian, and 'Astyages' in Greek? Or that the man known to Greeks as 'Kyros' ('Cyrus' in its Latin form) was 'Kuruš' in Old Persian and 'Kuraš' in Elamite? Where eastern names are concerned, I have used the Latinized Greek forms; these forms have become familiar because the western readers who constitute the primary audience for this book are more likely to have

read their Classics, or books based on Classical learning, than they are to have read transliterations of ancient eastern inscriptions or cuneiform tablets; and because Greek historians are still one of our most important sources (along with archaeology, art history, linguistic history, and so on) even for the less familiar lands and peoples covered in this book. Similarly, where Greek names are concerned, I have suppressed my pedantic urge to transliterate the original Greek, and have again used the more familiar Latinized/anglicized forms. I happen to think there is value in readers' knowing that 'Aeschylus' should really be 'Aiskhylos', that 'Scillus' was 'Skillous', and so on. But the danger in such pedantry is that friends may be turned into strangers. There is, as is often lamented, no policy on the writing of ancient names that will please everyone, but I hope at least, on utilitarian principles, to please more people than I offend.

In the autumn of 2004 I drove as much of the route taken by the Ten Thousand to and from Iraq as geopolitical circumstances and time made feasible. My thanks go to the manufacturers of my Land Rover Discovery, and to Ingrid Gottschalk, who shared the pleasures and the stresses of the journey. I would also like to thank my agents, Bill Hamilton and Emma Parry; my editors, Walter Donohue of Faber and Faber and Peg Fulton of Harvard University Press; and my readers, Paul Cartledge, Kathryn Dunathan, Andrew Lane, and the two anonymous reviewers consulted by Harvard University Press. I count myself particularly fortunate to have the friendship of Professor Cartledge, whose tireless energy and vast knowledge of both primary and secondary sources on ancient Greek history make him the perfect recipient of requests for advice and information. Wendy Toole, Alex Lazarou and András Bereznay demonstrated meticulous skill at, respectively, copy-editing, design and cartography. Others have helped too in various ways, especially Nazan Alsan, Martin Buckley, Tenir Demirbulut, Bill Murray, Tim Rood and Christopher Tuplin. Once again, the Royal Literary Fund supported my work by awarding me teaching fellowships. Researching the book would have been far more arduous were it not for the patience and skill of staff at the following London libraries: the Institute of Classical Studies, the British Library, the School of Oriental and African Studies, and the Warburg Institute.

Lakonia, Greece, December 2005

CHAPTER ONE

The Battle of Cunaxa

Late in September 401 BCE, two huge armies faced each other on a dusty plain, baked hard by the sun of a long summer, on the eastern bank of the River Euphrates, in what is now Iraq. One of the two armies was commanded by Artaxerxes II the Mindful, King of Kings, the Great King of the Persian empire; the other side was led by his younger brother Cyrus, who intended to commit fratricide and rule in Artaxerxes's place. The battle was the climax of Cyrus's campaign, long plotted from his domain in what is now western Turkey. A young Greek writer from Athens, Xenophon the son of Gryllus, who had joined the expedition out of a restless need for adventure, as an observer rather than a soldier, was on hand to record what happened, in the world's first and greatest eyewitness campaign narrative, known as *Anabasis* (the march inland from the sea) or *The Expedition of Cyrus*.

The exact location of the encounter is unknown: the battle came to be named after a nearby village called in ancient times Cunaxa, a version of the Aramaic *keništa*, 'synagogue', because this was a Jewish area of ethnically diverse Mesopotamia. The two best bets for the location of the ancient village, assuming that the name has been somewhat preserved over the centuries, are both obscure, and you will look in vain for them on most maps. There is a mound formed of layers of historical debris close to the Euphrates west of Baghdad, called Tell Kuneise, and somewhat closer to Baghdad there is a village called Al Nasiffiyat, a shortened version of the original Kuneise-safyatib. At present Al Nasiffiyat is some distance from the Euphrates, but in ancient times the river took a different course, and the village would have been close to its eastern bank.

Artaxerxes commanded an army of 45,000, a formidable force (ancient estimates, wildly inaccurate for all the assurance with which they are delivered, mention 400,000 or even 900,000). He had marched to meet his brother even though his forces were still mustering: one was to be led west by a half-brother as soon as enough men had assembled, and the other was already on its way from Phoenicia.

Most of the king's men were foot soldiers and the dreaded Persian archers, but there were also hundreds of cavalrymen and dozens of chariots. The Persians had a standing army (largely of Persians and Medes, supplemented by mercenaries rather than by local troops) to police some of the provinces and patrol the borders of the empire, but they also conscripted and hired others for special occasions such as this. Residents of the empire might expect military service to be rewarded with a land-grant, and a census was kept of the beneficiaries and their descendants, who were obliged, in perpetuity, to serve in the army when called upon to do so. Efficient bureaucracy and the ancient world's best system of roads before the Romans ensured that large armies could be raised with impressive speed.

Foremost among the Persian infantry were the Immortals. As the old conundrum implies, even if you first change the haft and then later the head of your axe, it is still the same axe. By the same token, the Immortals were so called because their number was never permitted to drop below 10,000: anyone who died or grew too old for service was immediately replaced by a fresh recruit. This, at any rate, was the Greek fantasy: it is more likely that the Greeks had mistaken the Persian word for 'attendant', which is similar to that for 'immortal'. The Immortals guarded the royal palace at Persepolis, and on campaign 1,000 of them, the *arštibara* or Spear-bearers, recruited from high-ranking subjects of the king, formed the royal bodyguard and were granted special privileges, such as the right to bring their slaves and concubines with them and to be supplied where possible with a richer diet. The Immortals' clothing was flashy, and each carried a spear of cornel wood with a silver-plated blade and a haft ending in a silver pomegranate (a golden one for the Spear-bearers' regiment), a bow and an elaborately decorated quiver.

The infantry came from all over the Persian empire, which extended from Egypt to Georgia, and from Pakistan to the Dardanelles. The fierce Saka tribesmen of Central Asia were prominent, but there was a fantastic display of regional differences in the army's gear: there were round, crescented and oblong shields of wood or wicker-reinforced leather, spears and lances of various lengths, bows of different sizes and shapes, straight short swords or wickedly curved sickle-like falchions, heavy iron clubs, axes, slings and even lassoes. A variety of different headgear, from turbans and pointed hats to helmets, completed a scene that the ancients found colourful and exotic or alien and terrible, according to their perspective. Many of the men were even wearing trousers, which the Greeks, without regard for the practicalities of a horse-riding people, considered effeminate.

The horsemen were particularly splendid. The Persian nobility rode caparisoned warhorses, invariably the world-famous Nesaean breed from the fertile plain of Media, which were larger and more powerful than the Mediterranean horses of the time. The horsemen wore armour under their surcoats and on their thighs, and each carried a bow, a spear and a sword. Their white cuirasses reflected the late-afternoon sun, which glistened on the tips of thousands of weapons. Three of the great satraps (semi-independent generalissimos and princelings of the Persian empire) – Tissaphernes, Gobryas and Arbaces – commanded divisions of the king's army. A fourth, Abrocomas, was on his way, but Cyrus had taken a difficult but fast route down the Euphrates, precisely in order to reach the battle zone before Abrocomas and his division could join up with the rest of Artaxerxes's army.

Cyrus's men, perhaps 30,000 in all, were outnumbered. There were somewhat over 14,000 infantrymen conscripted from Cyrus's subjects in Asia Minor, and 2,500 Paphlagonian and other horsemen. But although Cyrus had hoped for more support from Persian nobles, he was not unduly worried about being outnumbered, because he had many more Greeks on his side, and the Greeks were the supreme warriors of the time. These Greeks, moreover, were battle-hardened – a rare event in the days of amateur soldiering – since many of them had seen action in Greece during the recently ended Peloponnesian War. Their arms, armour and tactics outclassed anything they faced, even the famous Persian cavalry: no horse, however passionately urged on by its rider, will hurl itself into a solid phalanx, bristling with spears – and in a tightly packed phalanx, the spears of the first three lines were long enough to project in front of the first line, if the soldiers had the necessary strength and skill. The most a horseman could do was ride up close enough to discharge a javelin, and even that was difficult to do effectively in the days before saddles and stirrups.

The war would be won with a single battle, so Cyrus hired the best soldiers in the known world. The Ten Thousand – the misnomer has been popular since antiquity – were actually about 10,600 Greek hoplites (heavy-armed infantry) and 2,300 peltasts (light-armed troops), the latter mostly from the margins of the Greek world.

Cyrus's battle formation disposed the Greeks on the right wing, himself in command of the centre, and his trusted Persian second-in-command, Ariaeus, on the left. Ariaeus was Cyrus's uncle (the brother of his mother), the governor of Hellespontine Phrygia, and a good source of both men and money.

Hoplite Equipment

Greek hoplites, the heavy infantry, were armed, typically, with a helmet (the designs of which found various ways to balance protection, sight, hearing and a fearsome appearance), a corselet with a short protective skirt, bronze greaves for the shins, and above all a large, round, concave shield, about 90 centimetres in diameter (more than half a man's height, especially in those days), made of bronze-covered wood with a rim of bronze, and weighing almost 7 kilograms. Each of them carried a long, but not very stout, thrusting spear with an iron head; and, to fall back on if his spear broke, a short sword of iron. A fully armoured hoplite would rapidly get hot and exhausted.

But there were opportunities for individual choice and home-made gear, and the Cyreans presented a motley appearance: leather or stiffened linen jerkins far outnumbered bronze or partially bronze breastplates, especially in the heat of Babylonia; greaves were on the way

A hoplite. Shields were, more typically, perfectly round, but otherwise this late-sixth-century statuette, found in the sanctuary of Zeus at Dodona in north-west Greece, gives an excellent impression of a hoplite's fighting stance and fearsome appearance.

4

out; smaller shields were in the process of being introduced to improve mobility; helmets were of various designs and materials (many even wore a conical cap made of felt, known as a *pilos*), and sported a variety of horsehair crests, or none; some but not all shields were blazoned with family or state insignia, or with emblems of prowess; there were several types of sword, for slashing or stabbing; many but not all spears had bronze butt-spikes, graphically known as 'lizarders', for offensive use if the head of the spear broke off, and especially for finishing off foes who fell before one's feet.

Although, to give them a more impressive appearance, Cyrus made sure that a good number of them – the first rank, at least – wore the red cloaks favoured by Spartan hoplites, there was no uniform. But in one respect they behaved exactly like all hoplites everywhere: they fought, wherever possible, in a phalanx – a rectangular formation that was as tightly packed as topography and manpower allowed. When there were enough soldiers, hoplites made a phalanx eight ranks deep: at Cunaxa, then, they formed more than 1,300 files, and they presented a bristling wall of shields and spears over 1,500 metres long.

The shield on a hoplite's left arm was held steady: the arm passed up to the elbow through a ring, to a hand-grip on the inside of the rim. The weight of the shield could be offset, if circumstances permitted, by resting its upper rim on the left shoulder. While advancing, the shield protected the left half of a hoplite's body and the right half of the body of his neighbour; even in combat, when the necessity of standing sideways-on in order to wield his spear at shoulder height meant that his shield offered less protection to his neighbour, it was vital for the line of battle to remain as closely packed as circumstances permitted. As long as no cracks appeared, the line was virtually impregnable, and the hoplite phalanx became one of the most successful military formations in history.

Xenophon's *The Expedition of Cyrus* is, at one level, an account of astonishing successes: every time the Greek hoplites charged an enemy, the enemy chose to run away rather than engage them at close quarters. The peltasts were occasionally defeated, and the army as a whole was vulnerable to guerrilla tactics while on the march, but it was invulnerable in formal battles – and the more they won, the more their confidence grew, and the more flexible and formidable they became. They found ways to adapt to varying terrains and various types of opponents, from skirmishing hill-tribes to Persian cavalry. Both on the march and in battle, they experimented with different formations and with different combinations of light-armed and heavy-armed troops. This flexibility was hugely enhanced by the structure of the army: its basic tactical unit was a company of 100 men, each of which could act independently of other companies or in concert with as many others as the situation required.

The Cyreans were professional warriors. Many of them had lived and fought in the east before, and they knew that the rules were different. In a battle of Greeks against Greeks, the point was to establish your superiority, and not necessarily by exterminating your opponents. But now they felt they were facing an all-out battle.

Hoplite Warfare

In fifth-century Greece, light-armed troops were used largely for foraging and the destruction of enemy farmland; their value on the battlefield began to be demonstrated or rediscovered towards the end of the century, during the Peloponnesian War, but only in the fourth century were they organized and used regularly for battle. There was also little cavalry until the fourth century: the topography of Greece lends itself neither to the breeding of horses (so that ownership of horses was the kind of sign of great wealth that ownership of a Ferrari is today), nor to cavalry engagements. Moreover, they had no horseshoes, saddles or stirrups, which made riding, especially under battle conditions, difficult and uncomfortable. In the fifth century, horsemen were used more for scouting, skirmishing, protection and pursuit than as a strike force in their own right. Siege warfare was rare until later in the fourth century, from lack of effective technology. For at least two centuries, the form of land battle most familiar to Greeks involved hoplites more or less exclusively.

Maintenance of formation was tactically so critical that hoplites infinitely preferred to fight on level ground. Gaps could begin to appear in the line as a result of any kind of awkward terrain, or because of a natural tendency for hoplite lines to stretch out to the right, as each man sought to nestle his exposed right side behind the shield of the man on his right, or (as nearly happened at Cunaxa) when some men advanced more rapidly than others. They could also occur through fear, if a man abandoned his position; the rarity of this was due as much as anything to the tactical arrangement of the phalanx, where more experienced fighters hemmed in those whose behaviour was open to doubt. Besides, in canonical Greek battles, your neighbours in the phalanx were likely to be fellow citizens, or even close kin (especially since a hoplite served between the ages of eighteen and sixty), so that shame too, that most Greek emotion, played a major part.

In a battle of phalanx against phalanx, tactics were limited to pausing a metre or so before your opponent in order to wield your weapon, or a head-on collision between the two masses. Each phalanx tried to outflank the other, while compromising between avoiding being outflanked and being stretched too thin. In the event of a collision, the soldiers in the front line literally pushed with their shields against their opposite numbers in the enemy line, while thrusting with their spears or stabbing with their swords above or below their opponents' shields, trying by all the means available to them to create a lethal gap in the opposing phalanx. There was very little skill in hoplite battle: until one of the lines broke, the fighters hardly had room for movement and the thrust and parry of single combat. It was ideally suited to the amateur nature of Greek warfare, where peasants

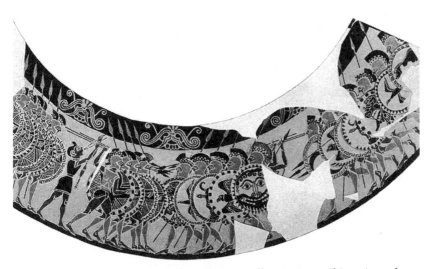

This detail from a panel of the Chigi Vase (actually a jug), a striking piece of proto-Corinthian ware from around 640 BCE, shows in a stylized form two Greek phalanxes about to clash. It was the pipe-player's job to try to regulate the speed of advance.

had little time for weapon training. In this kind of hand-to-hand fighting, where soldiers could even resort to hands and teeth, survival depended less on technical skill with weapons, and more on a distinctly less trainable ability – the intuitive ability to guess where your opponent was going to strike next, in order to defend yourself against him.

Hoplite armour was not so thick that it could not be pierced by a hard enough strike, especially when delivered on the run at the first moment of impact, and helmets were so inadequately padded that a heavy blow to the head could lead to concussion or even death. A skilled hoplite, however, more usually aimed for the exposed parts of the body, especially the face, where terrible wounds would render the victim almost unrecognizable, or the groin, the thigh or the neck, where a wound would bring a man down and open a breach in the line. The seventh-century Spartan poet Tyrtaeus, who was never one to shrink from the minutiae of hoplite battle, has left us a gruesome picture of an elderly hoplite's death:*

> With head already white and grizzled beard, gasping his brave last
>   in the dust,
> Hands clasping blood-soaked genitals – a shocking sight, offensive
>   to the eyes –
> And body stripped of armour.

Ancient Greek medicine had more weaknesses than strengths. Battlefield doctors could staunch light wounds, but were helpless in the face of major traumas. The fate of the seriously wounded was in the laps of the gods: though mutilated, men did survive terrible wounds, but it was far more common for infection to set in, guaranteeing a painful and lingering death, or for death to follow quickly as a result of shock or loss of blood.

Phalanxes charged at each other as fast as they could while maintaining good order. If one line did not turn in terror before contact, they crashed into each other, at a combined speed of about 15 kilometres an

---

*References for direct quotations and for paraphrases of named authors (and some unnamed ones), ancient and modern, can be found on pp. 224–31. Unattributed facts about the expedition are most likely to derive from Xenophon's *The Expedition of Cyrus*, or from my own or others' understanding of that text; otherwise they derive from a variety of sources, which can be tracked down via the bibliography on pp. 232–41.

hour, with a terrible din of shield on shield, of spear piercing shield and armour, of spears parrying and snapping. These inhuman sounds were raised to the level of a terrifying din by the grunts and shouts of men exerting themselves, soon to be augmented by the screams of the wounded. Quite often the sheer momentum of one phalanx was enough to destroy the formation of the other more or less immediately; if not, the two phalanxes could become packed to a stifling tightness as the rear ranks rammed into those in front.

Isolated within his metal helmet (if he wore one), an individual hoplite was preyed on by terrible fears. If he was in a middle rank, the chances were that his knowledge of what was going on came only from the shifting of the bodies around him. How could he interpret these movements? Did they mean that his side was winning, or was about to be overrun? If panic infected even a few men, potential victory could be turned into defeat. The terror of impending impact was such that it was universally recognized that your best fighters had to be posted not just in the front rank, where they belonged for obvious reasons, but in the last rank too, where they could urge on anyone in the middle ranks who was showing signs of reluctance to engage the enemy – and from where they could turn to face any onslaught that came from a hostile encircling movement.

The company commander often took the exposed position on the far right corner of the front rank. Until the fourth century, there were few professional generals, and no full-time officers. Men were elevated to a position of responsibility at the start of a campaign because of their experience, and they were expected to lead from the front: they and those in their company that they considered to be the best fighters would occupy the front and rear ranks. Generals and other officers were directly involved in combat, rather than in just the management of the battle, with important consequences for the morale of their troops. One of the main reasons Alexander the Great's men were so utterly devoted to him was that they had all witnessed his personal heroism on the battlefield.

A hoplite in the front two or three ranks was no less prey to fears. He could see better than those behind him – but what he saw was another fearsome phalanx, whose members were determined to try to kill him. He was going to have to summon up his courage and charge this other phalanx, for all its apparent impregnability. Sometimes a terrible silence gripped the ranks as they observed their enemies before them – a silence that could spread and sap confidence in a moment. The mantra-like paean, chanted just before the charge, distracted such chill fear. Another remedy was alcohol: all armies carried supplies of wine or foraged for it during their expeditions, and officers might issue their men wine, diluted in the Greek manner, before battle. The pre-battle sacrifice – the religious shedding of blood prefiguring the vile blood-letting that would follow – may have promised victory, but that did little to allay a hoplite's fears.

Hoplite battle tactics gave the Greeks their conception of courage: as the Athenian general Laches says in Plato's dialogue named after him, a man is courageous if he stands firm in battle. For all that Plato's Socrates found the idea woefully inadequate as a definition of courage, it was so entrenched in the Greek mind that fighting at a distance (with sling or bow or even javelin) was considered cowardly. The playwright Euripides, who loved paradox, even had a character hold the archetypal hero Heracles up to scorn on these grounds:

> He never held a shield on his left arm or came within range of a
> spear. He carried a bow, a weapon of utter cowardice, and was
> always ready to run away. A bow is no test of a man's courage:
> a brave man is one who, without flinching, keeps his place in the
> ranks while facing squarely a spear-cut furrow racing towards him.

The snobbish Greeks considered it part of a predetermined pattern that the upper classes, those who could afford to buy the full set of hoplite armour, were those who had to display courage, while light-armed troops, who were either from the poorer class or from peoples who were not fully Greek, wielded the weapons of cowardice. But upper-class Greek men were conditioned to bravery by a barrage of cultural rhetoric that stressed manliness and patriotism and more or less totally ignored the brutality and violence of war. In this rhetoric, winning was all that counted and winning seemed easy. The reality was terrifyingly different.

It was not uncommon for one phalanx to crumble before taking many casualties, but if both phalanxes survived the initial impact more or less intact, the hoplites would then shove at one another with their shields – those that had not been broken in the first clash – using their weight, if the soldiers were close enough packed, like some terrifying scrum, digging in their heels while jabbing their swords at their opponents. Many spears were broken at the point of impact – which was precisely what made it possible for the two phalanxes to get close enough to shove at each other. It was the work of only a moment, but a potentially fatal moment, to draw a sword or change grip on a broken spear shaft in order to wield its butt as a weapon. Movement forward or backward was limited at times to ragged shuffling. Sweat and dust obscured the vision, another cause for fear. The two opposing front lines were so close that, in addition to the stench of blood and guts and terror, they could smell the garlic and onion and wine on their opponents' breaths, and a successful strike was likely to be rewarded with a spurt of warm blood on the face and arms.

Here and there, men in either phalanx fell and the lines wavered and swayed, provoking manic fighting at the weakest points, until one side gained enough of these small-scale advantages for the other side to begin to fall back as a whole. Both courage and cowardice were tempted by the knowledge that the sooner this happened, the fewer the casualties. It was so important to win the first thrust that there were (at any rate, until the fourth century) usually no reserves and battles were often little more than fleeting, ghastly nightmares. A battle between two hoplite phalanxes provoked extremes of emotion – a short, sharp rush of adrenalin followed by the elation of victory or the terror of fleeing with the feeling that faster runners were on your tail. This is a species of battle that is unfamiliar in the world of computer-guided distance killing. Today we get that close to other human beings 'only at cocktail parties or tennis tournaments', as John Keegan genteelly put it.

Panic – so called because it was attributed to the god Pan – can spread with the speed of a flash flood, and once a phalanx began to crumble, disorderly flight soon followed. Men turned and ran, discarding their cumbersome shields, and the battle was lost. The effect of fear was to turn a phalanx from a gestalt entity into a mob of terrified individuals, each having to choose exactly when to give up fighting and turn to flight, few concerned with more than self-preservation. It was almost impossible for the losers to withdraw in good order, and a hoplite falling over at this stage risked death from trampling or an enemy 'lizarder'. Even so, casualties were rarely heavy: the winners could expect to lose an average of 5 per cent of their force, the losers around 15 per cent (in the ratio of half in the killing zone of the immediate battlefield and half while fleeing). But these simple figures disguise the horror of bloodied corpses piled up at the point of collision, of losers and victors alike covered in gore, of the grotesque postures of the corpses fanning out from the battlefield where they fell during flight. 'With the fighting over, the battlefield presented a vision of blood-soaked earth, corpses of friends and foes lying intermingled, shattered shields, splintered spears and swords bare of their sheaths – some on the ground, some sticking out of bodies, some still clasped in hands.'

The victorious hoplites, if disciplined, did not pursue the losers far, for fear of scattering and becoming vulnerable to a rally. Light-armed troops and horsemen gave chase to prevent rallying, killed as many as they could of the fugitives and those who, in their terror, were shamming death, and rounded up prisoners. While they were within killing range, the only safety for those retreating was to maintain some kind of order, as small bands if not in larger numbers. Escape was aided by the practice of stripping the armour off the dead or dying as booty, which delayed at least some of the pursuers.

Battles between two phalanxes of hoplites were in some ways formal, almost ritualistic – or rather, 'Greek hoplite warfare existed in perennial tension between battle conducted according to understood rules and the crafty subversion of those rules.' But casualty rates tended to be low, because the point was not to annihilate your opponents, but to take possession of the battlefield and especially of the enemy corpses, as symbols of victory. This is not to say that massacres and bloodlust were not aspects of Greek warfare, but the battle usually ended in formalities rather than in massive loss of life. The losers requested permission to collect their dead for burial; this request was formally equivalent to defeat and its acceptance to victory. The losers then joined the winners in post-battle tasks such as collecting the dead and identifying corpses that quickly ripened in the heat, and might have been vilely disfigured.

The victors were left in possession of the blood-soaked field, where they erected a 'trophy' (in Greek, *tropaion*, cognate with the verb meaning 'to turn') at the point where the enemy had turned and fled. A trophy was usually a tree trunk, on which enemy armour was hung. To mock the losers and to magically symbolize the winners' inheritance of the losers' might, the structures resembled armed mannequins. The setting up of the trophy was accompanied by prayers for success in future battles too, and by a thanksgiving sacrifice.

Thereafter, until the dynamics shifted again, your state occupied a

On this red-figure vase from Athens (c. 450 BCE), the name vase of the Trophy Painter, the goddess Victory is shown putting the finishing touches to a battlefield trophy. She is drilling a hole, probably to hang the shield, to complete her selection of enemy weaponry with which to dress the mannequin.

higher place in the hierarchy of honour than that of your opponents, and this delivered significant advantages for your diplomatic and other dealings with the defeated state. The hierarchy was an extension of the old Homeric culture, with states having replaced proud and combative heroes. Apart from the inevitable border disputes, one of the most common causes of war was the feeling that a state lower in the pecking order than yours had slighted your superiority. This amateur or stylized approach to warfare lasted as long as the citizen farmers of a state remained proud to defend their land by themselves, and as long as standing armies were considered suspect, as actual or potential instruments of tyranny. Mercenaries – professional soldiers such as those hired by Cyrus or would-be Greek tyrants – were less constrained by such traditional rules and regulations.

Cunaxa

Two days earlier, Cyrus and his men had left behind the thousands of camp followers – responsible for the animals, the baggage and the creature comforts of the fighting men – and in battle order, preceded by the horsemen, they had approached a great trench, which Artaxerxes had dug as a first line of defence against such attacks, or perhaps even against this specific invasion. The trench ran north-east for about 65 kilometres, from the Euphrates to the ruins of the sixth-century defensive wall that had linked the Euphrates to its eastern partner, the Tigris, and had been built in the early sixth century on the orders of Nebuchadnezzar II of Babylon, when his domain was being threatened by Medes from the north-east.

Cyrus expected that the enemy would be waiting by the trench, but he passed it unopposed, and he interpreted this as another sign of his brother's weakness. It now seemed distinctly possible to the overconfident pretender that his brother would not even offer battle. His mood trickled down through the ranks, and discipline became lax as the troops defiled through the narrow gap between the river and the deep trench, waited for the camp followers to catch up, and then continued south along the river bank.

Two days later, a Persian nobleman on Cyrus's staff galloped up, his horse in a lather, and shouted out that Artaxerxes was approaching with a huge army. Cyrus leapt down from his chariot, armed himself and mounted his horse Pasakas, while his men, who were strung for kilometres back across the plain in a loose column, picked up the pace and hurried to the front. They faced south, with the Greeks on the right wing, hard by the Euphrates, under their commander, the renegade Spartan Clearchus. In the heat, the dust and the confusion, Cyrus's men took hours to deploy.

At last the noise died down to a sound like the murmur of distant waves on a shore – only to turn again to cacophony when the enemy army drew close, because in the desert heat men naturally waited as long as they could before donning their heavy and ill-fitting armour. But before putting on their gear, they relieved themselves to the accompaniment of soldierly jokes, so as not to be taken short with their armour on – and to decrease the chances of fear causing an involuntary emptying of the bowels. At last their attendants, who had brought the gear from the transport wagons and had helped the hoplites on with their armour, withdrew from the battle lines and the fighting men were on their own. Their fresh hopes of an easy victory were replaced by a rush of fear, which at least served to banish their tiredness. As the afternoon drew on, a dust-cloud began to stain the sky to the south, and soon the whole plain was black with distant men.

As Artaxerxes's army approached, the Greeks could see that the enemy were preceded by deadly scythed chariots, whose sharpened blades projected not just to the sides of the axles, but swept the ground underneath, so that nothing could escape their onslaught. These chariots were a recent Persian invention, specifically designed for the destruction of hoplite phalanxes. The terror of the sight was magnified by a horrible silence: the Persians were not whooping and shouting, but marched on steadily in an eerie quiet and with far more discipline than the Greeks had been led to expect. The Magian priests who accompanied the army had promised the king victory, and he and his men were certain of it. There were so many more of Artaxerxes's troops that their right wing reached beyond Cyrus's left, and some hasty redeployment stretched the men of Ariaeus's division out to face them but left the ranks thin.

As far as Cyrus was concerned, the battle was little more than single combat, massively multiplied, between him and his brother: with Artaxerxes out of the way, the usually fickle satraps could reasonably be expected to give in – or at least not to organize any rebellions until the new king had had time to consolidate his position. Cyrus rode up and ordered Clearchus to make a direct assault on the Persian centre, where his brother was. But Clearchus felt strongly that he should not leave the river and expose himself to being outflanked – an exposure that would become acute in the kind of oblique advance that Cyrus had in mind – and he refused to obey this direct order from his paymaster. Short of more sinister interpretations, we have to believe that he knew how important the Greeks were to Cyrus's aspirations, and felt that he could get away with disobedience. Besides, he had the old soldier's suspicion of last-minute changes. Cyrus had always known that his brother would be in command of the centre, because that was the traditional position for Persian kings in battle, and he had always known that the Greeks were his best troops. His original plan had been for the Greeks to wipe out the Persian left wing, and then swing round to take the Persian centre in the rear.

The day's watchword 'Zeus the Saviour' and its response 'Victory' were passed through the Greek ranks, so that even in the confusion of battle they could distinguish friend from foe. They dressed their lines and waited, at first at ease, with their arms grounded. Then the company commanders called out the familiar commands: 'Up shields! Take distance! Up spears!' When the enemy were less than a kilometre away, at the sound of the trumpet, the Greeks struck up their repetitive chant of *iopaian* – the paean, sacred to the god Apollo in his capacity as protector of men, and designed to instil courage and foster comradeship – and advanced, with the support of 1,000 of the Paphlagonian horsemen. They started at a walk, but the phalanx began to bulge, and those who were being left behind picked up speed to catch up with the others and prevent gaps appearing in the line.

This acceleration proved to be contagious. Soon they were all running forward, shouting and screaming and banging their shields with the shafts of their spears, in an attempt not just to demoralize their opponents, but to overcome their own terror at the imminent, brutal shock of contact. But even before they had closed to about 150 metres – the most dangerous point, within range of the enemy bows, although at this distance the arrows lacked much penetrative power – most of the Persian left wing, under the command of Tissaphernes, caved in. Charioteers abandoned their vehicles and ran, horsemen turned tail, foot soldiers dropped their weapons and fled. The heavily armed Greeks pursued for a while, perhaps driven by their eagerness for booty further than they should, slaughtering the wounded left by the Paphlagonian horsemen as they harried their fleeing foes. Only two Greeks suffered minor injuries: one was bruised by an out-of-control chariot and the other was grazed by an arrow.

Tissaphernes himself, however, rallied some of his horsemen and charged along the river bank towards the Greek peltasts. The light-armed peltasts carried no more than a javelin or a bow, a short sword and a light, crescented shield called a *pelta* (after which they were named, just as hoplites were named after *their* shield, the *hoplon*). They stood no chance against such an assault, and their captain quickly ordered his men to open up their ranks and let the cavalry through. As Tissaphernes and his horsemen hurtled by, the peltasts inflicted what damage and delay they could.

In the centre and on the left, Cyrus had his men advance more slowly, waiting to see what tactics his brother would employ. He was pleased to see the success of the Greeks on the right, and some of the less stable courtiers in his entourage were encouraging him to think that victory and the throne of Persia were already his. With the Greeks off the immediate battlefield, however, Artaxerxes's cavalry galloped forward, followed by the Immortals and the rest of the infantry, in an attempt to encircle Cyrus's right flank, now exposed by the forward movement of the Greeks. Cyrus had to act quickly to come up with a significant counter-threat. He spotted the Persian royal standard with its spread eagle, and led his elite horsemen in a reckless, headlong gallop straight for his brother. They broke through Artaxerxes's cavalry, but at the cost of becoming scattered, and by the time Cyrus's impetus had carried him deep into the enemy ranks he was accompanied by rather too few of his bodyguards.

As is common in warfare, what happened next is not entirely clear: the surviving accounts are riddled with bias, none of the authors was an eyewitness, and the action was an untidy mêlée. It is possible that with his own hand Cyrus killed the commander of Artaxerxes's personal guard and pierced his brother's breastplate, though this tale of single combat seems too Homeric to be altogether plausible. At any rate, Artaxerxes was certainly wounded, and his guards closed ranks and carried their fallen king to a nearby hillock. Meanwhile, Cyrus himself had been wounded in the temple. Bleeding profusely, he slumped forward and soaked the protective felt frontlet his horse wore over its head, which was later recovered and presented in triumph to Artaxerxes. Dazed and weak from loss of blood, Cyrus fell to the ground and lost his horse. Staggering around the battlefield with an ever-decreasing number of retainers, he went unrecognized for a while by the enemy, because the force of the javelin thrust that had wounded him had also knocked off the royal tiara he was already presuming to wear. Finally, one of Artaxerxes's camp followers, playing wretched Paris to Cyrus's noble Achilles, brought him down by stabbing him behind the knee. Already weak from loss of blood, it took only a few moments for Cyrus's life to ebb away on the tide of blood that briefly stained the dry desert dust.

The death of the pretender spelled defeat, whatever happened elsewhere on the field of battle. No doubt this was why Clearchus had earlier warned Cyrus to stay out of the fray, but the young pretender, with typical impetuosity, had dismissed his advice. 'Here I am,' he said, 'reaching for a kingdom. Would you have me prove myself a coward, unworthy of kingship?' Persian propaganda constantly emphasized the warlike prowess of kings. With hindsight, Clearchus's decision to disobey Cyrus's command to attack Artaxerxes in the centre may have been a mistake. For all the huge numbers of men involved, the contest really was just between the two brothers. Cyrus's personal involvement in the battle may have been rash, but Clearchus's caution turned out to be disastrous.

Perhaps, though, the critical factor was not Clearchus's caution so much as Tissaphernes's cunning. After the battle, Tissaphernes was raised high and showered with rewards. Would the king have smiled with such favour on the only one of his commanders whose men performed badly in the battle? Tissaphernes had spent at least fifteen years in Asia Minor, in close contact with Greeks: he knew how dangerous hoplites could be. When you think that on another occasion, just a few years later, during the Spartan king Agesilaus's campaign in Asia, it took only two scythed chariots and 400 Persian horsemen to rout 700 Greek hoplites, it is hard to imagine that Tissaphernes would have given up so readily.

It was a feint. The Persians did not turn and flee: they disguised deliberate withdrawal as flight and drew the Greeks on, well away from the rest of the battle, in order to prevent them turning and attacking the Persian centre. Tissaphernes knew that the Greeks expected to defeat the lightly armed Persians, provided they could survive the chariots and the archers; he played to this expectation by feigning a terrified retreat. He knew that it was the job of the peltasts and the cavalry to follow his fleeing men, while the hoplites should have wheeled around and taken the king's centre in the rear; that is why he himself attacked the peltasts. He knew that it is common in battle for soldiers to be aroused to unreasoning lust for blood by the sight of their enemy's backs, and so he left the job of ensuring the utter 'defeat' of the king's left wing to the hoplites, who clearly lacked the discipline to cut short their pursuit. In short, Tissaphernes's tactics neutralized his king's most dangerous opponents.

Artaxerxes was attended by his Greek doctor, Ctesias of Cnidus, who was to write in his *Persian Tales* (now mostly lost) his own account of the battle and its aftermath. But the Great King was not too badly wounded. News of his brother's death was brought to him and before long he returned to the battlefield to see the corpse for himself. Artaxerxes ordered that his brother's head and right hand be chopped off and impaled on a stake within sight of his troops, to stiffen their resolve and remind them of where their loyalty lay. He and he alone was the Great King.

Meanwhile Cyrus's left wing, commanded by Ariaeus, also fared badly. Their attention was divided, since they were constantly in danger of being outflanked by the longer Persian line, and although at first they resisted as best they could – with Ariaeus himself wounded during the fight – the news of Cyrus's death broke their spirits and they fled all the way back to the staging-post where they had spent the previous night. A desperate fight took place among the baggage carts of the Greeks, where their plucky camp followers seized whatever weapons came to hand and fought off the marauding Persians. They managed to save themselves and some of the baggage – including one of Cyrus's concubines, a Milesian woman, who ran naked from her ordeal at the hands of the enemy soldiers who had captured her – but plenty of precious food and equipment was lost. So was Cyrus's other Greek concubine, a Phocaean woman called Aspasia, whose beauty and grin-and-bear-it attitude towards being fondled by Cyrus were celebrated in later Greek literature. She was no better off with Artaxerxes, however, who was said to get her to cross-dress in his favourite eunuch's clothes after the eunuch had died.

With Cyrus dead, victory belonged to the king; there was still the problem of the Greeks, however. Tissaphernes and his cavalry joined up with those of the king's men who had been plundering Cyrus's baggage train and together they marched back south, in the fast-fading light, to face the Greeks once more. As the enemy approached, the Greeks drew themselves up in battle lines, this time with the river on their left, and charged forward, just as they had, seemingly with such success, earlier in the afternoon. Once again, the Persians fled before these fearsome foreigners, and once again the Greeks set out in pursuit. This time, however, darkness intervened and put an end to any further action: as a rule, neither the Greeks nor the Persians favoured night-fighting. The Greeks did not yet know that Cyrus was dead; they had no idea that the battle was lost. Given their own apparent success, they probably assumed they had won. Weary and hungry, with bodies chafed sore from the abrasive blend of dust and sweat inside their armour, they returned to the plundered camp.

CHAPTER TWO

Greeks and Persians

The Greek mercenaries who performed so ambiguously for Cyrus at the battle of Cunaxa were a long way from home, but Greeks and Persians had a long history of official and casual intercourse. Warfare, at every temperature from outright hostility to diplomacy in times of uneasy peace, played a large part in their interactions, but there were also many cultural contacts. Greek artists, engineers, labourers (female as well as male), stonemasons, doctors, secretaries, engineers, envoys, mercenaries, athletes, entertainers, explorers, traders, translators and political exiles passed through or were resident in the domains of several of the satraps, and even occasionally in the court of the Great King himself. In the fifth and early fourth centuries, for instance, four Greek doctors tended the king or members of his immediate family. They were, so to speak, the king's general practitioners and surgeons, while Egyptian healers filled more specialist roles. Greek styles and techniques are evident in even the earliest, sixth-century art of the Achaemenid dynasty to which Cyrus and Artaxerxes belonged. The traffic was not just one way, however: in the fifth-century heyday of Athenian interest in Persia, eastern artistic motifs and styles decorated Athenian pots, clothing and luxury items, and references to the Persians, especially to the Greek victories over them, abounded in all forms of entertainment – in literature, sculpture, painting and rhetoric.

Thousands will remain forever nameless, but we know the names of some 300 Greeks who served Persians in various capacities in the 200 years before Alexander the Great occupied and Hellenized the east. After the Persian invasions of Greece in 490 and 480 BCE, even more Greeks were at least superficially acquainted with the appearance of various eastern peoples, chiefly Persians, and with their belongings, which were captured in huge quantities: parasols and personal jewellery, arms and armour, bedding and cloaks, gold and silver tableware, bullion and coins. Over the next fifty years of intermittent warfare, some Persian prisoners of war may even have ended up as slaves in Athens and elsewhere, and at least one high-ranking turncoat Persian lived for a while in Athens and died fighting against Persian allies in the early 420s.

Trade between the two peoples had always flourished through middlemen, carrying goods that ranged from expensive slaves to cheap pots. As always, ideas and technology were transmitted along the trade routes. The Greeks learnt (or re-learnt, after the Dark Age) from the east how to work bronze and construct monumental buildings. It is harder to assess in detail the archaic Greeks' intellectual debt to the east, but a few facts are certain. The alphabet came to Greece from Phoenicia, and coinage from Lydia; early Greek didactic poetry, represented by Hesiod of Boeotia around 700 BCE, was heavily indebted to Babylonian and other eastern models; the Greeks learnt theogonical and cosmogonical speculation, which led ultimately to the development of science, from the Near East; and some medical knowledge (or theories) trickled west from the older civilizations.

Where intellectual rather than technological achievements are concerned, the differences between the two cultures are as important as the similarities. The alphabet may have come from the east, but the Greeks added vowels and by the middle period of the Achaemenid empire literacy was far more widespread among Greeks than among their neighbours. In astronomy, the Babylonians had a long tradition of observation of the heavens and had built up copious lists of regular and irregular occurrences, but they rarely took this to the next level and developed theories. Most eastern mathematics was arithmetized and practical, the servant of some other domain such as land measurement (literally, 'geometry') or accountancy; it was the Greeks who developed non-arithmetical mathematical models and an interest in pure rather than applied mathematics, which led to the notion of proof, of showing how one fact followed from another or others.

Some Greeks even learnt to regard things with the eyes of protoscientists: they were reductionists, who looked to natural phenomena rather than to the gods for more economical explanations of the world. Philip of Opus, a pupil of Plato and his literary executor, asserted that 'Greeks improve everything they take over from barbarians'. Such jingoistic generalizations are hazardous, but it may be safe to say, as long as one focuses on intellectual achievements, that the Greek genius lay in the propensity to abstract and generalize, and in a tolerance of rational criticism and debate: since these factors allow knowledge to progress, in all such fields the Greeks were far more innovative, far less conservative, than their eastern peers.

The Origins of the Persian Empire

The Persian empire began with the ambition of our Cyrus's illustrious namesake, Cyrus II, the hero of Xenophon's fanciful and over-earnest *The Education of Cyrus the Great*. This Cyrus came to the throne of mountainous Parsa in 559 BCE. Parsa ('Persis' to the Greeks – hence 'Persia' – and modern 'Fars'), south-east of Babylonia and the other side of the Persian Gulf, was at the time a subject state of Media and its king Astyages. With tireless determination, energy and charisma, Cyrus united the Persian tribes and principalities, and launched his rebellion. By 550 Astyages was dead and Cyrus had taken control not just of Media, but of all the regions where the Medes had exercised some degree of hegemony: Mesopotamia, Assyria, Syria, Cappadocia and Armenia. Media itself, north of Persis and north-east of Babylonia, was reduced to the first satrapy of the new empire, and in a great symbolic act Cyrus developed the site of the battlefield where he had defeated Astyages as his new capital, Pasargadae, famed for the beauty of its open spaces and the majesty of its monumental buildings. The visions granted in legend to Astyages were beginning to come true: first he dreamt that his daughter urinated a huge lake of water, which flooded all of Asia, and later, just after he had married her to Cambyses, the father of Cyrus, that a vine sprouted from her womb and overshadowed the entire continent.

Cyrus had entered Media more as a natural heir than as a conqueror: Medes remained in important administrative posts and their customs were hardly changed. The Medes were no more a subject people than the British were when William of Orange landed to take over the throne in 1688, and to later Greek historians the terms 'Persians' and 'Medes' were almost interchangeable. But Cyrus was still surrounded by powerful kingdoms, and King Croesus of Lydia, of legendary wealth, saw Cyrus as a threat: in 585 he had agreed with Media that the Halys river would form the border between their domains, but he had no confidence that Cyrus would respect this agreement. The famous story is that Croesus consulted the oracle at Delphi in Greece, which returned a typically ambiguous answer: 'If you make war on the Persians, you will destroy a great empire.' Assuming that the empire to be destroyed was Cyrus's, in 547 Croesus attacked. The empire that was lost, by the following year, was his own; Lydia became the satrapy of Sparda, with its capital still at Sardis.

Croesus of Lydia had exacted tribute from the Greek cities of the north and west coasts of Asia Minor, which at the time constituted the wealthiest and most cultured part of the Greek world, and so the Persians inherited these Greek dependencies – or 'enslaved' them, as the Greeks put it. At a stroke, a substantial portion of the Greek world was in Persian hands. In the short term, the Asiatic Greeks were compelled to demolish any defensive fortifications they had erected; in the long term, they had to pay tribute and provide troops if called upon to do so, but they retained a degree of autonomy in selecting their own local rulers and making their own laws. To be on the safe side, successive Persian kings colonized the Greek coastlines by giving favoured barons large estates close to the most important cities. These dislocated Persians tended not to absorb much Greek culture, but tried to maintain a Persian way of life in the west, with palatial mansions and *paradeisoi* (walled parks and hunting-grounds) – and also with enough of a local garrison to ensure that the Asiatic Greeks saw sense, kept the peace, and appointed not too many anti-Persian governments. Cyrus's annexation of Lydia brought Greeks and Persians into contact for the first time as peoples, as political units with broad agendas and, however dimly at this stage, their own sense of identity. For the next two centuries, until the conquest of the Persian empire by Alexander the Great, the histories of Persia and Greece intertwined.

Next it was the turn of Nabunaid of Babylon, formerly the ally of Lydia. In 539, following severe losses in battle, the disaffected and defeated Babylonians opened the gates of the city to Cyrus's commander. Cyrus gained the most fertile region of the Near East and consolidated his conquest by means of clever propaganda (such as that inscribed on the British Museum's Cyrus Cylinder) portraying him as the favourite of the Babylonian gods and the proper heir of their ancient kings, and by prudent generosity towards those who had supported him.

Cyrus was no less successful in expanding his dominion eastwards as far as, in modern terms, Afghanistan, Turkmenistan, Uzbekistan and Tadjikistan. Following his death in 530, fighting a border war in the far north-east of the empire against the wild Massagetae under their savage queen Tomyris, his son Cambyses II inherited both the throne and the task of conquering Egypt. This he had achieved by 522, with the help of the venal commander of the Egyptian king's Greek mercenaries, who was easily induced to defect. Along with Egypt came the island of Cyprus; the Libyans and the Greek cities of north Africa submitted too. Attempts at further expansion in Africa were largely disastrous, but the Near Eastern world had been turned upside down, as empires and kingdoms, old and new, fell before Persian ambition and ruthlessness. The only quasi-survivors were the sensible Cilicians, who had given Cyrus free passage through their land from Syria, and in reward were permitted semi-independent status, under kings each of whom was given the throne-name Syennesis.

Darius I and the Administration of the Empire

Cambyses did not live long enough to consolidate the newly expanded Persian empire, though he laid an important foundation by making it the duty of his Egyptian and Phoenician subjects to supply future kings with a navy. Consolidation was left to steadier and more popular hands (there were rumours that the king was insane), but not until a period of near chaos had loomed and passed. In 522, while Cambyses was still in Egypt, his brother Smerdis, satrap of Media and Armenia, declared himself king in Cambyses's place and proclaimed a programme of undermining the power of the Persian oligarchy.

On his way back from Egypt, Cambyses died of a gangrenous wound, leaving the throne to the usurper. Smerdis did not last long, however: after only a few months of rule he was assassinated by his cousin Darius, who had served alongside Cambyses in Egypt and whose father had gained one of the eastern satrapies. This is the simpler and more plausible version of events. Darius, however, on the Bisitun inscription told an implausible fable whereby, unknown to the general populace, Smerdis (whom Darius calls 'Bardiya') had been killed many years earlier, before Cambyses went to Egypt, but then a lookalike, calling himself Smerdis, had usurped the throne and was dealt with by Darius. This was Darius's attempt to portray himself simultaneously as a pious avenger and innocent of shedding royal blood.

Darius had stolen the throne from a man who had a better claim to it than he did; he had to act fast to gain legitimacy. With the help of fellow Persian nobles and Cambyses's battle-hardened troops, as well as propaganda, assassination and the brutal quelling of the oppor-

The Bisitun Relief. Darius I is the larger-than-life figure to the left, showing mercy to the bound captives, who represent the nations he has conquered. The inscription narrates in three languages the king's struggles to obtain and secure the throne. The winged figure on high represents Ahuramazda. This nineteenth-century engraving, by an unknown artist, well captures the impressiveness of the monument, which was carved into a high rock face, and measures about 25 x 35 metres.

tunistic rebellions that broke out all over the empire, he rapidly consolidated his position. In 522–521 alone he fought nineteen battles and made nine kings his prisoners. On the Bisitun inscription – the original carved into a cliff face overlooking one of the main caravan routes of the empire, near Ecbatana, and copies disseminated throughout the provinces – in which he regaled his subjects with a boastful list of his conquests and a vivid depiction of representatives of the various races subject to him, he presented himself as kin to Cyrus the Great by tracing Cyrus's family back to his own direct forefather, Achaemenes. In fact, though, the Achaemenid dynasty truly began with Darius; it would end almost 200 years later with the death of Darius III in 330, during the invasion of Alexander the Great.

Once peace had been restored, Darius I devoted himself to the task of administration, and proved so gifted at the fiscal aspects that those of his subjects who dared to tease called him a 'shopkeeper'. He reformed the empire's legal systems, reorganized the tax-paying satrapies and the contributions of the tribute-paying vassal states, introduced coined money, and standardized weights and measures across the empire to facilitate the movement of goods. The main job of the satrapies was to pour huge amounts of gold and silver bullion into the king's coffers – the annual total being equivalent, according to Herodotus, to 14,560 talents of silver, when just three or four talents would have made an individual a millionaire. Then there were gifts and tribute from vassal states, and some tax was paid in kind. But satraps were also required to maintain order, raise an army if necessary, and defend or even extend the empire.

Given the vast size of the empire and the consequent problems of rapid communication and central control, satrapies were run as semi-independent kingdoms. Satraps (from a Median word meaning 'protectors of the kingdom') wielded both civil and military authority in their provinces. Although they were viceroys, answerable, in theory, to the Persian king, in fact they tended to consider themselves monarchs in their own right, since they had at their command the income and armies of large and wealthy countries. The king held the ultimate authority, not least because anyone who held land anywhere in the empire held it for him in fief, as a kind of tenant, but the stability of his empire required satraps he could trust. Satrapal rebellion was not unusual, and in order to counter the threat – in order to remind the satraps that they might be kings, but he was the King of Kings – Darius and his successors saw to it that they personally were the final court of appeal, and that the most senior members of the satraps' civil services could, if need be, report directly to them rather than to the satraps. 'The king,' they said, 'has many ears and many eyes' – though the existence of a secret service consisting of agents called 'the king's eyes' and 'the king's ears' may have been little more than a Greek fantasy, stemming from the commonplace that despots suffer from paranoia.

Darius also oversaw irrigation projects all over the empire, repaired the old Egyptian canal approximately equivalent to the modern Suez Canal, and improved the empire's roads, which served chiefly to speed armies on their way. Communication was vastly aided by a network of well-maintained roads (consisting at best of a packed gravel surface) with way stations and pontoon bridges, by the relative scarcity of brigands, and by an extraordinarily efficient messenger service. Herodotus likened these couriers to relay racers and in praising them gave the US Postal Service its unofficial motto: 'Whatever the conditions – it may be snowing, raining, blazing hot, or dark – they never fail to complete their assigned journey in the least possible time.' They could speed a letter from Sardis to Susa, a distance of over 3,000 kilometres, in as little as seven days.

It may also have been Darius who initiated, or at least developed, the system that pervaded and unified the Persian empire, whereby almost everyone, however high or low their station, received rations. The king or his local representatives gathered in all the produce, and then redistributed it according to the perceived merits of the recipient. Tokens of merit were not just loyalty and hard work: men who fathered many children were also rewarded. Those held in the highest regard received so much more than they and their dependants could possibly consume that they resold it for profit; others received barely enough to live on.

One result of Darius's administrative reforms, necessitated by the logistics of running a vast empire, was that bureaucrats and court officials came to occupy an intermediate level of government, between the king and the general populace. The most commoners or even lowly nobles could do was try to get a petition read to the king, perhaps by cultivating the acquaintance of a powerful eunuch or the *hazārapatiš* (chiliarch, or 'leader of a thousand'), a kind of Grand Vizier who had command not only of the king's bodyguard, the elite thousand of the Immortals, but of all the minor court bureaucrats, and who therefore virtually controlled access to the royal person. Greek envoys learnt well that, even after the lengthy journey to the new capital city, Susa, gaining access to the king himself involved tiresome and insulting delays and negotiations with a complex hierarchy. The king's word was law, but he consulted an inner circle of nobles and officials (such as the 'royal judges', who were experts in traditions) before declaring the law.

As an absolute monarch, and as one who enjoyed the special protection of Ahuramazda (the Wise Lord, the one great god, though there were lesser deities beneath him, such as Anahita and Mithras), Darius was portrayed performing superhuman feats, and later kings inherited this habit of self-aggrandizement and tolerance of flattery. But the weakness of absolute monarchy is its dependence on the personality of the monarch: all too easily flattery can lead to treachery, and therefore to all the court intrigues and harem scandals that plagued successive Persian kings and destabilized the empire. Although in theory the eldest son was supposed to inherit the throne, the succession was frequently contested, and undisguised murder and scheming rendered the theory difficult to put into practice.

Whereas Cyrus and Cambyses had adopted the policy, common to most empires, of favouring local elites in their territories, Darius exalted the Persian nobility, especially those families that had helped him gain power, and members of his own family. The members of this ruling elite of future satraps and high courtiers were educated at special schools, which trained them in Persian customs until they were ready for power within the empire. Henceforth, it was not impossible for non-Persians to reach the highest levels of the hierarchy, but it was harder. Darius suppressed local kingships and baronies, but in other respects tried to create an empire that, for the first time in the world, brought a large number of different races under a single government in a way that left them a degree of autonomy. There were military

The north stairway of the *apadana* (royal reception hall) of Persepolis, evidently designed to overawe the king's visitors. Each column is about 20 metres tall, and the figures lining the stairway represent the king's subject nations.

garrisons at key locations throughout the empire, but they were not too heavy-handed.

Darius also laid the foundation for the Great King's notorious aloofness and inaccessibility, as marks of his majesty and unique status. In his eulogistic biography of the Spartan king Agesilaus, Xenophon claimed that Persian kings actually prided themselves on being inaccessible, even rarely seen in public, and slow to grant petitions and conduct business. The king's exalted position was reflected in his attire, which, at least by the time of Artaxerxes II, was said to be worth 12,000 talents. Slaves had to wear masks so that their breath would not displease the king: these were the days before dental hygiene. Areas of his palaces were covered in purple-dyed rugs that none but the royal feet could press, and he had his own special wine, bread, salt and scented oil. His meals were incredibly sumptuous, the tables laden with gifts provided by his subjects and so reflecting his power and reach. Out on campaign, in a combination of privilege and the Zoroastrian emphasis on cleanliness, he drank only purified water from the river that flowed through Susa, which was transported on special carts, and he slept and held court in a tent that was little less than a movable palace.

Driven by the bizarre logic of imperialism and perhaps by an aggressive interpretation of the Zoroastrian imperative to defeat evil, Darius then turned to further expansion abroad. In 513 he made a historic crossing of the Bosporus into Europe and attacked the Scythian tribes on the steppes to the north and north-west of the Black Sea. Though this campaign was not altogether successful, he left a bridgehead in Europe, and by 512 the Persians occupied most of Thrace (roughly, Bulgaria and north-eastern Greece), including the Greek cities on the north coast of the Hellespont. A few of the most easterly Aegean islands were also absorbed. By 510 the Macedonian tribal rulers too had submitted in the Persian fashion, by offering the king or his envoys earth and water (a symbolic representation of territory), and much of what we think of as northern Greece was in Persian hands. Under Darius, the empire grew both eastward and westward to its greatest extent; subsequent kings maintained rather than expanded their inheritance.

At around two million square kilometres, this was the largest empire the world had ever seen. It included the most fertile and densely populated areas of the ancient world, and was so large that it had several mother cities, in addition to the capitals of each satrapy: Susa, Ecbatana, Babylon and Persepolis (the 'city of the Persians', developed by Darius to surpass Cyrus's Pasargadae) all vied for the Great King's presence. Sardis or Dascyleum, in the satrapies of Sparda and Phrygia, were his preferred residences when he was campaigning in the west, against Thracians or Greeks; Bactra, capital of Bactria, when he had to be in the far east.

In order to protect his western border, Darius or his satraps began placing puppet rulers in Greek coastal or island cities. Darius's intentions were suddenly an issue on mainland Greece, as the city-states there found themselves on the borders of the largest and most aggressive empire in the world.

The Persian Invasions of Greece

In the last decade of the sixth century, the relatively insignificant Greek city of Athens was rocked by a revolution whose ideals have spread and utterly transformed our world. In the teeth of opposition from Spartan-backed reactionaries, who wanted to maintain the aristocratic status quo, Cleisthenes, though no less of an aristocrat than his rivals, pushed through a series of popular reforms that turned Athens into a fledgling democracy. But Sparta was anxious to include Athens in its burgeoning land empire, and seemed prepared to use force to crush this unwelcome turn of events.

Cleisthenes sent envoys east to Sardis, to ask the Persian satrap, Artaphernes, for an alliance with Darius, to counter the Spartan threat. It is hard to guess what was going through Cleisthenes's mind; he must have known that the Persians would offer assistance only if Athens agreed to become a vassal state. And this was indeed what Artaphernes demanded, prompted no doubt by Hippias, the exiled Athenian tyrant, who was resident in his court. Far from home, the Athenian delegates had to make a quick decision: they agreed to Artaphernes's terms. In the event, the Spartan invasion came to nothing, and by the time the envoys got home the threat had evaporated. In their new confidence the Athenians punished the envoys and foolishly refused to acknowledge that they were now officially vassals of Darius.

The issue came to a head in 499, in Asia Minor, when Aristagoras, the ruler of Miletus, stirred his city into rebellion against their imperial overlords. Many of the Greek cities of Ionia and the Hellespont, and of the Hellenized cities of Caria, followed. Some wanted to rid themselves of puppet rulers, some wanted an end to tribute-payment, but

This scene from the magnificent red-figure name vase of the Darius Painter (c. 325 BCE, southern Italy) shows King Darius I, seated on his throne in the centre, overlooked by deities, and receiving a delegation of Greeks – the figures who are less exotically dressed. Scholars have guessed that it represents an episode from the Ionian Rebellion. The men in the bottom right corner of the unwrapped vase are prostrating themselves in the way the Greeks imagined Persians paid homage to their king.

their common cause was simply to throw off Persian rule. Aristagoras tried to enlist the help of the Spartans, the supreme military force on the Greek mainland, but the Spartans were justifiably daunted by the task, so he next turned to Athens.

The Athenians were happy to flex their new democratic muscles and to show the world that they were no longer ruled by a pro-Persian tyrant. They agreed to support Aristagoras with twenty ships, fully half of their fleet at the time, and they were joined in this doomed venture by five ships from the small town of Eretria on the neighbouring island of Euboea. In 498 Aristagoras launched an ill-judged assault on Sardis, in which he and his allies succeeded only in setting fire to residential areas of the city before being turned back: the sheer acropolis of Sardis proved, as often, impossible to capture. The Athenians were defeated in battle just as they were about to embark for home at Ephesus.

It was, in the words of Herodotus, 'the beginning of misfortune for both Greeks and barbarians'. This action of theirs meant that they came to the attention of the Great King himself, not just of his brother Artaphernes:

> Meanwhile, news reached King Darius of the Athenian and Ionian capture and burning of Sardis, and he was told that the man who had gathered the troops together, and was therefore the instigator of the whole affair, had been Aristagoras of Miletus. It is said, however, that his first reaction to the news was to discount the Ionians [the Asiatic Greeks], because he was confident of punishing them for their rebellion, and to ask who the Athenians were. On hearing the answer, he is said to have asked for his bow; he took hold of it, notched an arrow and shot it up towards the sky. And as he fired into the air, he said, 'Lord Zeus [Ahuramazda], make it possible for me to punish the Athenians.' Then he ordered one of his attendants to repeat to him three times, every time a meal was being served, 'Master, remember the Athenians.'

Cyprus joined the rebellion, but hopes that it would spread to Egypt, invariably the least stable part of the western Persian empire, were dashed. Cyprus was defeated in 496, Aristagoras made himself scarce and soon died, and one by one the rebel cities, which never fully united, were besieged and captured. Miletus was the last to fall, in 494, and the city was razed to the ground. Many of the inhabitants were slaughtered, many others enslaved or deported; other towns, and several of the islands, suffered hardly less. The news stunned the Greek world, and especially the Athenians – so much so that in 493 the tragic dramatist Phrynichus was fined for putting on a play entitled *The Fall of Miletus*, which reminded the Athenians of their friends' disaster and their own impending doom.

With an uneasy calm once more restored to the Asiatic Greek cities, Darius turned his attention to mainland Greece. He had indeed not forgotten the Athenians. A naval expedition of 492, under one of his sons-in-law, Mardonius, was wrecked off the coast of the Athos peninsula (famous today for its timeless monasteries), where sharks dealt with at least some of the floundering sailors. White doves, it was said, first appeared in Greece shortly after this miraculous storm. Doves or no doves, by the summer of 490 the Great King's military commanders had assembled a fleet of warships at the Aegean island of Samos, which had been in Persian hands since 519. Mardonius had been replaced, for his earlier failure, by Datis the Mede and Artaphernes, the son of the satrap of Sardis. The Persian mission was to annexe as many of the Aegean islands as possible, devastate Eretria and capture Athens. With Hippias re-installed in Athens as its tyrant, the Persians would have a foothold in mainland Greece.

The first part of the mission went well: the armada sailed across the Aegean, stopping at island after island to punish or conscript the inhabitants, and Eretria was burnt to the ground after being betrayed to the invaders by the pro-Persian faction within the town. Just across the narrow strait separating Euboea from mainland Greece lay the village of Marathon, on Athenian soil. The shoreline there was perfect for beaching the fleet, and the level plain beyond the shore suited the deployment of the highly trained cavalry with which the Persians expected to overcome any armed resistance. They landed only 40 kilometres from Athens.

Terror and determination to resist gripped the Athenians in equal measure. They dispatched a runner to summon Spartan help, but the Spartans procrastinated: the phase of the moon was wrong, and there was danger of a slave rebellion if a full contingent of their fighters left. Only a handful of troops from the tiny Boeotian town of Plataea, an ally of Athens, came to reinforce the outnumbered Athenian hoplites. In a display of boldness that must have seemed outright stupidity to fainter hearts, Miltiades and his fellow generals chose to march out against the overwhelming Persian army. They encamped on rising ground to dissuade a Persian attack, and the two sides watched each other for several days.

The Persians became bored with the stalemate, and decided to re-embark and sail around the Attic peninsula to attack the city more directly. Miltiades saw his opportunity. When the formidable Persian horsemen were out of the way, boarding the ships, the Athenians and Plataeans moved down the slope, 10,000 facing 20,000 or more, and charged, to minimize the amount of time they were vulnerable to Persian arrows. In the centre the Athenians only just managed to hold their ground before beginning to disintegrate and fall back, but the two wings – Athenians on the right and Plataeans on the left – were victorious. They routed the enemy, but with admirable discipline turned to assist the centre, rather than pursuing their fleeing opponents. Before long the entire Persian army was withdrawing in disarray to their beached ships. After some bloody hand-to-hand fighting right by the ships, the Persians managed to take to the safety of the sea. A signal from pro-Persian elements among the Athenians – those who wanted to see the restoration of the tyranny, overthrown in 510, or at least to get rid of the more radical democrats in Athens – warned the Persians against sailing around to Athens. The Athenians raced home to defend their city, and the Persians sailed away. The raid on mainland Greece had brought the Persians nothing, but they still had the strategically critical Aegean islands.

The Athenians lost 192 men, while the lighter-armed Persians lost over 6,000; the ghosts of dead men and horses were said in later years to haunt the battleground every night. The miraculous victory elevated Athens to the front rank of Greek states, so that from now on she was a direct rival of Sparta. Although, from the Persian point of view, it was no more than a minor engagement on the fringes of the empire, Marathon really is one of those great 'what-if' battles whose outcome decides the course of history for a substantial region of the world. The nineteenth-century philosopher John Stuart Mill famously quipped that English history had been more radically affected by the battle of Marathon than by Hastings. If the Greeks had lost there (or, since they won, if they had lost any of the cardinal battles of the subsequent Persian invasion), European culture as we know it would have been strangled at birth and autocracy would have swamped the fierce independence of the Greek states.

Darius vowed revenge, but was delayed by rebellions in both Egypt and Babylon. On his death in 486 he bequeathed the task to his son Xerxes I. The seriousness of the third Persian invasion was marked not just by the scale of the armament and the personal presence of the king, but by two huge engineering works: the entire 2-kilometre width of the Hellespont (the Dardanelles) was bridged by a double pontoon of boats, and a canal was dug through the Athos peninsula. The way was clear for the invading army of perhaps 150,000 land troops and a navy of 600 warships.

In 481, faced with this imminent invasion, the Greeks convened an emergency conference in Corinth. It was poorly attended, because many Greek states, not unnaturally, preferred to capitulate to or side with the Persians, or to maintain an uneasy neutrality. The amount of pro-Persian feeling in Greece should not occasion surprise. It was not quite treason or treachery, because there was no Greek nation to betray; in any case, the Persian empire tolerated cultural diversity. The delegates from thirty-one states – fewer than 5 per cent of the mainland Greek states – agreed to put aside their mutual and often long-standing differences, and chose the Spartans, with their military expertise and leadership of a powerful coalition of Peloponnesian states, as the overall commanders of the Greek forces. They formed two lines of defence: one in the north, directly in the line of the Persian approach, at Thermopylae and Artemisium, and one to fall back on in the south, around the isthmus to the Peloponnese.

Following the betrayal and glorious defeat of the Spartan king Leonidas and his vastly outnumbered troops at the narrow pass of Thermopylae, which gave Xerxes his first taste of the passion with which love of freedom inspired the Greeks, it was the turn of the largely Athenian navy at Artemisium. Perhaps they could check the inexorable advance of the Persian forces south through Greece. The Athenian leader was Themistocles. Even though quite a few Persian ships had been destroyed in a storm, the Greeks were still hugely outnumbered, but they held their own in an indecisive battle, before falling back south to the island of Salamis, in the Saronic Gulf near Athens.

Nothing could now stop the Persian advance, and the Athenian fleet was used, on Themistocles's orders, to evacuate the city and ferry its inhabitants to safety on Salamis and elsewhere. It must have seemed to be the end of the world: no one knew whether they would see their native city again or whether, if they ever did return, it would be as insignificant members of an increased Persian empire, slaves to the Great King. The Persian fleet was stationed in the bay of Phalerum, right by Athens itself, while the army marched on, through Boeotia and into Attica. The Acropolis was besieged and soon taken. The few defenders, those who were too stubborn or too poor to have evacuated, were massacred and the temples were plundered and burnt to the ground.

Many of the Greeks saw their position at Salamis as a dead end, a trap, and regarded the capture of Athens as the end of the war on the mainland. They were now concerned only to retreat to the

Peloponnese and make a last stand there. In fact, the Peloponnesians were already in the process of building a defensive wall across the isthmus near Corinth. But this was a futile strategy, engendered by desperation: even if the wall succeeded in holding up some of the Persian troops, others could be landed beyond it, since the Greek fleet could not patrol the whole coastline of the Peloponnese.

Themistocles, however, understood that the Greeks had to risk all on a single battle, and he saw that their position at Salamis, though it looked hopeless, could work in their favour. There is even a story that he sent a message to the Persian king, pretending to be a traitor and encouraging him to bottle up the Greek ships in the stretch of water between the island and the mainland. Whatever the truth of this story, that was exactly what Xerxes did. The Persians divided their fleet by night into two parts, with each part blocking one of the channels on either side of Salamis. The Greek fleet was confined to the water on the landward side of the island, and the Persians rowed into the attack at dawn. They expected to find the Greeks in disarray, but were faced with a small but disciplined and determined force. The Greeks pulled back, to draw the Persians further into the narrow straits where their superior numbers would be a disadvantage, and then attacked. The battle was desperate and fierce, but in the end the Greeks won and did so decisively.

Xerxes, who had watched the battle and the massacre of his men from a vantage point, was utterly dejected. In a rage, he executed his naval commanders for their failure, and many of the alienated Phoenician and Egyptian sailors deserted. Xerxes took what was left of his fleet back to Asia to forestall opportunistic rebellions at home, to secure his line of retreat, and to guarantee provisions for the bulk of the land army, which stayed behind to continue the campaign the following year. On the same day in 479 Greek forces annihilated the Persians on the mainland at Plataea and on the coast of Asia Minor at Mycale. Many of the Asiatic Greek cities rose up once more in revolt. With half of their army and most of their fleet lost, the Persians withdrew, to lick their wounds and prepare for the future. Although Xerxes rarely lost a battle, his successes elsewhere in the empire were unknown to the Greeks: as far as they were concerned, the Persians had lost the aura of invincibility that had served them well in the past.

CHAPTER THREE

Xenophon and His Times

Xenophon, son of Gryllus and Diodora, was born in Athens a year or two after 430 BCE and died around 354, probably in Corinth. It is not unusual for us to know little about an ancient Greek's life, however famous his deeds or voluminous his creative output. Xenophon is no exception. He revealed little of himself in his books, and though he became famous enough to attract biographical attention, the only Life that remains, by Diogenes Laertius, was written in the third century CE, is lamentably brief, and may be less reliable than we are sometimes forced to assume.

Maybe he had siblings or close relatives who died in the plague that decimated Athens when he was an infant: we shall never know. Maybe he himself served as a young man in the Athenian cavalry, at home and abroad: all we have to go on is the impression we gain from *The Expedition of Cyrus* that he already had experience of the battlefield.

Busts of Xenophon are rare. This one, dating from a couple of centuries after his death, probably gives little idea of his actual features, since such busts tended to convey a general impression of what types of people, such as historians (as here) or philosophers or statesmen, were supposed to look like.

He was said to be good-looking, and perhaps as a young teenager he was taken in hand by an older man of the same social standing, who in return for a fairly innocent degree of homosexual licence acted as his mentor, with the promise of ensuring that he would be introduced into the right circles later in life. However, in his later writings he showed himself to be more averse to homosexual liaisons than many of his upper-class peers. One thing that we can be sure of is that, as a well-born young man, he was naturally destined to play a part in his city's political life. But events, and his own lack of sympathy with Athenian democracy, put paid to any such plans.

His early years were dominated by the Peloponnesian War between Athens and Sparta, the two superpower states of classical Greece. The war ran intermittently from 431 to 404, after decades of tension and skirmishing, and resulted in the defeat and humiliation of his native city, whose reputation had become tainted by years of abuse of imperialist power and wealth. As a member of the privileged class, the young Xenophon would have led a somewhat pampered life, but when war is all one knows, wealth does not imply security. Nevertheless, at an age when other boys were being apprenticed to their fathers' trades, he was attending school. Athenian education was pretty basic, by our standards, and not least because its function was to mould character, rather than to impart information or develop critical thinking. It was a way of acculturating a young man (never girls, in the fifth century) into his society. Xenophon attended three teachers: a *paidotribēs* in a gymnasium to teach him sports and the value of physical effort; a *kitharistēs* to teach him a musical instrument and the softer virtues hymned by the lyric poets; and a *grammatistēs* to teach him the practicalities of reading, writing and basic arithmetic, and with whom to learn substantial amounts of the Homeric poems, with their emphasis on martial prowess and the aristocratic values of competition.

Though by the end of the fifth century there were *nouveaux riches* merchants, bankers and manufacturers in Athens, most of the wealthy families were landowners. Xenophon was surrounded in his youth by family anxiety, since estates outside the defensive walls of the city were vulnerable in wartime to invasion by the Peloponnesians, whose prime purpose was to steal or destroy crops, to damage property and to do their best to mutilate trees, in order to try to entice the Athenians into a foolhardy attempt to offer pitched battle. In addition, Xenophon's family may have owned property abroad, attached to an outpost of the empire and rented out to a local tenant farmer: this too would have been lost as the empire crumbled in the last decade of the fifth century. But in the years of uneasy peace that occupied much of the middle period of the war, Xenophon accompanied his father to his nearby estates, and that is undoubtedly where he learnt to ride. He was a good rider, and much later he wrote two pertinent treatises: *On Cavalry Command* and *On Horsemanship*.

We are afforded a glimpse of such a life, for an estate owner whose land was close to Athens, in his book *On the Management of an Estate*:

> If there's no need for me to be in Athens [says Xenophon's mouth-piece, Ischomachus], my slave takes my horse on ahead to my farm, and I use the journey out of town as an opportunity for a walk. ... Out on my farm I may find planting, ploughing, sowing or harvesting taking place, and I oversee all aspects of the labour and make any changes I can to improve what's going on.
> Next, I usually mount my horse and put him through his paces: since I imitate as closely as I can the equestrian skills needed in battle, I don't steer clear of uneven or steep ground, or ditches or streams – although I do my best not to lame my horse during these exercises. When this is over, my slave lets the horse have a roll and then takes him back home along with anything we need in town from the country. I walk some of the way home and run the rest, and then scrape myself clean with a strigil.

The city and its politics were the focus of these leisured landowners: it was their duty and their pleasure to make what contribution they could to the administration of Athens. So Xenophon, like many of his class, was being trained to be more of an absentee landlord than a hands-on farmer. He was able to discourse at length about the generosity of the soil and about how to manage the workforce, but he left the skilled work to his foreman and labourers, who were all slaves. The land provided him with a good living, allowed him to practise his horsemanship and gave him the opportunity to hunt – these were its main advantages.

Hunting was another topic to which Xenophon devoted a treatise. Again, it was one of the typical pursuits of young men of the Athenian leisured class, who had the time and money to occupy themselves with it. And so in his treatise Xenophon defended the activity against the charge of aristocratic self-indulgence by stressing that it was a tough, even dangerous sport, undertaken on foot across difficult terrain, and occasionally involving face-to-face confrontations with a beast as savage and unpredictable as a wild boar, and by arguing that it promoted qualities useful for the community as a whole, especially physical fitness and courage. Whether this was uppermost in his mind as he went out with his youthful peers into the Attic countryside in pursuit of hares, however, is another question.

As a citizen of Athens, Xenophon was inculcated with certain values. He grew up in a city that was still clinging to the pride, now fading, that had led it to initiate a programme of adorning itself with monumental public buildings; he grew up in a democracy that, for all its flaws, encouraged every citizen to feel himself a part of his city's destiny and future. An Athenian citizen combined privilege with obligation. After the age of eighteen, he participated in the civic religious rites, which kept the gods smiling on the city, and he could attend meetings of the popular Assembly, where at the age of twenty he could make his voice heard. At thirty he could serve as a juror in the law courts (which, in addition to dealing with criminal cases, provided the legal muscle to support the city's democratic institutions) or on the Council (which prepared the agendas for the executive Assembly), and he could have his name put forward for selection by lot to any of the public offices of Athens. He was expected to serve in the army or navy, and, if rich, to perform certain services ('liturgies'), such as financing a religious festival or maintaining a warship, that served in Athens as a form of taxation. In return, an Athenian citizen enjoyed the protection of the laws. In most or all of these respects, he was sharply distinguished from Athenian women and children, and from resident foreigners (slaves and businessmen), all of whom had fewer or no rights. He learnt that the gods valued dutifulness towards one's community, hospitality towards strangers, respect for elders and care for parents, kindness towards friends and reasonable hostility towards enemies, and that they would punish criminals and humble the proud. The cardinal virtues of Greek men were personal integrity, self-restraint (knowing one's place in society), piety towards one's human and superhuman superiors, shrewdness and courage.

Xenophon's Religion

The plague, a strain of typhoid fever, that struck Athens in the summer of 430 and lingered for three years had a powerful effect on the minds as well as the bodies of Xenophon's parents' generation. The Greeks of the classical period had always lived in an insecure universe, where early death, warfare, pestilence and hunger were all too frequent visitors. The Homeric pantheon of fickle gods whose whims were invariably beyond the comprehension of mortal men was a projection of this insecurity on to its supposed causes. But in Athens the plague became part of a larger pattern of events that threatened the old moral order. In a famous passage, the historian Thucydides analysed and catalogued the moral decline caused by the plague:

> People had fewer inhibitions about self-indulgent behaviour they had previously repressed, because they saw how rapidly fortunes could change – how those who were well off suddenly died and how those who had formerly been destitute promptly inherited their property. The upshot was that they sought a life of swift and pleasurable gain, because they regarded their lives and their property as equally impermanent. No one had the slightest desire to endure discomfort for the sake of what men deemed honourable, because they doubted whether they would live long enough to earn a reputation for honour. In fact, what was held to be honourable and beneficial was whatever contributed to the pleasure of the moment, regardless of its source. Fear of the gods and human laws were equally ineffective as deterrents: the sight of the religious and the irreligious dying equally made people conclude that piety made no difference, and no one expected to live long enough to be taken to court and punished for his crimes.

There is a degree of exaggeration in this account – not everyone in Athens succumbed to lawlessness – but only a degree. Things would not have got so out of hand if there had not already been a cultural tendency in the direction of subverting the old moral order. The upper strata of Athenian society in the last quarter of the fifth century were rocked by a moral and religious crisis, with intellectuals casting doubt on the existence of the gods and the value of traditionally moral behaviour. Sophists, and those they influenced, questioned the very foundation of morality. Why, they asked, should an individual have to endure discomfort and sacrifice for the greater good? If a man can get away with behaviour that, although not sanctioned by the moral code, makes him prosperous and happy, why should he not do it? They taught that there were no gods, or that if there were they had no concern for mortal men, and that prestige and material success were the most important values. The Athenian reaction to such subversive ideas was to attempt to muzzle intellectuals, by mocking them (as comic playwrights did before the assembled people at dramatic festivals) or even by legal means: the famous trial of Socrates in 399 was the culmination of a series of actual or threatened court cases and decrees aimed at buttressing tradition.

In addition to suffering from relative material insecurity, then, Xenophon was born into an era of moral change. But he never questioned the religion of his youth. Greek religion was based on the performance of certain rites – chiefly sacrifice, prayer and libation – not on a creed. The gods were ever-present, potent forces who could and did influence one's life in all things, great and small. It followed that your prime duty was to try to win the gods' favour for yourself, your friends and family, and your community. Xenophon's very first instruction to a would-be Cavalry Commander (a high military office in Athens) is this:

> Before all else, you should offer up a sacrifice and ask the gods to
> ensure that the way in which you conduct your command – your
> thoughts, words and deeds – not only may afford them particular
> pleasure, but also may be particularly effective in bringing
> yourself, your friends and your state alliances, honour and general
> benefit. Once you have secured the favour of the gods, you next
> have to recruit horsemen . . .

Xenophon was blessed with the fortunate ability to believe that if the gods did not answer your prayers, or did not do so immediately, they had some reason for not doing so, and that if they did answer them, that only demonstrated their magnanimous nature. Most Greeks held that even though the gods were not entirely reasonable (they both were and were not like human beings), you still had to act as if they were; Xenophon, by slight contrast, believed in the ultimate comprehensibility of divine will. The gods, he thought, were essentially benign – for instance, they had created the world and all its contents for the good of humankind – and one aspect of their benevolence was that they chose to communicate with mortal men.

The way men in their turn uncovered and tried to decipher these often enigmatic messages was divination. For all that its results could be ambiguous, Xenophon placed enormous trust in divination. At one point towards the end of the retreat from Babylonia, when the remaining Cyreans had reached Bithynia, the men were critically short of food: it was imperative, you would have thought, that they either abandoned the place to find fresh pastures, or at least left their defences and raided nearby villages. Yet in the face of near mutiny, Xenophon showed an almost Spartan obsession with the niceties of religion and refused day after day to let the troops make a sortie, because the omens from repeated sacrifices showed that the gods were opposed to their departure.

There is something odd about this particular case. On the battlefield or out on campaign, responsibility lay with the commanding officer. The diviners could read the entrails and make stronger or weaker suggestions, but it was ultimately up to the general to decide whether to go along with them. Dreams were one of the more common ways in which the gods communicated with mortal men, and so we may compare the ominous dream Xenophon had that prompted his change of role from passive observer to active participant in the Cyreans' affairs, until finally he became their leader:

> Xenophon was as agitated as everyone else and found sleep impossible. When at last he did fall briefly asleep, he had a dream, in which thunder rumbled and lightning struck his family home and brilliantly illuminated it all. He woke up terrified. From one point of view, he was inclined to put a positive interpretation on the dream, since a great light from Zeus had appeared in the midst of trouble and danger; but from another point of view, he found it alarming, because he assumed that the dream had been sent by Zeus the King, and the fact that in the dream the fire had cast its light all around suggested that he might not be able to escape from the king's territory, but might be hemmed in on all sides by various difficulties.
>
> But the true meaning of a vision such as this can be judged by the events which followed the dream. What happened was, first, that as soon as he woke up he fell to thinking: 'Why am I lying here? The night is passing and at dawn the enemy will probably arrive. If we fall into the king's hands, we'll inevitably die

inglorious deaths, after witnessing all the most ghastly scenes one could possibly imagine and suffering the full range of the most gruesome tortures. Yet no one is showing the slightest interest in defence or doing anything practical about it; we're just lying here as if we were in a position to take it easy. From what other city do I expect a general to come and organize things? Why am I waiting? How old do I have to be? I won't get any older at all if I just surrender to the enemy today.'

Xenophon clearly chose, for human reasons, to give an ambiguous dream an optimistic interpretation. Where the sacrifices at Calpe Harbour in Bithynia are concerned, it is hard to believe that eight sacrifices in a row produced such unambiguous warnings – misshaped, diseased or even missing organs, flames that swirled in a menacing fashion, too much or too little blood – that the diviners would have absolutely insisted on the troops' staying put. There must have been points at which they told Xenophon, 'Well, it doesn't look too good, but you might be able to risk it.' But he never led the men out.

When he came to commit the story to writing, he chose to make his firm refusal an example of good leadership: a good general always obeys the gods. The pages of Xenophon's writings are littered not just with traditional religious advice and with pious heroes, but also, somewhat more distastefully, with 'I told you so' examples of how things go wrong for people who ignore the gods. In the case just mentioned, one of Xenophon's fellow commanders among the Cyreans, a man for whom Xenophon shows nothing but contempt, ignored the omens and, in search of popularity, took 2,000 men out on a foraging expedition: a quarter of them never returned and Xenophon's men were faced a few days later, when the gods had at last given permission for a sortie, with the gruesome task of burying their comrades' decomposing bodies.

Xenophon was always a practical man, and his religion too was oriented towards results. It was not just that the gods were the givers of good things, so that if one behaved correctly towards them one would receive good things. More subtly, throughout *The Expedition of Cyrus*, he stresses how religious observance welds the army into a unity and increases morale. The men regularly chant a paean to Apollo before battle; they celebrate their (apparent) safety with games in honour of the gods; they are unanimous in agreeing to dedicate a portion of the spoils to the gods; and after the action of a few men has brought collective guilt down on the army as a whole they agree to a mass purification. These acts (and other examples could be given) are moments of joy in otherwise dark, dangerous and confusing conditions. Surrounded in his youth by instability, Xenophon clung to the one thing that appeared to offer a secure foundation. There is a sadness reflected in his work, a nostalgia for the values of a bygone era.

Xenophon and Socrates

Xenophon's childhood education was no more than barely adequate, and some time in the 400s, in keeping with the new mood in Athens late in the fifth century, he attached himself to the circle of mostly privileged, mostly young men who felt themselves to be followers of Socrates. The anecdotal tradition retains a very nice story, consonant with conversion stories throughout the ages, of Xenophon's first encounter with Socrates. Xenophon was walking down one of the narrow streets of Athens, and Socrates blocked his way, engaged him in conversation and asked him where various mundane commodities could be acquired in Athens. Xenophon politely answered each of the older man's questions. Finally Socrates asked, 'And where can one get goodness?' When young Xenophon looked puzzled, Socrates said: 'Follow me, and find out.'

One of the chief respects in which Socrates differed from his Sophist cousins (as far as we can tell from the seriously biased writings of Socrates's followers) is that, although he too taught his followers to question tradition, he went further than they did in the attempt to place morality on a new, rational foundation. His thinking was that it is only by uncovering basic principles that morality can be rebuilt after a period of the sort of crisis that Athens faced at the end of the fifth century. Above all, Xenophon was quick to learn from Socrates the ideal of self-sufficiency built on self-discipline, not least because he could readily harmonize such a concept of virtue with the Spartan values he was more and more coming to admire. And so all his heroes, at least as refracted through his writings, are characterized by this ideal. Many of Socrates's followers had or were suspected of pro-Spartan inclinations. The comic dramatist Aristophanes described them as hippies: 'In those days everyone was mad about Sparta: they grew their hair long, starved themselves, never washed, Socratized.' Hair worn long in the Spartan fashion became in Athens the characteristic fashion of the social class to which Xenophon belonged. In fact, though, the link between Socrates and Sparta was tenuous: he never encouraged his followers to approve of the enemy's culture or politics, but he had the misfortune to attract members of the wealthy upper class who were precisely those who felt least satisfied with Athenian democratic institutions and looked with some envy upon the less egalitarian, more structured set-up in Sparta. Their minds were apt at translating into mundane political terms any philosophy that stressed the importance of discipline.

In 399, in one of the most infamous trials of world history, one of Socrates's three prosecutors was a prominent democrat: there was undoubtedly a political subtext to the trial, which was preceded by a wave of politically inspired pamphlets denouncing the philosopher. Only fifty or so years later the Athenian orator Aeschines could say bluntly that the Athenians put Socrates to death because he had been the teacher of the bloody oligarch Critias.

Socrates himself wrote nothing, and because of the nature of his approach to philosophical and political issues – largely through raising questions rather than answering them definitively – it is hard to pin down his positions. But he certainly questioned the lack of professionalism of Athenian democratic politics, especially its use of the lottery, rather than consideration of ability, in the selection of officers. The legal system, with its mass juries, lack of judges and advocates, timed speeches and vaguely worded laws, was also flawed, and at one point Plato gives his Socrates a nicely ironic *mot*: if he were ever taken to court, he says, 'My trial would resemble the prosecution of a doctor by a manufacturer of sweets before a jury of young children.' Socrates thought, however, that while Athenian democracy could be improved, it was better than most constitutions; if he did not criticize Spartan society, that was because he lived in Athens and was concerned to improve his fellow citizens. But in keeping with the bipolar mentality of the times, some of his enemies read his criticism of Athens as approval of Sparta. The trouble was that some of his friends read it the same way.

Socrates was charged with not recognizing the gods of the state, with introducing new gods, and with corrupting the younger generation of Athens. Even apart from the religious issues mentioned in the indictment, there was a further religious subtext to the trial.

Traditional societies such as fifth-century Athens, in which religion permeates civic life, are notoriously paranoid about failure to conform. Socrates was not a conformist. The corollary of the traditional belief that a pious society will prosper is that a state with a significant number of impious individuals might not prosper. Athens had just lost a disastrous war; Socrates was the chief scapegoat. His trial was a response not just to his specific friendships with notorious anti-democrats such as Critias and Alcibiades, but to the traumas of recent Athenian history. Socrates was felt to personify the moral rot that had undermined the Athenian way of life. Aristophanes had portrayed him exactly this way twenty-four years earlier, in his comic masterpiece *Clouds*.

The trial of Socrates was a cardinal moment. Before long, none of the charges would have made much sense. Greek religion had always been open-minded about new gods – after all, even the familiar gods were ultimately unknowable, and came with different titles and different cults – and soon, under the influence of mercenaries returning from abroad, and then of Hellenistic cosmopolitanism, the state began to sanction the wholesale introduction of foreign gods; and the disintegration of values meant that it was not only the younger generation that had been 'corrupted' by new ideas.

The central issue of Socrates's trial was the old conflict between the individual and the state. It was widely known that Socrates received communications directly from the gods, and although many Athenians might have been happy to accept the sacredness of the experience, the trouble was that Socrates's link to the divine was not publicly accessible. Whatever god or gods he was in touch with (Socrates would have said Apollo) were not available for public worship or communication, could not be influenced by the usual means (prayer, sacrifice and offerings), and showed no interest in the welfare of anyone but Socrates and his immediate circle. At the time of his trial, individualism was still deeply suspect, on both religious and political grounds, but within thirty or forty years private and personal forms of worship had become far more acceptable. Socrates was not only a transitional figure himself, but passed this on to his followers, including Xenophon, who came to see the army's experiences during the retreat from Babylonia as reflecting a general retreat from the supposed certainties of the fifth century to the relativism of the fourth.

Xenophon Leaves Athens

The instability of Xenophon's upbringing bore dramatic fruit in his momentous decision, aged twenty-seven or so, to leave Athens and accompany his Boeotian guest-friend Proxenus, from oligarchic Thebes, on his journey east with Cyrus. 'Guest-friendship' translates the Greek *xenia*, a kind of hereditary, ritualized friendship between aristocrats from different communities. Xenophon consulted Socrates, his guru and his mentor, about the plan:

> Socrates thought that friendship with Cyrus might well be actionable in the eyes of the Athenian authorities, because Cyrus was widely believed to have wholeheartedly supported the Spartans in their military operations against the Athenians, and he advised Xenophon to go to Delphi and consult the god about whether or not he should go. Xenophon went and asked Apollo which of the gods should receive his sacrifices and prayers to ensure that the journey he had in mind would go honourably and well and to guarantee a safe return after a successfully completed endeavour, and in his response Apollo named the gods to whom he should

Overlooking the sea of olives from the heights of sacred Delphi, where Xenophon consulted the oracle before setting out to join Cyrus's expedition.

sacrifice. Back in Athens, Xenophon reported the oracle's response to Socrates, who told him off for having failed to ask the preliminary question whether it would be better for him to go or to stay – for having already decided that he was going to go, and then asking Apollo how to ensure a successful journey. 'However,' Socrates said, 'since that was the question you put to the god, you had better carry out all his instructions.' So once Xenophon had sacrificed as instructed to the gods named by Apollo he set sail and caught up with Proxenus and Cyrus in Sardis just as they were about to set off inland.

This story tells us a lot about Xenophon's character at the time: he was restless and optimistic enough to disobey even as august an authority figure as Socrates. He was a wilful young man, but underlying his disobedience lay a correct intuition. Readers of *The Expedition of Cyrus* see him mature in the course of the expedition, as he discovered, with the pleasure that always accompanies the emergence of competence, his native courage and capacity for command. As he himself says, by the end of the expedition he had become such a hardened soldier that he had gained in confidence and courage – and could hold his wine better! He had stumbled, more or less by accident, upon a role that disconnected him from his own and others' expectations, and led him into a way of life that was quite different from anything he had experienced in Athens.

There was certainly another factor contributing to his restlessness in 401: he was disillusioned with the state of Athenian society. Although there were no political parties as such, the politics of all the Greek states were largely dictated by two opposing factions. There were those who favoured limiting political power, and even the franchise, to a favoured few, defined by the value of their property or their income; and there were those who favoured some form of democracy, of which the Athenian constitution was the most radical example. Whatever the slogans, these were the true underlying issues of the Peloponnesian War: the Spartans tended to support oligarchy and to impose it on those states under their control; the Athenians tended to support democracy and to ensure that their allies throughout the empire were governed by friends of democracy.

In theory, the renewed Athenian democracy of 403 was conciliatory: politicians of all stripes mouthed the words about healing the factional wounds that had torn the city apart immediately after the end of the war, when for a few months a vicious, oligarchic junta, soon to be known as the Thirty Tyrants, had employed the timeless tactics of terror under the pretext of restoring stability to the city. The leader of the junta was Socrates's friend Critias, and even though Critias was killed in the civil war that followed the welcome uprising, the oligarchs remained a menace until 401 from their stronghold in the town of Eleusis, just 35 kilometres north-west of Athens. In practice, then, the old divisions remained, and there were plenty – Xenophon included – who thought that democracy was a mess. The assembled people were fickle and easily led by unscrupulous demagogues (there were notorious cases to support this line of argument); the lottery did not allow for expertise or intelligence, but favoured the average; democracy was supported by an unsatisfactory legal system and encouraged a society in which everything and anything was permissible; democracy was undermining the traditions that had made the city great; democracy had taken the city into a disastrous war.

In addition, there were financial issues: although everyone suffered in war, the poorer classes, whose interests were best represented by a democracy, had more to gain and less to lose by victory and so tended to be more belligerent than their better-off fellows, whose income plummeted in times of war just as their expenditure shot up as a result of war taxes. In short, there were many who felt it was time for power to be returned to those few men who, by long-conditioned training within the right families, were the city's natural leaders. Later scholars were wrong to ascribe to Xenophon the *Constitution of Athens*, which has been preserved among his works and was written in the last quarter of the fifth century, but it contains sentiments he would have endorsed:

> The contrast between aristocracy and democracy is universal. It is based on the fact that intemperance and injustice are more or less unknown in the best men, who have the highest degree of concern for decency, whereas ignorance and unruliness and dishonesty are in the highest degree qualities of the masses, who are tempted towards immoral conduct by their poverty.

Nor was Xenophon the only Athenian of the well-to-do cavalry class to leave his native city and join Cyrus. There were several Athenian officers in Cyrus's army, and army ranks reflected social status at home, so it is likely that these Athenians were well off, the kind of men to find themselves at odds with democracy. They left either, like Xenophon, out of dissatisfaction with the state of affairs at home, or because their families had been ruined or impoverished by warmongering democratic politics, or because they had been banished for their political views. Xenophon's friend Lycius, the commander of the small cavalry squadron hastily cobbled together after Cunaxa to counter the threat posed by the mobile troops of the enemy, is a good example. Lycius's father had worked closely with the oligarchs who briefly ruled Athens in 411, after the first of Athens's two oligarchic coups, and Lycius sympathized with his father's views enough to defend him in court in 410 (if the anonymous author of the defence speech 'For Polystratus', mistakenly preserved among the speeches of the eminent Athenian orator Lysias, is indeed our Lycius). He was Xenophon's political twin; they were 'partners in prejudice', as Robin Lane Fox has put it.

It is quite likely that Xenophon and Lycius became acquainted, if they did not know each other before, as members of the cavalry unit that helped to police Athens during the rule of the Thirty Tyrants of 404–403. Xenophon's narrative of these events in his main historical work *Hellenica* is redolent of first-hand experience, and he displays more knowledge of the machinations of the Thirty than he does of their opponents. However, the brutality of the oligarchs alienated him as thoroughly as the inefficiency of the democracy: ideologically, he had no home in Athens, and this is why he seized the opportunity for adventure in the east.

Banishment

The critical moment of Xenophon's relationship with his native city came with the city's unexpected decree of banishment. Though the date of the decree cannot now be determined with as much certainty as one would like, it happened while he was away from Athens in the 390s, still serving abroad as a mercenary general. He mentions it in *The Expedition of Cyrus* in a typically understated, unemotional, third-person passage: 'Meanwhile, Xenophon stayed away and made no secret of the fact that he was getting ready to go home – for there was no sign yet in Athens of any proposal that he should be officially banished.' For all his impassivity, however, it is not reading too deeply between the lines to find a sense of shock, and there is a poignant undercurrent in that, even at the time of writing *The Expedition of Cyrus*, about thirty years later than the actual events, he still considered Athens to be 'home' – a home from which he had long been debarred.

Exile was a common punishment in ancient Greece for crimes against the state. There were two main reasons for Xenophon's banishment; either of them could have been decisive, or they might both have contributed to the disfavour in which he was held in the city of his birth. First, Socrates might have hit the nail on the head: joining the expedition of Cyrus might in itself have been enough to turn the Athenian authorities against Xenophon. Cyrus had spent the last few years of the Peloponnesian War in Asia Minor, with the job of supporting the Spartan war effort – a task at which he succeeded admirably. There was considerable bitterness in Athens about Persia in general and Cyrus in particular.

Second, the early 390s was a time of fervent, renewed democracy in Athens. There was in those days no middle ground between oligarchy and democracy, just as in 1930s' Europe politics became polarized between communism and fascism. The Thirty Tyrants had been imposed on Athens, and aided and abetted by Sparta. Throughout his life Xenophon showed distinct pro-Spartan leanings, not just in the subjects he chose to write about (especially his *Spartan Society*, with its praise for the stability of the constitution there), but also in his expressed admiration for Theramenes, one of the Athenian oligarchs (though more moderate, or slippery, than some), and in the wide vein of snobbery that lay just below the surface of his writings. Xenophon believed that the most able men should have power – but also that the most able men were bound to be those who had been groomed for generations to wield power. He was even at some point made the Spartan *proxenos*, a position that allowed him to represent Spartan interests in Athens, but was no more than an honorary position in his case, since exile prevented him from taking it up. He could have been exiled, then, because he preferred the way of life and the politics of Athens's enemy; his association with Socrates would have done little to lift the cloud of such suspicion.

If Xenophon was exiled earlier rather than later – immediately following the retreat of the Cyreans from Baghdad to Byzantium – the first of these two reasons is more plausible than the second, because in

399 Athens was still officially allied with Sparta, so Xenophon could not overtly have been banished for his pro-Spartan inclinations. But 394 is another good possibility, preferred by some scholars: the outbreak of hostilities against Sparta in 395 (in what came to be called the Corinthian War) encouraged the Athenian authorities in a desire to placate the Persian king and satraps, who needed little encouragement to resume their role as power-brokers and paymasters of wars between mainland Greeks.

These were favourable conditions for Xenophon's exile: by then he had spent years fighting for and alongside Spartans, and he had of course participated in an invasion of Persia. The final straw for the Athenian authorities would have been Xenophon's return from Asia with the Spartan king Agesilaus and his presence, if not his actual participation, on the Spartan side at the battle of Coronea in 394, where the Spartans and their allies beat the army of a confederacy that included Athens. In addition, there was at the time widespread anger at the cavalrymen in general, as a social class, on the possibly genuine ground that they had not performed as well as they might in the two great battles fought in 394 against the Spartans – Nemea River and Coronea. There was even talk that they had held back at Coronea because there were Athenians of their class on the other side: not only Xenophon, but other remnants of the Cyreans (including Lycius, if he was still alive) and of a force of 300 Athenian cavalrymen who in 399 had been sent to Asia by the restored Athenian democracy to fight for the Spartans, as a punishment for their oligarchic politics.

A relatively neglected piece of evidence to my mind just tilts the scales towards the later date for Xenophon's banishment. At one point in *The Expedition of Cyrus*, he tells us that, after the Cyreans' booty had been sold at Cerasus and he had received his share of the cash, he dedicated some of it to Apollo. The offering, perhaps a statuette, that he commissioned with the money was inscribed with his own name and that of his friend Proxenus, and then set up in the Athenian Treasury at Apollo's most important centre, Delphi. Since it is impossible to imagine that he could have done this unless he was either an Athenian citizen still, or at least in good standing in Athens, it becomes critical to ask when this dedication was made. Assuming that he saw to it himself, rather than using intermediaries, the earliest he could have visited Delphi was in 394, since he was abroad until then. This rules out the possibility that Xenophon had been banished and was already out of favour in Athens earlier in the 390s. We know that Agesilaus visited Delphi in 394, shortly after the battle of Coronea. Perhaps Xenophon accompanied him, and managed to squeeze the dedication in just before the Athenians passed the decree of banishment.

Whatever the precise date of the decree, and however surprised Xenophon may have been at the time, with hindsight there is an aura of inevitability about it. Xenophon felt himself to be out of place in Athens; hence his restlessness. Although he continued to regard the city of his birth as his home – just as any of us feel a strong attachment for those places, usually only one or two in a lifetime, where we have stayed long enough for fusion to occur – and although he must have felt upset, he probably did not feel too badly displaced, because he was already displaced. His father was dead (we may assume, though we lack concrete evidence, on the basis that the average life expectancy for an ancient Athenian male was thirty-five years) and he had not yet started his own family; Socrates had been executed in 399, and there is no sign that Xenophon had any close friends remaining in the city. And so banishment did little more than put a seal upon a sequence of events that was already in motion, and that had already committed Xenophon to spending the prime of his life as a wandering adventurer, a soldier of fortune.

CHAPTER 4

The Intrigues of Cyrus

The removal of the immediate Persian threat in 479 encouraged Greeks to see one another as kin, as friends united against the common enemy. Under the dual leadership of Athens and Sparta, they could lay aside their petty squabbles, keep the sea free of pirates and Persians, and share in a new prosperity. But this was wishful thinking. The Spartan regent Pausanias, in charge of land operations against the Persians in Asia Minor, was an arrogant, unlikeable man, and he made the mistake of appearing too familiar with his supposed enemies. The rumours spread thick and fast. They said that he had contracted to marry the daughter of a Persian satrap, that he had agreed to abandon Asia Minor to the Persians, that he had 'gone native' and had been promised the satrapy of the Greek mainland once the Persians achieved their goal of conquest. By 477 leadership of the Greeks against Persia had devolved on to the Athenians alone.

Over the next thirty years, the Athenians led an aggressive coalition of, chiefly, Aegean and Asiatic Greek states in an offensive and defensive alliance against Persia. At its peak the league, which came to differ only in name from an Athenian empire, boasted over 170 states. With their coffers overflowing with allied tribute, most of which helped the Athenians to maintain a navy (at any rate, until they chose to spend it also on glorifying their city with monumental buildings such as the Propylaea and the Parthenon on the Acropolis), the Athenians, under the command of Cimon the son of Miltiades, achieved some notable successes. The northern Aegean was cleared of Persians, who were also driven back from Caria and Lycia, and in the early 460s the Persian fleet was wiped out and the land army routed at the mouth of the river Eurymedon in Pamphylia.

Campaigns in Cyprus, however, were inconclusive, and Athenian support for a rebellion in Egypt in the 450s cost them an entire fleet. Disaster was averted only because the Spartans were dissuaded by their Peloponnesian allies from taking up a Persian offer to finance an attack on Athens in its weakened state. The Peloponnesians, lacking

A Greek hoplite (a Spartan, to judge by his long hair) dispatches a Persian archer on a vase from the middle of the fifth century. The Persian is wearing trousers, which the Greeks considered effeminate.

an effective fleet, appreciated that the continued protection of the Aegean was best left to the Athenians, and so by 449 the Athenians had worked themselves into a position to negotiate a favourable treaty with Artaxerxes I, Xerxes's youngest son, who had been placed on the throne as a teenager in 465 after the murder of his father and his brothers.

This peace, named the Peace of Callias after the chief Athenian negotiator (one of a number of Greeks who became experienced envoys to Persia), did not dissolve tension between the two sides, nor put an end to occasional skirmishes and threats. The most serious incident came when Pissuthnes, satrap of Sparda and the king's cousin, loaned his (Greek) mercenaries to the islanders of Samos, during their attempt to secede from the Athenian empire in 440. By the terms of the treaty, the Athenians agreed to cease military operations in the eastern Mediterranean and, in return for retaining undisputed control over Egypt and Cyprus, Artaxerxes agreed not to venture west of Pamphylia. Though they necessarily had to maintain relations with the local satraps, and with Persian grandees who had been given estates in the area, the Asiatic Greeks no longer feared revival of their status as tributary subjects of Persia – but they had replaced it with membership of the Athenian empire.

The long-standing rivalry between Athens and Sparta finally erupted into full-scale war in 431. Each side had such extensive alliances that almost the entire Greek world was involved, including Sicily and southern Italy. During the first part of the war – the Peloponnesian War, as it has come to be known – the Persians largely watched gleefully from the sidelines, but only partly out of honour for their treaty with Athens: they were also distracted by rebellions within the empire. Sparta had military superiority on land, but Athens ruled the sea from an impregnable base and controlled a large empire. But the Athenians had a critical weakness: they were heavily reliant on grain getting through to them from the entrepôts and colonies of the northern Black Sea. The Spartans' best hope lay in finding a way to deprive their enemy of this resource – but for this they needed a navy. Ancient navies, however, were incredibly expensive to maintain, and the Spartan alliance, which never had surplus money or men, was facing financial ruin thanks to the war. They needed Persian cash.

Early in 424, the Athenians (who had a good track record at this kind of counter-intelligence) intercepted a messenger carrying a letter from the king to Sparta. The Athenians had the letter translated and found that the king was asking the Spartans to make up their collective minds: no two of all the Spartan agents he had seen, complained Artaxerxes, offered or announced the same policy. Although not expressly stated, the underlying question was this: in return for Persian help against the Athenians, were they, or were they not, prepared to sacrifice the Greek cities of Asia Minor, still coveted by successive Persian kings? Before long it was clear that they were. The Spartans had gone to war with Athens, they claimed, in order to free the Greek cities from imperialism, and yet, in the vague terms of an early draft of the agreement they would soon enter into with the Persians, 'All the territory and all the cities held now by the king or held in the past by the forefathers of the king shall belong to the king.'

Faced, then, with the one true threat against their superiority in the war and with the knowledge that the Spartans had been negotiating for some time with the Persians, the Athenians hastened to renew the Peace of Callias with the new king after the death of Artaxerxes I later in 424. Following several months of the usual intrigues and feuds (including the 45-day reign of Artaxerxes's only legitimate son as Xerxes II, before he was murdered), one of his sons by a secondary, non-Persian wife secured the imperial throne as Darius II, and retained it by force of arms and with the help of the judicious assassinations of his courtiers and their families. But war makes politicians fickle, and before long the Athenians made two bad mistakes – displaying, as an eminent Athenian politician later put it, 'our usual bad habit of constantly abandoning stronger friends and siding with the weaker ones'.

First, they violated the treaty with Persia. When Pissuthnes and his son Amorges tried to win independence from the Persian empire in 415, the Athenians sent help, and the unsurprising consequence of this was that the Persians considered the treaty null and void. Tissaphernes, a member of a great Persian family that owned substantial estates in Caria and had a long familiarity with Asia Minor, was sent out to open negotiations with the Spartans, to bring the Asiatic Greek cities back into the empire, and to deal with Pissuthnes. This last task was achieved with relative ease, once Tissaphernes had bribed the Athenian commander of the satrap's mercenaries to change sides; Amorges fought on ineffectually for a while from a base in Caria.

Second, some Sicilian cities sent a plea for help in resisting further Syracusan expansion on the island, and the Athenians hugely overstretched and overcommitted themselves by sending a vast armada west in 415. The size of the Athenian response showed that in fact they wanted to wrest control of Sicily from Syracuse – they were beginning to despair of winning the war in the eastern Mediterranean – but the long and savage campaign came to an end in 413 with the virtual annihilation of the Athenian army, and the loss of the entire fleet. The Spartans would never have a better chance to challenge Athenian mastery of the Aegean.

Not unnaturally, since the Persians could now see that the Athenians were not just a hostile force, but soon would be a spent one, within a few months a trained Phoenician fleet was hovering off the southern coast of Turkey. In the event, however, this fleet was ordered back because of trouble in Egypt, and the Great King was compelled by instability elsewhere in the empire to leave his two main western satraps to get on with the job. But Persian effectiveness was blunted by rivalry between Tissaphernes (now satrap of Sparda in Pissuthnes's place) and Pharnabazus II, who had become satrap of Phrygia in 414.

The post had by then been in his family for ninety years, despite the fact that even such hereditary succession was not automatic but needed the king's approval.

Both Tissaphernes and Pharnabazus tried to persuade the Spartans that the Athenian weak underbelly lay in their territory. Pharnabazus argued that the Athenians depended critically on their grain ships getting through the Hellespont, but Tissaphernes prevailed by reminding the Spartans of the propaganda value of demonstrating a willingness to fulfil their old promise – now little more than a slogan – to liberate the Greek cities from Athenian imperial rule. So the Spartans began with the cities and islands of the Asia Minor coast, and many of them, long disaffected with Athenian rule, defected more or less willingly.

In addition to the loss of manpower in Sicily and the loss of unquestioned control of the sea for the first time in the war, every state that withdrew from the empire exposed Athens's lack of cash. The vast resources with which they had started the war were exhausted. They needed money, and they needed to drive a wedge between the Persian satraps and Sparta. This was the moment for Alcibiades of Athens to put his enormous wealth, charm and talents to use. In 415 he had chosen exile rather than face a politically inspired trial at home, and had even treacherously lived in Sparta, where he had offered the enemy valuable military advice. By 412, however, he had made himself unpopular in Sparta – not least because it was widely known that he had had an affair with the wife of one of the two Spartan kings. In Sparta, it was possible in certain cases, for eugenic reasons, for men to father children on other men's wives – but all the parties concerned had to be Spartiates, true-blue Spartans. Alcibiades found it expedient to take refuge in the court of Tissaphernes.

Alcibiades chose a double game. Presenting himself to Tissaphernes as a supporter of Persia, he advised him to play Athens and Sparta off against each other, and pick up the pieces in the end. Tissaphernes was happy with this scheme, because the Spartans were showing distinct signs of wanting to go back on their agreements with Persia: despite explicit promises, they already had in mind the possibility of incorporating Athens's former dependencies into an empire of their own, rather than handing them back to Persia. At the same time, however, to the Athenians Alcibiades could portray his dealings with Tissaphernes as a way of stifling the relationship between Tissaphernes and the Spartans.

Only part of the plan worked. Alcibiades did succeed in ingratiating himself with the Athenian authorities, but as soon as Tissaphernes reduced the flow of cash to the Spartans, and indeed showed signs of being prepared to finance the Athenians, the Spartans abandoned Tissaphernes and put themselves in the hands of Pharnabazus. But Pharnabazus ultimately proved just as half-hearted and erratic in his support of the Spartans as Tissaphernes had been, and the war lurched onward indecisively, with Athens generally doing better than Sparta, until Darius became exasperated with the two satraps. In 407 he sent his son Cyrus, aged only sixteen, west to Asia Minor with special powers.

There were four satrapies in western Anatolia: semi-independent Cilicia, with its capital at Tarsus; Cappadocia, with its capital at Mazaca; Sparda, with its capital at Sardis; and Phrygia, with its capital at Gordium. These were the four largest territorial units, though they were subdivided for various administrative and tax purposes. Sparda, for instance, the wealthiest western satrapy, included a region incorporating both Lydia and Ionia, and another consisting of Lycia and Caria; Phrygia contained both Hellespontine Phrygia (also known as Dascyleum, after its picturesque main city on the south-eastern shore of Lake Dascylitis) and Greater Phrygia. The satrapies were not tidy geographical units that between them covered the entire region. In a pattern that was repeated here and there across the empire, large tracts of western Anatolia were never fully under the Persian king's control: the tribes of Mysia were more or less independent, and troublemakers included the Pisidians, the Lycaonians and the Bithynian Thracians. The plains were easier to dominate than the mountains.

Darius gave young Cyrus military and administrative oversight of the western satrapies of Sparda, Dascyleum and Cappadocia – a rare but not unprecedented post, and commensurate with Cyrus's royal standing – and instructed him to crush the hill-tribes of Pisidia and Mysia, to bring the war between Athens and Sparta to an end by supporting Sparta, and to ensure that the royal treasury would once again be swelled by Greek tribute. Tissaphernes and Pharnabazus were far from delighted at being sidelined and reduced from full satraps to governors of subordinate regions (Tissaphernes of Caria, Pharnabazus of Western Phrygia) and advisers to a mere boy. In any case, Cyrus ignored Tissaphernes's advice: the former satrap wanted the prince to continue Alcibiades's policy of playing the Spartans and the Athenians off against each other, but Cyrus preferred to stick to the original plan and see Athens brought low.

Cyrus may have earned himself some notable enemies, but he also gained an important friend. The chief Spartan commander in the region was now Lysander, a man as ruthless, as charismatic and as hungry for power as Cyrus himself. Lysander was pleasantly surprised to discover that underneath Cyrus's effete exterior, typical of a member of the Persian royal family, lay a young man who was not afraid of hard work. Cyrus's support for Lysander's endeavours in Asia Minor was both generous and effective: he had brought 500 talents west with him, and he extravagantly promised that if this princely sum were not enough, he would draw on his own resources, and even melt down his gold and silver throne.

Alcibiades had been restored to official command by the Athenians, but was again banished for his failure to live up to his promises: Tissaphernes was not in his pocket, and he was not doing as well on the military front as the Athenians expected. Within a year or two, hired assassins brought to an end his chequered life. By the end of 405 Lysander had devastated the Athenian fleet in the Hellespont and made it impossible for Athenian grain ships to get through. Before long people were dying of starvation on the streets of Athens, and Lysander was negotiating the humiliating terms of the city's surrender. The war would probably have ended in Sparta's favour before long anyway, but Cyrus could take credit for hastening the downfall of Athens.

Cyrus in Asia Minor

Cyrus was sent west in 407 with a near-impossible job. His father had ordered him to end the war between the Greeks in favour of the Spartans, so that his coffers could once again be swelled by the tribute of the wealthy Greek cities of Asia Minor. The first part was easy enough: with Persian money it did not take the Spartans long to finish off the crippled Athenians. But regaining the tribute was another matter, because it was clear that the Spartans were already casting covetous eyes on the Asiatic Greek cities and hoping simply to take over the Athenian imperial territories after the war. The Athenian empire had at least been established as a coalition to combat the Persians, but the prospective Spartan empire would be a travesty, established with no grander or more plausible motive than sheer imperialism, by a state that was prepared to betray the promises of freedom it had given to the Asiatic Greeks and the treaties it had made with the Persians.

Despite the speed and effectiveness of Cyrus's support for the Spartans, his loyalties lay entirely with himself. He was a pampered boy, brought up to believe in his own abilities and right to high command. His mother Parysatis encouraged him in all his ambitions and it was she who had helped him gain such a powerful position in Asia Minor despite his youth. She may well already have been looking ahead to a struggle over the succession when Darius died, and wanting to give her favourite son a power base; she may have been the one who seeded in his mind the notion that the Spartans would one day make useful allies. At any rate, Cyrus would carry out his father's wishes as long as it was in his own best interests to do so, and in the meantime he kept himself in readiness. He continued a personal regime of physical fitness, and began to win over powerful dynasts, both Persians and others, in the region.

On one critical occasion, however, Cyrus's youth got the better of him and came close to spoiling his campaign. By 406, not long after his arrival in the area, Spartan prospects looked good and Cyrus was making successful forays against various hill-tribes. Flushed with success, he assumed that his father would be too pleased to take much notice of anything else he got up to. When two close relatives, his father's cousins, appeared before him with their hands exposed from their long sleeves – an infringement of court protocol only in the presence of an actual king – out of pique or paranoia Cyrus took this to signify lack of respect, and he had them both put to death. Using a period of ill health as an excuse, Darius deprived Cyrus of his command and summoned him back to Susa, to remind him that he was not the king. For the long journey home, Cyrus took a bodyguard of 300 Greeks, commanded by Xenias of Arcadia, and Tissaphernes, the young prince's senior adviser, also went with him.

The rebuke Cyrus received from Darius rankled, and Parysatis continued to pour her brand of sweet poison into her favourite son's ear. She not only favoured her younger son, but loathed his brother's wife Stateira, whose mind was almost as cunning and as full of schemes to promote her husband as Parysatis's was to promote Cyrus. Things were moving fast, because by the time Cyrus reached his father's side, the aged king clearly had not long to live. Aware of the history of assassinations and satrapal unrest that plagued succession to the Persian throne, Darius's urgent message to Cyrus was that he should let his elder brother Arsaces reign in peace.

It took several more months for Darius to die, and he was finally laid to rest early in 404. Cyrus remained in Susa the whole time, listening to his mother and subtly testing the loyalty of the Persian nobles. Did he entertain wild hopes that his father might name him as his successor? It is unlikely, for all that the Greek historians liked to imagine the possibility, based on the specious argument that although Arsaces was the eldest, Cyrus was the first to be born after their father had ascended to the throne, and was therefore the eldest son of an actual king, born in the purple. Apart from illegitimate children, the offspring of Darius's liaisons with concubines, there were also two younger brothers, Ostanes and Oxathres, and a sister called Amestris; other siblings had died young.

So the eldest brother, Arsaces, came to the Persian throne as Artaxerxes II. The ceremonies, designed above all to ordain the new king as the gods' representative on earth, were long and complex. One of the many rites Artaxerxes had to perform to sanctify his accession was to present himself at Pasargadae, 600 kilometres south-east of Susa; Cyrus the Great, the founder of the Persian empire, had made his residence at Pasargadae and it was still an important religious centre. Here the new king had to be dressed in rough clothes and take part in a ritual in the temple of the goddess Anahita, involving the eating of fig cakes, the drinking of yoghurt and the chewing of turpentine wood, all symbolic of the simple life of the Persians' nomadic past. Artaxerxes's younger brother and most of the court accompanied him on his journey. Not long before the investiture was to begin, Tissaphernes brought to Artaxerxes one of the priests, who had an astonishing tale to tell. Cyrus, he said, was planning to hide himself in the sanctuary and kill Artaxerxes when an opportune moment presented itself. What made the story especially credible was that this priest was close to Cyrus; he had been his boyhood tutor.

This story is highly implausible: it is unlikely that Cyrus would have done his own dirty work, and committing fratricide in a sacred temple would hardly have been the way to win the hearts and minds of his putative future subjects. The tale is undoubtedly later propaganda, put about by Artaxerxes after Cyrus's failed coup, to tarnish his dead brother's memory. But the smoke was generated by the fire of Cyrus's ambition, which had long been smouldering and was now fanned into flames by Parysatis. Another grain of truth in the story is the likelihood that Tissaphernes spoke to Artaxerxes of his concerns about Cyrus's intentions, and that the tenuous friendship between Cyrus and Tissaphernes – which Cyrus saw as no more than the condescension of a superior towards a subordinate – had irretrievably broken down. Artaxerxes was tempted to keep his brother by his side in Susa. Cyrus's friends at court, assiduously cultivated over the last few years, melted into the background. Stateira joined her brother Tissaphernes in warning Artaxerxes about Cyrus. But Parysatis won: she persuaded Artaxerxes to let her favourite return to Asia Minor and resume his good work there with the Spartans.

The rivalry between Parysatis and Stateira formed one of the critical dynamics of the Persian court at the time. In a Persian king's court, senior women could be immensely powerful – and the two most senior women at any time were the king's mother and his wife, usually in that order. Parysatis's quarrel with Stateira was not just petty and personal, but political: Stateira's family, the Hydarnids, was immensely powerful and was becoming more so thanks to its close association with the ruling Achaemenid dynasty. Parysatis wanted to keep the Hydarnids down. The vendetta had begun a few years earlier, when Terituchmes, the Hydarnid satrap of Hyrcania, fell in love with his own sister (another sister, not Stateira) and tried to kill his wife, Amestris, the daughter of Darius and Parysatis, and sister to Arsaces/Artaxerxes and Cyrus. The plot (which was combined with an attempt at full-scale rebellion) was foiled; Terituchmes and many of his close relatives paid with their lives. To Parysatis's annoyance, two members of the family were spared: Tissaphernes, because of his great services to Persia, and Stateira, because she was married to the heir apparent. This may have been the point at which Parysatis gave up on Arsaces and made Cyrus the object of her vicarious ambitions.

Parysatis was a patient woman, and a few years later, in 400, she took her revenge on Stateira, coolly poisoning her at a dinner at which Artaxerxes too was present. Feigning politeness, Parysatis graciously cut up a small bird they had been served. The knife had been treated with poison, but only on one side of the blade. Parysatis took the unpoisoned portion of the bird and ate; Stateira confidently took the other half and died in agony. Parysatis's part in the murder was universally known, though unprovable, and she was banished to

Babylon, but only for a year or two. She was certainly back in court in time to oversee Tissaphernes's fall from grace in 395.

Planning for Rebellion

Having agreed that Cyrus could return west, Artaxerxes had to find a way to restrain him. He adopted the rather crude method of cutting his allowance. As supreme commander in the west, Cyrus was naturally owed allegiance by the Greek cities of Asia Minor, who channelled their tribute to the king through Cyrus's personal coffers. It was a common system in the Achaemenid empire for towns to be given in this way to powerful individuals, as a way both of rewarding someone and of avoiding the nuisance of taxing such towns centrally and then having to redistribute the appropriate portion of the revenues; for instance, Xenophon twice mentions occasions on which the Cyreans passed through land belonging to Parysatis. Artaxerxes, by royal decree, removed the Asiatic Greek cities from Cyrus's control and returned them to Tissaphernes's personal fiefdom, where they had been until Cyrus first appeared on the scene.

The exact status of the prosperous Asiatic Greek cities is unclear. They had been more or less contented members of the Athenian empire; then for a few years they were controlled by Sparta, and especially by the notorious 'decarchies' – juntas of ten men, who were usually loyal to Lysander himself – that Lysander imposed on them as he gained control of them between 407 and 405; then, a little later, the Spartan authorities saw sense and restored their right to choose their own governments. After the collapse of the Athenian empire, they paid tribute to Persia, and may have had an obligation to supply troops if called upon to do so, but that seems to have been more or less it, except that in order to ensure a steady supply of tribute and troops the Persian authorities liked to see their friends in power: relative subservience was the price of relative freedom.

Tribute-payment was, however, enough for Artaxerxes's purposes. Without this source of income, Cyrus would find it hard, if not impossible, to maintain his courts in Sardis and Celaenae, pay his Greek bodyguards, and in general act with the generosity expected of a royal satrap. Gift-giving underpinned Achaemenid society in a large number of ways: gifts conferred prestige on the recipient but simultaneously marked the donor as the higher authority. To deprive Cyrus of this ability was to humiliate and unman him. The personal animosity between the two brothers occasioned no surprise: a family history of intrigue and assassination had not taught them the virtues of brotherly love.

This was Artaxerxes's unsubtle but non-violent attempt to defuse his brother's aspirations. Cyrus was no fool, however; he knew that his light would remain dim unless he could get rid of his brother once and for all. If Parysatis were to die, he would lose his best advocate – and probably his life. He returned west determined never again to be in his brother's power, and committed to finding a way to rule in his place. Throughout the long journey back to Asia Minor from Susa, he was weighing up possible courses of action, goaded by a sense of injured pride. If he had not already done so, he now, in 404, began to put in motion his plans for fratricidal rebellion. Did Artaxerxes remain ignorant of what his brother was up to? Sifting through the anecdotes, we arrive at a picture of widening knowledge of Cyrus's plans, and of Artaxerxes's response.

The first story dates from late in 404. The most plausible of the confusing accounts of Alcibiades's assassination given by our sources is as follows. If it is a somewhat shabby tale, that is normal for events involving Alcibiades. Not long after Cyrus's return, Alcibiades got wind of the young prince's intentions, or at least his ambitions. Wanting to ingratiate himself with the new king by informing him of the threat posed by his brother, Alcibiades was preparing to travel east with the news. Pharnabazus, however, wanted to be the one to gain the king's gratitude for this information, and he was in any case being urged by the Spartan authorities to deal with the renegade Athenian, so he had his agents murder Alcibiades.

The second story is frustratingly undatable, but tells of a more severe response by Artaxerxes to his wayward brother. Perhaps it began in 403; perhaps it was a response to Pharnabazus's information. One of Cyrus's lieutenants in Sardis, from the start of his western command, had been a cousin called Orontas. Artaxerxes at some point ordered Orontas to occupy the almost unassailable citadel of Sardis and hold it against Cyrus. Artaxerxes clearly by then perceived his brother as a direct threat and was taking steps to curtail him. Cyrus besieged Orontas into submission, however, and Orontas once again swore loyalty to the young prince – only to take his men and join the unruly Mysians in raiding Cyrus's territory. Cyrus again defeated him,

and again Orontas rejoined Cyrus's fold; a third act of treachery, however, during the actual march east, was rewarded with a military tri-
bunal and execution. It may seem strange that Cyrus did not have
Orontas put to death on either of the earlier two occasions, but the
ancient Persians had the pleasing habit, instituted by Darius I, of letting a person's whole life count: if he had performed sufficient good
deeds in the past, they were taken to counterbalance his present bad
deeds. Cyrus himself probably benefited from this way of thinking
when he was restored to Asia Minor despite his evident antagonism
towards his brother.

Finally, the chief symbol of the enmity between Tissaphernes and
Cyrus became the Asiatic Greek cities. Although these cities had been
re-assigned to Tissaphernes, the largely oligarchic rulers preferred,
when Cyrus returned west in 404, to put themselves into Cyrus's
hands, suspecting that Tissaphernes would like to see the cities under
democratic government. All but Miletus refused to acknowledge
Tissaphernes as their master, and Miletus was the exception only
because Tissaphernes executed or expelled the aristocratic ringleaders
before they were able to act. The Milesian exiles found their way to
the court of Cyrus, who gave them men and *matériel* to besiege
Miletus and try to take it back from Tissaphernes's faction.

These hostilities fell short of open warfare between Cyrus and
Tissaphernes only by virtue of the fact that the fighting was taking
place between proxies. Artaxerxes was undoubtedly delighted by
Tissaphernes's resistance to Cyrus's annexation of the Asiatic Greek
cities: it was a way of keeping his brother too busy in Asia Minor to
turn his greedy attention eastward. Hostility between satraps was one
of the dynamics of the empire that successive kings exploited to their
advantage. Artaxerxes may have given Tissaphernes the explicit go-
ahead, or may just have known that he could rely on the satrap to
make life difficult for Cyrus.

In short, then, Cyrus's preparations were not unknown to the king;
he was never going to take his brother by surprise, and Artaxerxes had
plenty of time to muster an army at Ecbatana (still largely awaiting
excavation under modern Hamadan in north-west Iran), where
Persian rulers spent the summer in the relative cool, 2,000 metres
above sea level on the slopes of Mount Aurvant, whose snow-melt
streams made the location both charming and fertile. The best Cyrus
could do was keep his brother guessing and seize the chance presented

by an Egyptian rebellion to prevent Abrocomas from joining forces with Artaxerxes.

Preparations for War

Cyrus heated many irons in the fire and found clever ways to keep his brother's suspicions from erupting into the kind of armed response that would pose a more significant threat than those of Tissaphernes and Orontas. In this he was helped by the opportune rebellion in Egypt, which diverted the king's attention and a substantial part of his armed forces. It is tempting to see the hand of Cyrus even here: did he stir things up in Egypt? It would be in keeping with his character, and one of his closest associates in Asia Minor was the Egyptian Tamos (who found it expedient to take refuge in his native country after Cyrus's death), but the idea is sheer guesswork, and it is just as likely that, as they had done before, the Egyptian dynasts took advantage of the temporary instability created by the accession of a new king. They will play little further part in this story, but it is worth mentioning that this was by far their most successful rebellion: the Persian empire did not regain control of the wayward province for sixty years, and then only briefly, before rebellion broke out again.

Apart from this stroke of fortune, if that is what it was, Cyrus personally moved matters forward on a number of fronts. In the first place, he began a propaganda war against his brother. He needed as many high-ranking Persians as possible on his side, or at least uncommitted to his brother, not just because of their private armies and networks of allegiances, but in order to be in a position to consolidate his rule as quickly as possible after he had killed his brother. He made his brother out to be a weakling and a drunkard, who might run a splendid court but would ruin the empire – look what was already happening in Egypt – and thereby lose the Persian nobility its lands and privileges. Xenophon tamely agreed with this assessment of Artaxerxes. By contrast with his brother, Cyrus made himself out to be the chosen of the gods, and a man of vigour – a great hunter and warrior, schooled in the Persian virtues and capable of holding his drink. He made a point of cultivating his parks with his own hands. Xenophon was impressed with this because it showed that Cyrus was not too high and mighty to get his hands dirty, but there was more to it than that. In Persian belief, if the king's garden prospered the land as a whole would prosper; Cyrus was performing one of the many ritual acts of a Persian ruler, based on the Zoroastrian belief that the human race bears responsibility for this world.

In the second place, Cyrus opened negotiations with Sparta. The Spartans were indebted to Cyrus for his crucial support at the end of the Peloponnesian War, and in any case it was in their interest to help him. After all, in attempting to establish an empire for themselves, they were breaking treaties with Artaxerxes; although they were still nominally allies of the Persians, anyone with any sense could look ahead to a time not far in the future when escalating tension would erupt into armed conflict. Cyrus promised them a free hand among the Asiatic Greeks if they helped him defeat his brother. Whether or not he knew it, he may also have been helping them in another way. He took pains to employ mainly Peloponnesian soldiers. It is undoubtedly true that Peloponnesian troops were the best fighters, but it was also true that, after the Peloponnesian War, there were many armed and dangerous troops in the Peloponnese or abroad who could have been organized by a disaffected state or an ambitious individual such as Lysander (who had become something of a loose cannon) and have threatened Sparta itself. Ultimately, Spartan help came to Cyrus in two forms, active and passive. Actively, they at least connived at his employment of Clearchus, if they did not actually order Clearchus to join him, and they also sent further hoplites under Cheirisophus; passively, although they were officially allied to Persia, they did nothing to hinder Cyrus's attempt to overthrow the legitimate king. In the turmoil of the last years of the fifth century, no one, not even the god-fearing Spartans, could afford to preserve all the diplomatic niceties.

In the third place, having secured promises of military aid from local dynasts, and especially from Ariaeus, the governor of Hellespontine Phrygia, Cyrus set about raising a considerable force of Greek professional soldiers. It was not at all uncommon for western satraps to have small mercenary units at their disposal, but a substantial army such as Cyrus required would rapidly have raised suspicions. Hence Cyrus took pains to disguise what he was up to, and hence the bulk of the mercenaries whose services he bought were engaged abroad, outside his territories, so that he could plausibly maintain that they were nothing to do with him, or at least no threat to Asian affairs. He arranged things so that he could claim that all he was doing was continuing to fund Greek battles, just as he had during the Peloponnesian War, even though this time the beneficiaries were semi-independent mercenary commanders rather than generals appointed by states.

The Greek communities of the Chersonese had a history of suffering from raids by Thracian tribesmen; having carved out space in Thracian lands, they had been unable to arrive at a peaceful modus vivendi with their fierce neighbours. They could not afford on their own to arm and maintain a large enough force to defend themselves, but the Spartan Clearchus, a guest-friend of Cyrus, took command, perhaps in a bid for rulership of the region, and brought from Cyrus sufficient funds to raise and maintain a sizeable army.

A second army was held in readiness for Cyrus in Thessaly, where the old ruling aristocracy, accustomed to power by centuries of privilege, was threatened by the forces of democracy, or at least of change. The end of the Peloponnesian War brought such political instability to many parts of the Greek world, as old structures crumbled and revolutionaries rushed to fill the gaps. One of the threatened aristocrats was another guest-friend of Cyrus, called Aristippus of Larissa, whose value can be estimated by the fact that, though Cyrus supported Clearchus to the tune of 10,000 darics, he gave Aristippus around 24,000 (about 100 talents in ancient Greek terms, or roughly $25,000,000 today), so that he could maintain a mercenary force of 4,000 men. In theory, each of these armies had valuable work to do; in fact, both Clearchus and Aristippus were in Cyrus's debt and were expected to bring their forces when summoned. Cyrus had clearly been using the Greek institution of guest-friendship to establish a network of men on whom he could rely, though in the event Aristippus let him down. Cyrus spoke Greek, and had assumed more than a little Greek culture and more than a few of its customs.

As well as these two armies, Cyrus also attracted men such as Xenophon's guest-friend Proxenus of Thebes to raise further troops in mainland Greece. Many recruiters were involved, both amateur and professional; some recruited hundreds, some only a handful, but it all added up. This was not as time-consuming a task as might be expected: each recruiter worked locally, in his own native territory, and, just as Cyrus made use of his network of guest-friends, so recruiters made use of the various kinds of formal networks and kinship groups that underpinned Greek society; they had to undertake only a certain amount of travelling from village to village and town to town, tempting recruits with attractive terms of service. As in Greece today, men wanting work gathered in town centres when they heard of an opportunity for being hired – and there were many potential recruits after the end of the Peloponnesian War. The reason Cyrus gave Proxenus and the others for his request was that he was planning to crush Pisidia into full membership of the Persian empire.

In addition to these mercenaries, most of whom were employed and probably hired abroad, Cyrus also took advantage of his conflict with Tissaphernes to recruit more Greeks within Asia. Greeks had served as mercenaries in the east for a long time: Greek-speaking Cretans worked for King David of Israel as far back as the tenth century, and Greek mercenaries were the 'bronze men' who were sent by Gyges of Lydia to help Psammetichus I of Egypt around 660; these Greeks subsequently settled in Egypt and their successors served many kings. Further east, they worked for Nebuchadnezzar II of Babylon early in the sixth century (the fine Greek poet Alcaeus, from the island of Lesbos, wrote some lines welcoming his brother back from the campaign); Persian kings used them against rebels, and the rebels (such as Pactyas of Sardis in 546, and Megabyzus of Syria in the late 450s) used them against Persian kings. In the third quarter of the fifth century, Pissuthnes of Sparda surrounded himself with Greek soldiers, both while he was a loyal subject of Persia and when he and his son tried to secede from the empire. The British Museum's Nereid Monument, sculpted around 400 BCE in Lycia, portrays Greek mercenaries storming a town there. In short, Greek hoplites had demonstrated time and again in the east that they deserved the respect of any opponent, or of any future paymaster.

In Cyrus's time, there were certainly several thousand Greek mercenaries, especially from the poorest regions of the Peloponnese, already serving in Asia Minor, having chosen military service in the east as a lifelong career. Many were not available for hire, since they were already employed by people whose suspicions Cyrus had no desire to arouse. But hundreds more were waiting in Asia Minor for recruitment, surviving in the meantime on casual labour or banditry. So Cyrus ordered all the commanders of garrisons in cities under his control to hire as many fresh mercenaries as they could, on the pretext that they might be needed to defend the cities against attacks from Tissaphernes. He also hired more Greeks for the siege of Miletus, which was held against him by Tissaphernes's men. Xenias of Arcadia and Pasion of Megara were in command of all these Asia Minor mercenaries.

CHAPTER FIVE

The Army Musters

When the time came and Cyrus called on his generals-in-waiting to bring themselves and their hired soldiers to Asia Minor, he did not tell them all what he had in mind. Only the most senior commanders – perhaps Clearchus and Xenias, and Cheirisophus, once he arrived – knew from the start that he intended to go against his brother; all the others were fobbed off with tall stories about Mysians and Pisidians, or, more cunningly, were led to believe that at the most Cyrus was determined to fight Abrocomas or to escalate his conflict with Tissaphernes.

On the face of it, Clearchus was an unlikely confidant. Born around 450, he was a natural choice as the Spartan naval commander in the Propontis in the later stages of the Peloponnesian War, since (following in his father's footsteps) he was the *proxenos* of Byzantium, which is to say that he represented the city's concerns to the Spartan authorities. The Athenians put Byzantium under siege while Clearchus was in command of the city, and Clearchus so thoroughly alienated the people of Byzantium that they took the opportunity presented by his temporary absence in 408 to open their gates to the Athenians. The near-starving Byzantines had particularly resented the way he preferred his soldiers to civilians when it came to sharing out food and other increasingly scarce resources.

In 403, after the war, the Byzantines again appealed to the Spartan authorities for help: they were suffering from Thracian incursions, and their city was torn apart by civil strife. As part of their post-war policy of being seen to be the protectors and liberators of all Greeks everywhere, the Spartans sent Clearchus with an army to help, despite having fined him for his failure to hold the city in 408. After all, he already had experience and contacts in the area, where he had somewhat redeemed himself in the last years of the war. But Clearchus was not liberator material; he saw himself as another Pausanias, the maverick Spartan commander in the Propontis in the early 470s, who had also made Byzantium his headquarters. Clearchus's solution to the city's internal troubles was to kill the trouble-makers, appropriate their property for himself and his favourites, and try to set himself up as sole ruler of the city.

Naturally, the Spartan authorities recalled him, but he refused to disband his largely mercenary army and return home. The Spartans sent a force against him, and he fought his fellow countrymen before realizing that discretion was the better part of valour and crossing over to Asia Minor, where he took refuge with Cyrus. The Spartan authorities, meanwhile, banished him and sentenced him to death. But Clearchus had unfinished business with the Thracians. He was not overly concerned whether or not they made life difficult for the Greeks living in the area, but he did want to have another stab at getting hold of some of their fabled treasures (of the sort that recent archaeology has unearthed). This was the dubious venture for which Cyrus paid.

Or rather, what Cyrus paid for was Clearchus's expertise as a general. Xenophon has left us a thumbnail sketch of the man, which stresses, above all, Clearchus's warlike nature: he was as devoted to war, Xenophon tells us, as others are to their soulmates; he found personal relationships difficult and was truly happy only when facing mortal danger. While, in his dealings with his fellow generals, he usually looked for consensus before implementing any strategy, his treatment of his men was quite different: he possessed the admirable ability to weld his men into an obedient fighting unit, but the only way he managed to do this was by making them frightened of him – of his quick temper and random, brutal punishments. Spartan officers were notoriously harsh disciplinarians, but many of the mercenaries were little more than thugs, eager for blood and booty, and a harsh disciplinarian may have been just what was needed to keep them in line.

In Clearchus's case, however, Spartan harshness may have been compounded by a less controllable factor. Historian and Vietnam veteran Lawrence Tritle has suggested that he was a victim of post-traumatic stress disorder (PTSD). By the time of Cyrus's expedition, he was fifty years old: he had been on active service more or less continuously for over twenty years, and had seen and participated in more than his fair share of atrocities. A particular trigger for PTSD is seeing the death of someone close to you – close emotionally, or just physically close at the time. As a long-serving front-rank hoplite, Clearchus would have seen this on a number of occasions; the horror accumulates. One of the common symptoms of the delayed reaction to such appalling shocks is terror at the realization that the enemy is indeed trying to kill you, and a consequent desire for revenge – or just to kill whoever the enemy may be before they kill you. The character of such people changes, until they may even perform horrors such as the mutilation of enemy corpses – something the Cyreans certainly did, though not Clearchus in particular. PTSD victims become enamoured of violence, are constantly ready for it, seek it out, and expose themselves to it, sometimes in ways that can seem crazy to others. The adrenaline rush provides a kind of 'high' that simulates oblivion, so that it is only in the midst of violence that such people can forget the horrors they have witnessed and carried out. Clearchus's character, as summed up by Xenophon, fits this profile very well.

The ambitious Clearchus did not start out as the Greek commander most highly valued by Cyrus, but he rose ever higher in the prince's estimation as they journeyed east. The turning point occurred at Tarsus when Cyrus was faced with mutiny by many contingents of the mercenaries. Their anger was justified: they had been hired for a specific task – to defeat the Pisidians – but by the time they reached Tarsus they had already passed the Pisidians and it was clear that Cyrus was breaking their contract. Clearchus manipulated the men into staying with Cyrus by pretending to be on their side (as opposed to the other generals, who were alienating their men by ordering them to continue with Cyrus) and to be prepared to lead them back home. 'It will never be said of me,' he declaimed, 'that I led Greeks into barbarian lands and then betrayed those Greeks by preferring the friendship of the barbarians.'

Then, cynically undermining the democratic procedures of the army, he got stooges among the assembled troops to stress the dangers of incurring Cyrus's hostility. The ruse was successful, and the men agreed to carry on – as Clearchus had secretly reassured Cyrus they would. Not only that, but 2,000 of them left their original contingents and put themselves under Clearchus's command, making him effectively the most important of the mercenary commanders. Cyrus would have been lost without these Greeks, but Clearchus too would have been lost without them. His whole future was predicated on the success of Cyrus's campaign, since he had nothing to look forward to at home except trouble from the Spartan authorities.

To judge by what little we know of some of the other mercenary commanders in Cyrus's army, they were cut from the same self-serving cloth as Clearchus. Meno, in particular, receives an obituary from Xenophon that is so hostile as to be little more than a caricature of a venal villain. Meno was Aristippus's lieutenant (and probably his lover). Aristippus himself felt unable to respond to Cyrus's summons, and sent Meno with only a quarter of the 4,000 hoplites Cyrus's generosity had allowed him to raise (though he sent 500 peltasts too). Aristippus, unlike Clearchus, refused to abandon those he had been helping with Cyrus's mercenaries; he remained in Thessaly with the rest of the mercenaries, only to be massacred a few years later in a battle that appealed to the Greek love of the bizarre and macabre, because it was said that the crows of even southern Greece were attracted to feast on the distant battlefield.

Despite his youth – he was little more than twenty at the time – Meno was at first the senior Greek commander, originally destined to be in charge of the privileged right wing of the army. It was he who was chosen, a few weeks into the expedition, to escort Cyrus's lover, Queen Epyaxa of Cilicia, back home by a route that would bring him round behind Epyaxa's husband Syennesis (the throne-name at the time of all Cilician kings), and so help Syennesis make up his mind which side he was on. After Clearchus had insinuated himself into Cyrus's good books, Meno constantly curried favour with Cyrus and tried to regain pole position. He was helped in this by the fact that he became the lover of Cyrus's greatest ally, Ariaeus. But he spoiled his chances by sowing dissension among the Greeks, and by allowing his men to rape, pillage and plunder, not least as a way of keeping them utterly loyal to him and less inclined to attach themselves to Clearchus.

We know less about the other mercenary generals. Proxenus of Boeotia appears to have been a weak leader, concerned more to win the approval of his men than to keep order; Xenias and Pasion, despite their long association with Cyrus as his mercenary commanders in Asia Minor, deserted only a few weeks into the expedition, piqued when about half their contingent put itself under Clearchus's command. Most of the rest of the generals are little more than names, who put in brief appearances in the narratives of the historians who covered the Cyreans' march and campaign; they were the Arcadians Sophaenetus and Agias, and Socrates of Achaea. Another Arcadian, Cleanor of Orchomenus, took over the remnants of Xenias's and Pasion's units after they deserted. Finally, Cheirisophus of Sparta,

A Thracian horseman, of the kind employed until their desertion by the Cyreans, and a light-armed Thracian foot-soldier, carrying the crescented shield, the *pelta*, that gave these peltasts their name. The soldiers are wearing the fox-skin caps and long cloaks mentioned with jealous approval by Xenophon (*The Expedition of Cyrus* 7.4.4) as Thracian winter wear. The vase was made in Athens around the middle of the fifth century BCE.

whom circumstances would later raise to brief prominence, arrived later, when the Cyreans had almost reached Syria, sent by Sparta with 700 further hoplites.

Some of the company commanders (responsible for a *lokhos*, a tactical unit that among the Cyreans consisted for as long as possible of 100 men) had also been busy with recruitment. It was not unknown for men to raise a company and then offer it to prospective employers – as the homosexual Episthenes of Olynthus, one of the company commanders in Cyrus's army, once formed an entire company out of good-looking men. Some generals and company commanders owed their rank to experience and expertise, some to the fact that they brought troops with them, some to a combination of these factors. Xenophon says bluntly that most of the generals were inexperienced –

or at least he says that Clearchus became, in effect, the commander in chief, *primus inter pares*, because the other officers recognized that he was the only one with valid experience. In addition to mercenaries, some brought javelin-wielding peltasts as well, who came especially from Macedon and Thrace (areas which, lacking the political infrastructure, had not developed the hoplite strategies favoured by the southern city-states), but there were also 200 archers from Crete and 200 men from the island of Rhodes, who came to be employed as slingers. Then there were forty Thracian horsemen to supplement Cyrus's Paphlagonian cavalry.

The Character of Cyrus

What about their paymaster and commander-in-chief? Cyrus's youth tells us a lot about him. He was only sixteen when he was elevated to high command by his father, and still only twenty-two at the start of his fratricidal expedition (but then Alexander the Great was the same age when he set out to conquer the Persian empire); he had the arrogance of youth, enhanced by an upbringing that served only to encourage high ambition; he had that combination of intelligence and natural, princely charm that has proved elusive to more than a few members of royal families. Even the scars he bore from a hunting encounter with a bear only added to his aura of attractive manliness. In his portrait of Cyrus, Xenophon painted a picture that was too good to be true: Cyrus was unfailingly honest, adopted a zero-tolerance policy towards crime, loved hunting and was the best in his generation at this and all manly pursuits, won the loyalty of all who met him, was generous and thoughtful to his friends. He may have deceived his brother as to his true intentions, and manipulated both his Greek and non-Greek troops by disguising for as long as he could the true object of the expedition, but that did not count as a character flaw: all Greeks were agreed that deception in war was justified; deceiving the enemy is after all a large element of what is known more grandly as 'strategy'.

This idealized portrait needs a little qualification. For a start, Cyrus chose some unfortunate friends: Clearchus the would-be tyrant, Lysander with his policy of imposing dictatorial juntas on the Asiatic Greek cities, the oligarchs of Miletus. He seems also to have been less than straightforward in paying the Greek mercenaries. They were three months overdue in Tarsus, and Cyrus claimed to be able to pay them then only thanks to the generosity of Syennesis of Cilicia, whose wife Epyaxa brought funds; later he promised them a pay rise, without handing over any actual cash, yet he was in a position to make the extravagant gesture of rewarding an accurate prediction by Silanus of Ambracia, a diviner attached to the Greek army, with the enormous sum of 10 talents, the equivalent of six or seven days' pay for the entire Greek mercenary force. But Xenophon came to dislike Silanus intensely, and he would have been inclined to accept the most exaggerated sum he heard mentioned. Even though it was common practice for generals to keep back some money, as a hedge against resentment, it begins to look as though Cyrus did not have a proper war chest. But the irregular payment of troops was always a recurrent theme in Greek relations with Persian satraps.

Xenophon was convinced that Cyrus would have made an excellent king. This may be true, but we should not forget that Cyrus was planning fratricide, and was moved to rebellion simply because he was dissatisfied with his lot, even though his life was luxurious to a degree unimaginable by most people, and even though he already had authority over a vast region. This was more than mere ambition: this was pathological greed. Nor was his contempt for his brother justified: Artaxerxes II enjoyed the longest reign of any Achaemenid (404–359), survived the revolt of Evagoras of Cyprus in the 380s and that of several satraps more or less simultaneously in the 360s, and in general coped better than most with the problems of managing a vast and unruly empire.

There are also indications that Cyrus was not as widely loved and admired as Xenophon claims. He seems to have been less than entirely certain of his Greeks: Xenias's and Pasion's families were hostages; he felt capable of telling only a few of the generals about his plans; he constantly had to bribe the Greeks to stay; and he kept the purchasable provisions among his own troops, leading to rumours that he had hundreds of cartloads of spare food. He was uncertain about his non-Greek troops too. During the trial of Orontas, Cyrus prudently had 3,000 Greek mercenaries surround his tent, where the trial was being held, to prevent an uprising in Orontas's favour. Nor was Orontas the only high-ranking Persian who was prepared to turn traitor: a man called Megaphernes, a 'Royal Secretary', holder of one of the most powerful positions in court, was executed while the army was in Cappadocia. At another point during the eastward march, Meno and Clearchus and their respective contingents came terrifyingly close to fighting, and Cyrus stopped them only by warning them that at the first sign of dissension among the Greeks the non-Greek troops would fall on them all and massacre them; for the non-Greek troops especially, it was one thing to go against Pisidians, another to take up arms against the king. On Cyrus's route, Syennesis of Cilicia was less than fully committed, the governor of Syria sided with the king, and no satrap joined him. In short, Cyrus met hostility wherever he went. He could count on the loyalty only of those who had been his immediate subordinates in Asia Minor, those whom he had cultivated for many years, and those whose friendship he had bought.

Greek Mercenaries

In all, Cyrus hired some 10,600 Greek hoplites, and about 2,300 peltasts. They came in several units, depending on their ethnic loyalties and on their recruiting officers, and each soldier's first allegiance was to the fellow members of his unit and to his commander, who secured his men's fickle loyalty by being the channel through which pay from Cyrus would reach them. Until they were forced by the defeat at Cunaxa to unite against the common enemy, relations with other Greek units tended to be tense and divisive (and the Greeks as a whole also kept themselves aloof from the Persian and other non-Greek troops – but then, members of elite regiments have always acted with haughty disdain towards other units). It was only after Cunaxa that the generals took joint command of the army as a whole, rather than being responsible for just their own units.

The quarrelsome and violent nature of the Greek officers was reflected in the ranks: the Greek mercenaries were an unsavoury bunch. For not a few of them, the main attraction of the expedition was the possibility of marauding their way back again afterwards. They were hardened fighters, prepared to risk their lives for the promise of rich rewards and to turn against their paymasters if they failed to give them their due, in terms of provisions, cash and respect. During the journey east, the men displayed a restlessness that once or twice came close to mutiny, and as soon as they felt themselves safe during the retreat they showed time and again that their chief motivation was greed.

Why would anyone entrust his future to such thugs? Because, with almost 300 years of experience of hoplite warfare, the Greeks were the supreme warriors of the ancient world, and therefore in demand as mercenaries. So high was the demand, in fact, that one of the main reasons Artaxerxes wanted to end internal fighting in Greece, in the decades immediately following his defeat of his brother, was to make more mercenaries available for his own use against Egypt. Ironically, the Cyreans advertised to Persians the value of Greek mercenaries, and both satraps and kings used them in increasing numbers in the fourth century, culminating in the 20,000-strong division of the army of Darius III that faced Alexander the Great at the Granicus river in 334.

The rise in international demand for their skills suited the Greeks, because socio-economic conditions in the Greek states were such that there was already a long and honourable tradition of professional sol-diering. The economy was preponderantly agricultural, and yet, as a drive around Greece still instantly demonstrates, Greek land was poor, and many Greeks had hardly enough land to live on (hence, at other periods of history, Swiss and Spanish peasant villages have been good sources of mercenaries); there were increasing numbers of political or voluntary exiles and refugees, especially after the Thirty Tyrants in Athens set an example of mass banishment; the end of the Peloponnesian War left many dispossessed peasants looking for alter-native means of employment, with soldiering as one of the preferred options. Hence poorer regions of Greece, such as Arcadia and Achaea, were famous sources of mercenaries, and indeed these two regions provided Cyrus with over half of his hoplite mercenaries: 4,000 from the Arcadian mountains and 2,000 Achaeans from the scarcely less rugged northern region of the Peloponnese. The Arcadians were such specialists as mercenaries that Cyrus's 4,000 represented about 8 per cent of the entire adult male population of Arcadia at the time; pro-fessional soldiers were their chief export. The rest of the hoplites came from all over the Greek world – the majority from the Greek mainland and the Peloponnese, some from further east or west.

By the early fourth century, Greek mercenaries were in such com-mon use that they were often regarded, especially on their return from service abroad, as a threat to Greek stability, as they roamed the land while waiting for the next Greek city to employ them, perhaps even for use against fellow Greeks. Some felt that mercenaries were unscrupulous enough to be capable of turning against their employer, and of either establishing a military tyranny in the city or turning to rape and pillage there. A few worried that they might involve their fellow citizens in unwanted wars.

The Athenian orator Isocrates described mercenaries as vagabonds, deserters and criminals, given to preying on others. Unattached mercenaries, exiles from their native cities, formed bands, lived in caves in the mountains of Greece or Asia Minor, and survived by scavenging and brigandage – much like their later counterparts, the notorious *klefts* of Ottoman Greece. Since mercenaries worked for pay, it was a common belief, with a solid factual foundation, that they would desert for better pay, or if they calculated that the odds against them were too great; they were thought to lack the discipline of citizen soldiers (though in actual fact they were far more professional than citizen soldiers). The heat of these charges was fanned by traditional snobbery: taking money for work was regarded as slavish by the Greek aristocracy, who lived off slave labour on their estates and therefore had the leisure to develop broader concerns than just making ends meet. Xenophon idealistically thought the solution was contingents of mixed citizen soldiers and mercenaries, because rivalry would then encourage each group to outdo the other in bravery.

Mercenaries had distinct advantages, however. Greek soldiers had traditionally been citizen peasants, who could not afford to be away from their farms or smallholdings for the months and even years demanded by modern warfare; mercenaries could provide more consistent effort – and since the peasants were usually the ones who legislated for the hiring of mercenaries, they naturally seized the opportunity to fight by proxy. This was particularly the case in states whose manpower had been severely reduced by the Peloponnesian War. Moreover, Greek states had traditionally relied on their allies to supplement their armies, and so, as alliances swayed in the winds of self-interest, the hiring of mercenaries became more and more common.

The chief advantage of mercenaries, however, was just that for these men fighting was a craft, their life and their livelihood. The fourth century saw amateur soldiering give way almost entirely to the professionalism of mercenaries, whenever there was an important battle or war to be fought. The contrast between peasant soldiers and professionals was recognized early. An otherwise unknown Cretan mercenary of the second half of the sixth century, called Hybrias, wrote a rebellious popular song, which drips with scarcely disguised contempt for the traditional agricultural way of life and celebrates freebooting:

My wealth is a stout spear, a sword
And a fine shield, protector of my body.
With them I plough, with them I reap,
With them I press sweet wine from the grape.
With them in hand I'm called master of slaves.
All those who dare not bear spear, sword
And fine shield to protect their bodies
Bend their knees before me in fear
And hail me as their master and their great king.

Conservatives lamented increasing reliance on mercenaries as a factor, even if one among many, that hastened the decline of traditional morality. Instead of patriotism and courage, the voting citizens of a Greek state at war now needed only to find ways to raise cash to pay for mercenaries to stand in their place. Citizen soldiers stood their ground, it was believed, because of the shame of defeat, while a hired soldier would retreat in order to live and fight another day. The Greeks liked to compare a hoplite phalanx to a building, where each stone contributes to the solidity of the whole. Fighting side by side in a phalanx, where your life depended in no small measure on the skill and bravery of your neighbour, had been one of the main glues that bound a community together, so that increasing reliance on mercenaries contributed to the unravelling of the fabric of the Greek states. But these conservatives were flogging a dead horse: more practical minds saw that it simply no longer made sense for states to rely entirely or even mainly on citizen soldiers, and that in any case the fifth-century version of the Greek citizen-state was rapidly becoming a dinosaur.

Pay and Booty

By the time of the Cyreans' expedition, there was a recognized pay structure for mercenary armies, which followed the basic threefold hierarchy of ranks: generals received twice what company commanders received and four times what ordinary soldiers got. The somewhat minimalist structure of ranks was better suited to the usual small contingents of mercenaries, who acted as a potentate's bodyguard or as the garrison of a town, than to Cyrus's massive army, and we do hear from time to time in *The Expedition of Cyrus* of a few intermediate ranks, though they were perhaps field commissions for specific tactical contexts.

The going rate for ordinary soldiers could be as low as 3 obols a day, but Cyrus paid them 5 obols a day: a gold daric a month of thirty days, where 1 daric – a standard weight introduced by Darius I – was approximately equivalent, in Greek terms, to 25 drachmas or 150 obols. Coined money, such as Cyrus's Hellenized darics, was used by Achaemenid rulers almost entirely for dealing with foreigners such as Greeks (that is, for paying mercenaries and bribing politicians), while internal payment was mainly in bullion or kind. The rate at which Cyrus paid the Greeks was increased to 7½ obols a day after the near-mutiny at Tarsus – or at any rate the increase was promised, even if not delivered. But a promise from Cyrus was good enough for the Greeks, because by then they knew they were going deeper into Persian territory, and Greek fables had always painted Persia as a land of immeasurable wealth.

Cyrus took full advantage of the Greeks' susceptibility to dreams of the future. Although mercenaries were usually paid at the end of each month, Cyrus got away with paying them only once, for four of the six months they served under him. When the Greeks finally learnt that they were going against the Great King himself, Cyrus kept resentment at bay by promising them a generous bonus and even said that he would pay them not only for the outward journey, but for their return as well – an exceptional step, prompted less by the unusually long distances involved than by a desire to discourage the returning Greeks from plundering lands that would by then be his. And just before the battle itself, Cyrus bribed all the Greek officers with the promise of a golden crown each once he had seized Artaxerxes's throne.

A few obols a day was subsistence-level pay, about what an unskilled labourer could expect to receive for casual labour in a prosperous city, but so many mercenaries were available for hire after the Peloponnesian War that paymasters could get away with offering little – not that the pay had ever been generous: there was always a buyer's market, and any kind of pay for military service was a relatively new idea, a break from the notion of voluntary service to the state by its citizens. Even the generals would not get rich from their wages, though this was a matter of less concern to them, since they came from more privileged backgrounds and most of them carried substantial amounts of personal money with them on the expedition. At any rate, even late in the expedition, when the remnants of the army had reached Cotyora, three senior officers were each fined 10 mnas, or 600 obols. But leaving aside personal wealth, the daily wage was regarded by the vast majority of the troops as a kind of retainer, to be topped up by pay increases, bonuses and, especially, booty.

As things turned out, of course, Cyrus was unable to fulfil these promises. Profit, however, remained a major issue, second only to survival. It is a good and revealing question to ask of any army at any time what motivates it, what gives the men the will to fight and risk their lives. In the case of the Cyreans, there were two prime motivations: survival and profit. Patriotism did not play a part, because they came from many different states; loyalty to their leaders was secondary, in the sense that they gave their loyalty to their leaders only if they helped them to survive and showed them where booty was to be had; honour had little to do with it, because they had harder, more urgent matters to attend to than abstract concepts. The Cyreans signally failed to value honour more than greed.

Mercenary pay covered little more than their daily expenses during the campaign. They bought quite a bit of their food, and in many cases there were dependants to maintain, prisoners to keep alive until they could be sold or ransomed, and the demands of fragile equipment to satisfy. Nevertheless, mercenaries generally expected to get back home wealthier than they set off – which meant that they expected, if they could, to profit from booty. It is a distasteful fact of war that soldiers loot: they steal from the corpses of fallen friend and foe alike, if there is no more substantial target available. All ancient armies looted, there was massive looting of corpses at Waterloo and, for all we know, the troops in Iraq now are indulging in a little surreptitious 'souvenir hunting'. After the death of their paymaster Cyrus, the only chance the Greeks had to make a profit was from booty, and the closer they got to home the more they looked out for such opportunities.

Although booty was the best way for mercenaries to make a profit, they were often not in a position to do as well as they might. Because they did not want the inconvenience of transporting prisoners and other bulky booty over long distances, they had to compromise and get the best price they could at the earliest possible market. As Xenophon said at one point: 'This enabled them to capture a great many slaves, sheep and goats, and five days later they arrived in

Chrysopolis, where they stayed for seven days selling their booty.'
Bargaining with the dealers took that long.

Prisoners taken in battle might be sold for ransom or, more likely,
for slavery. A skilled man or an attractive woman could fetch a considerable sum of money. In the east, captured boys were highly prized,
especially if they were good-looking: Persian grandees were prepared
to pay a high price for potential eunuchs. The historian Herodotus
delights in a story in which a slave-dealer who castrated boys and sold
them to Persians received his come-uppance when one of his former
eunuchs gained enough power to force the slave-dealer personally to
castrate all four of his sons. Greeks commonly expressed horror at the
eastern practice of castration, but Cyrus's Greek mercenaries certainly
did not pass over opportunities to profit from the sale of beautiful
boys.

Booty also commonly included livestock, personal belongings and
furnishings, clothing, tableware and works of art. Bullion and coined
money were of course highly prized. Generally speaking, booty
acquired by the communal action of the army was pooled, and the
profit distributed in the same 4:2:1 ratio as pay to the three main
ranks. At the same time, though, it was always possible for men to
keep small items for themselves and soldiers certainly felt that if they
had acquired something by their own initiative they had a right to
keep it for themselves and not pool it. The tension between these two
systems spilled over into a violent riot at least once during the
Cyreans' retreat. A tenth of the booty or profit was traditionally kept
aside and given to the gods, in the form of gifts of cash or kind to the
appropriate temples, which had usually been identified in an earlier
vow. During the retreat, the generals also reserved some booty as a
public purse with which to reward acts of distinguished bravery and to
bribe local politicians and warlords along their way, on one occasion
by laying on a magnificent banquet for them, with lavish entertainment.

Cyrus's army was the largest body of mercenaries anyone up until
then had ever employed. Normally, mercenaries were expected to provide their own equipment, just as anyone hiring artisans expected
them to come with the tools of their trade, but Cyrus wanted hoplites
above all, and there simply were not that many hoplites available,
even allowing for the fact that their panoply consisted of fewer and
lighter – and so cheaper – pieces than a century or so earlier. 'Hoplite'

was a social as well as a military term: in their native Greek cities, hoplites were those who could afford to purchase the panoply, as it was called, which cost on average between 75 and 100 drachmas (450–600 obols, four months' pay for a skilled worker). No doubt there were many Cyreans who did belong to this middle class, and there were others, such as Cheirisophus's 700, who must have been equipped by Sparta, since they were an official Spartan contingent; but there were many more who came from poorer stock, especially those whose livelihood had been damaged or destroyed by the Peloponnesian War and who were desperate for employment. In order to ensure enough heavy-armed troops, Cyrus had to move down the social scale and supply the poorer men with at least the rudiments of a hoplite panoply – a shield, a spear and a sword.

Xenophon Joins the Army

When summoned to Sardis, most of the mercenaries came in ready-made units, led by their recruiters, though stragglers also trickled in. Several weeks passed between the arrival of the first troops and the actual start of the expedition. Before long, Tissaphernes could tell that this marked a new phase of Cyrus's ambitions. He no longer believed that this huge army was being raised for even the complete subjugation of the Pisidian raiders, and he made himself scarce. It was not just the size of the army, but its inappropriate composition: to fight hill-tribes you need fewer hoplites and more peltasts. Tissaphernes took a cavalry troop of 500 and fled or raced east to tell the king what was going on, to give his master as much time as possible to finalize his preparations.

This was the army Xenophon set out to join. By the time he wrote *The Expedition of Cyrus*, he was at pains to distance himself from the mercenaries themselves. 'There was in the army,' he said, 'a man called Xenophon, from Athens. He had come along not as a general, nor as a company commander, nor as a soldier, but because Proxenus, a long-standing guest-friend, had invited him to leave home and join him.' He was motivated, in other words, by a sense of adventure and by the constant pressure on a young man of noble birth to prove himself, but not by the desire for booty and he certainly did not need to work for pay. Despite these disclaimers, he would discover before long how well suited he was to the vagabond life of a mercenary, and he set himself

86

up for many years from booty he acquired during and immediately after the expedition. Certainly, by the time Cyrus and Artaxerxes met on the plain of Cunaxa, Xenophon was playing a part in the ranks, not just as an observer.

Xenophon took ship in Piraeus, the port of Athens, and disembarked on the Asia Minor coast at Ephesus. No doubt he lingered for a day or two to rest from his voyage and to take in the far-famed spectacle of this glorious and wealthy city, of all the Asiatic Greek cities the one where eastern influences were most pervasive. When he left, he was seen off by a diviner: the beginnings of any action, such as a journey, were considered especially important, and a diviner could interpret any omens that might occur. And indeed they were vouchsafed an omen: Xenophon saw an 'eagle' (more likely a buzzard, in modern terminology) perched off to his right and heard its cry. Although the right was the direction of good fortune, the diviner's prediction was not entirely positive: 'The eagle is a magnificent bird,' he said, 'but in this case it signifies suffering, because other birds are liable to attack an eagle when it is perched. Moreover, it is not an omen of profit, because the eagle generally gets its food on the wing.' He scored one hit and one miss: Xenophon did profit, but he certainly suffered along the way.

The journey of 100 kilometres or so from Ephesus to Sardis was not arduous, since the Persian Royal Road linked the two cities. Xenophon was accompanied by his slaves and perhaps by a military escort sent by Proxenus to protect and guide him. But the keen edge of his anticipation of adventure was blunted somewhat, not just by the diviner's pessimistic tone, but by the familiarity of the countryside, which, with its low, shrub-covered hills and intensively farmed valleys, was little different from what could be found in many parts of Greece. Before long, however, the countryside started to stretch – Turkey is built on a more generous scale than Greece – and the final leg of his journey to Sardis took him across a broad and fertile plain. As he drew closer to the city, he saw the jagged and wooded crags of the Bozdağ, one of which had acted recently as Orontas's stronghold, though Xenophon had little idea at the time of such intrigues. All he saw was the splendour of Croesus's old palace on the hilltop, the well-watered plain, dotted with the tumuli of long-dead Lydian kings, and in the distance a blue lake and the far-off mountains of northern Lydia. It was spring, and wild flowers grew in profusion everywhere.

Sardis at this time was not so much a Lydian or Persian city, but multi-ethnic and cosmopolitan. Though the rulers of the satrapy of Sparda tended to be high-ranking Persians – even, in Cyrus's case, a member of the royal family – the elite included Lydians as well. The city had a rich Lydian heritage and the Persians had wisely not stamped out the old culture, but had absorbed it and overlaid it with a Persian veneer. In time, Greek elements too had entered both the racial and the architectural mix. With its long tradition of high culture, independence and self-importance, it was a natural base from which Cyrus could foster rebellion. After the original Persian annexation of Lydia in the sixth century, the old fortifications had been largely dismantled, but by the time of Xenophon's arrival it had a lesser defensive wall, and the acropolis was fortified with a triple wall. The foot of the hill was crowded with residences, temples and official buildings, and outside the city walls were houses of mud brick with reed roofs, and two ornate walled parks for shade and recreation. Sadly, little apart from Roman and a few Hellenistic remains now grace the quiet farming village of Sart, near Salihli.

Xenophon arrived just as the army was about to set out, but in time to be introduced to Cyrus by Proxenus. The plain outside the city was in a state of barely contained chaos. Not only was the main army of non-Greek soldiers, led by Cyrus himself, encamped there, but thousands of Greeks had arrived as well. They had already formed themselves into units: Xenias commanded 4,000 hoplites, Sophaenetus another 1,000, and Socrates about 500; Proxenus's unit consisted of 1,500 hoplites and 500 peltasts, and Pasion's 300 hoplites and 300 peltasts. When the army set out, it spread across and along the plain for many kilometres.

They headed east for a while over the plain of Castolus, making good progress over the easy terrain, before turning south-east to avoid some hills, and reaching Colossae (modern Denizli) in four days. They had covered some 150 kilometres, which included crossing the Meander river by a bridge of boats (such as was still used there in the nineteenth century) a day's march north-west of Colossae. The town became famous later for its early Christian community, addressed in a letter by St Paul, but to the ancient Greeks it was known for the river that rose right in the middle of the town. At Colossae they were joined by another band of mercenaries, 1,000 hoplites and 500 peltasts, under the command of Meno, and the combined force then marched

Lake Acıgöl, from the quiet modern road between Colossae (Denizli) and Celaenae (Dinar), which follows the route of the ancient road.

100 kilometres east to Celaenae (modern Dinar), past the beautiful Lake Acıgöl. At Celaenae they were joined by the remainder of the mercenaries, who came from various assembly points in the north. Clearchus of Sparta led a contingent of 1,000 hoplites, 800 Thracian peltasts and 200 Cretan archers, and others arrived with smaller numbers. There were now some 9,500 Greek hoplites, and 2,300 light-armed troops.

They stayed in Celaenae for a full month while the men assembled and were divided into their companies; officers were appointed where necessary and cereal crops ripened in the fields they would pass through further east. In imitation of the decimal system of the Persians, they chose the 100-strong company as their basic tactical, social and administrative unit. While the men drilled and bonded, Cyrus sent out last-minute spies and messengers, awaited their return, fine-tuned his plans and dreamt of kingship. In fact, Celaenae rather than Sardis was the true starting point of the expedition: it was one of Cyrus's centres – the rich, red soil there was easily capable of supporting one of his favourite ornamental parks, and the town was the centre of a network of major roads to the west, south and north – and by the time he left he had all the troops he could reasonably expect. The force was enormous, and already rumours were circulating of Cyrus's generous nature, while some spoke more guardedly of his ultimate objective. The sense of anticipation when they set out was intense.

CHAPTER SIX

The Journey Begins

From Celaenae the full army marched north-west to Ceramon Agora (modern Uşak). The landscape was undulating, gradually rising to 900 metres above sea level, occasionally boggy, and blessed with fertile plains. The name Ceramon Agora means 'Pottery Market', and the main roads into and out of Uşak are still lined with factory outlets for ceramic wares, made from the rich local clay. Then they turned east and arrived in Cayster Field (possibly the modern town of Çay) ten days after leaving Celaenae. They were in no hurry, and the twists and turns of their journey were dictated by the desire to keep to the main roads, to avoid rugged terrain and, above all, to recruit or press-gang more troops. Besides, the warm weather alone encouraged a slow pace. Their route took them past some beautiful lakes, fringed with deep green reeds and teeming with fish and fowl. With boar and other countryside creatures, and villages rich in grain and orchards, the army flourished.

Although the pace was leisurely, the Greeks were unhappy. Many of them had assembled in Asia Minor ten or twelve weeks previously, having journeyed there at their own expense, yet so far none of them had seen any pay. Cyrus had kept them going largely on promises, and at Peltae, on the road between Celaenae and Ceramon Agora, he had called a halt while the Arcadians celebrated their most holy festival, and had himself provided gold crowns as prizes for the athletic contests which, in a typically Greek fashion, formed part of the festival; but now the troops wanted to see hard cash. At Cayster Field there were the rumblings of mutiny. But just as the situation was getting ugly, an ornate caravan arrived in camp. Epyaxa, the wife of the aged king Syennesis of Cilicia, had arrived with her entourage and, more importantly, with plenty of money from her husband. Cyrus was able to pay the troops four months' wages, no fewer than 215 talents.

This was not the first time Cyrus and Epyaxa had met, and the older woman made herself available to the young man for far more than official negotiations. Under the guise of being an ambassador from her husband, she resumed a casual affair with the Persian pretender. Cyrus knew the value of combining what is pleasant with what is practical: it would be useful to have an ally right in the heart of Syennesis's court and he badly needed to know where the Cilician king's loyalty lay, since he would have to pass through his kingdom. The army travelled for four further days, past the town of Thymbrium (now the small market town Akşehir), stunningly dominated by the lofty peaks of the Sultan Dağlari, and on to Tyriaeum (Ilgın). Now at last they were heading south-east, towards the Pisidians – and towards the heartland of the Persian empire.

At Tyriaeum, the queen asked her lover to have his army put on a display, and the Greeks decided to make it a memorable occasion; this was, after all, the first time all of them had been in full battle array. The Greek section of the army marched past the spectators in a normal review, but carried on until it was a good distance away, when the hoplites took up battle lines. The phalanx began its slow advance towards the spectators, weapons at the ready, shields blazing in the sunlight and red cloaks flashing. As they got closer and showed no signs of stopping, the mood of the crowd changed from laughter to apprehension; when the Greeks broke into a run, apprehension gave way to fear. Whose side were the Greeks really on? Had Epyaxa's cash pacified their resentment? Did they still have a point to prove? Merchants upset their stalls as they fled; Epyaxa ran for her comfortable carriage and drove a safe distance away; members of Cyrus's retinue turned and ran. The disciplined Greeks, capable of drilling to a high degree of precision, charged right up to the royal throne before stopping. They enjoyed their edged joke, and Cyrus longed for the day when the mercenaries would rout his enemies as easily as they had his friends.

The army continued south-east across an enormous, gently rolling, dry plain, swept by the occasional buzzard, towards Iconium (the modern holy city of Konya, famous for its whirling dervishes). Iconium, whose sense of a long and illustrious past made it the legendary seat of antediluvian kings, was an outpost of Persian influence within the otherwise unsettled territory of the Lycaonians – which made it the perfect place for Cyrus to permit the army for the first time to plunder the land, rather than buy their provisions. They needed to replenish their supplies, vent their frustration and get their first loot. Rape and pillage were and still are such horribly familiar features of warfare that ancient writers tend not to bother to give us the details, but Shakespeare was more honest:

If not – why, in a moment look to see
The blind and bloody soldier with foul hand
Defile the locks of your shrill-shrieking daughters;
Your fathers taken by the silver beards,
And their most reverend heads dashed to the walls;
Your naked infants spitted upon pikes,
Whiles the mad mothers with their howls confused
Do break the clouds, as did the wives of Jewry
At Herod's bloody-hunting slaughtermen.

Up until then, the official version of the army's mission was still that Cyrus intended to subdue rebellious Pisidian hill-tribes. At Iconium, however, with Pisidia now to the south-west, Cyrus gave the order to continue south-east. In response to the Greeks' puzzlement, Cyrus told them that he was planning to attack Abrocomas, the military governor of Syria and Phoenicia. Given the long history of intense and bloody rivalry between the satraps of the Persian empire, this was a plausible mission, but not all the Greeks were convinced, and talk of Cyrus's hatred for his brother began to circulate more openly.

Despite the fact that Cyrus's intentions were an open secret, he was right to make as much use of disinformation as he could. Desertion was endemic in ancient armies, and deserters were one of the best sources of information about the other side (hence Greek commanders regularly employed the tactic of supplying the enemy with false deserters, primed with misleading information), so Cyrus restricted the number of people who knew his plans. As a rule of thumb, 'When the number of accomplices in a conspiracy exceeds three or four, it is almost impossible for it not to be discovered, through treason, imprudence or carelessness.' In Cyrus's case, his true intentions were known only by the very few commanders of both his Greek and his non-Greek troops that he felt were entirely trustworthy. But why should he still want to conceal them? After all, he must have known that he was no longer fooling his brother, if he ever had. He must still have been uncertain of the reaction of a significant number of his troops, especially those who had long been subjects of the Persian king. Everyone who knew also knew that the king would respond in force; after all, what with the rebellion in Egypt, Artaxerxes had lost control of a substantial portion of his western empire.

The information Epyaxa had given Cyrus about her husband disturbed him: although Syennesis had provided him with a generous amount of money, it looked as though he was hedging his bets. Cyrus had no choice about crossing the formidable Taurus mountains in order to enter Cilicia, but it would be easy for Syennesis to hold the narrow pass, the famous Cilician Gates at modern Gülek, against him. Over the centuries, many armies have found to their cost how easy it is for the pass to be blockaded, and the ruins of the fortress with which the Genoese controlled the Gates are still visible. In Cyrus's day the road through the pass was little more than a cart track past steep, pine-covered slopes and jagged peaks, though today one is faced with the easy choice between a scenic route and a motorway packed with sluggish lorries belching diesel smoke.

Cyrus decided to help Syennesis make up his mind. First, he found a way to insert a force behind his back, so that if Syennesis did choose to blockade the Gates he would himself be trapped between two armies. So while the main army continued east and north-east, skirting the

The formidable Taurus Mountains, around the middle of the pass taken by the bulk of Cyrus's army.

foothills of the mountains, Cyrus sent Meno's contingent through an obscure and undefended pass, south of modern Ayrancı. The main army, with all its carts and gear, could not negotiate this trackless pass, but a lightly equipped force could make it. The second aspect of Cyrus's plan for entering Cilicia safely concerned Epyaxa. Meno was also to escort Epyaxa back home to the capital of Cilicia, the great city of Tarsus. Now, Cyrus undoubtedly wanted Epyaxa to get home quickly to work on her husband's allegiance, so the queen presumably went willingly, despite the risks of a more hazardous route – but while she might think she was a willing participant in a plot against her husband, she was in fact a hostage, another lever on Syennesis's loyalty, in case diplomacy failed. Cyrus was prepared to sacrifice Epyaxa's open arms for those of her husband.

While Meno's detachment was crossing the mountains to the west, the main army took the easy route across the plains to Dana (possibly Ereğli), in the south-western corner of Cappadocia. There they turned south. Though they were already 1,000 metres above sea level, the massive bulk of the Taurus range, with its highest peaks standing at over 3,500 metres, slowly appeared through the dust and haze of the plain. The travel was fairly easy, at least until they reached the lumpy foothills of the main mountain range, but the plain became increasingly barren as they drew closer to the mountains. It was a disheartening stage of the journey, because the distant mountains seemed hardly to draw any closer and they had no idea whether or not the pass was held against them.

At the pass, it became clear that Syennesis had indeed been planning to block their way – but also that the appearance of Meno's men in Cilicia had had the desired effect. Syennesis had withdrawn, his decision aided by news of the fortuitous approach of a convoy of warships, some temporarily withdrawn by Cyrus from service in Asia Minor against Tissaphernes and some belonging to Sparta. Cyrus had, of course, known they were on their way, but the hazards of ancient seafaring made it impossible for him predict the time of arrival.

The combination of the threats posed by Cyrus in front of him, and Meno and a fleet behind him, was enough to get Syennesis to withdraw his troops from the pass, but he was still afraid – naturally enough, since he had intended to oppose the pretender – and even after Cyrus reached Tarsus, it took a few days of negotiations and generous tokens of friendship before Syennesis was prepared to come down from his mountain stronghold and deal face to face with the prince. But Syennesis's neutrality or friendship was important to Cyrus: he could not afford to divide his army to face a threat in his rear. Syennesis, however, continued to play a double game: while appearing to be Cyrus's friend, and accepting his gifts, he sent a report to Artaxerxes about the strength of Cyrus's army. Whichever way the dice ultimately fell, he could plausibly claim that he had always had the victor's best interests at heart. But it did him no good: once the threat of Cyrus was behind him, Artaxerxes had the Cilician king replaced by another Syennesis.

Cyrus and the main army reached Tarsus to find the place somewhat the worse for wear. Meno's men had not crossed the mountains unscathed: the Greeks had suffered their first losses.

> Two companies from Meno's force had perished during the passage over the mountains and down to the plain. Some said they had been annihilated by the Cilicians while they were out foraging, others that they had fallen behind and got lost, and died without being able to find the rest of the army or the roads. Whatever the facts, each company had consisted of 100 hoplites. When the survivors reached Tarsus they were so angry about the deaths of their comrades that they looted not only the city, but the palace too.

By the time Cyrus arrived, only those civilians with food or sex to sell remained in the city.

Surrounded by lush, almost sub-tropical countryside, Tarsus offered a stark contrast to the other side of the mountains. It was already a prosperous city (though not as grand as it was by the time St Paul was born there, when it rivalled Athens, Alexandria and Antioch as a centre of culture), and the Cyreans stayed there for twenty days. However, they did not stay just to relax and replenish their supplies: rumbling Greek discontent erupted into mutiny. Their orders were to march east, into the heat of the Syrian desert, but they felt they were not being paid – or offered – enough to compensate for such a gruelling expedition. At any rate, this was the pretext for mutiny, though in truth it was prompted by greed: the greater their certainty that Cyrus was aiming for the throne, the greater their insistence that Cyrus could afford to pay them well. All the senior Greek officers urged their troops to carry on, but they simply refused. Clearchus's men even pelted him with stones when he repeated the order. The next day Clearchus summoned his contingent to another assembly. With tears in his eyes, presenting himself as just a common soldier like his men, he told them that if push came to shove, if he had to choose between them and Cyrus, he would always choose Greeks; if they wanted to return home, so be it.

With the rest of the Greek officers still insisting that their men carry on, Clearchus's apparent climb-down swelled his contingent with substantial numbers of Greeks from other units, especially those of Xenias and Pasion. Cyrus, understandably disturbed at the prospect of losing thousands of his best troops, sent an angry message, demanding Clearchus's presence at an urgent meeting, but to the delight of the men Clearchus publicly refused. This game continued for most of the day – and it was a game. Clearchus had secretly told Cyrus to be patient and to continue to send messengers for him to reject in public, and had assured him that he would win over the Greeks. The situation was absolutely critical – and yet this was the moment when, at Clearchus's instigation, the two commanders coolly played a bizarre and audacious game of manipulation. Clearchus had also already primed the assembly of the men under his command with stooges to impress upon the assembled soldiers the folly of arousing Cyrus's hostility at this juncture. This cynical manipulation of a democratic institution was an aspect of the same tyrannnical nature that had led Clearchus to try to take Byzantium for himself. Eventually Cyrus promised a pay rise (though he continued to pretend that only Abrocomas was his target), and the Greeks united behind Clearchus and agreed to continue east. The contest among certain of the Greek generals for the position of Cyrus's favourite had gone Clearchus's way.

The Approach to Cunaxa

In five days of easy travel across rolling, fertile countryside, with the Taurus range receding behind them, they crossed the Pyramus (Ceyhan) river at Mopsuestia (Misis), before turning east-south-east through the Kara Kapu pass between the Adana plain and the Plain of Issus. And so they came to Issus (at or near modern Dörtyol), one of the great crossroads of the ancient world and later the site of one of the most critical battles in Alexander the Great's campaign to conquer the Persian empire. There they met up with the convoy of ships, which brought welcome supplies and 700 fresh hoplites, under the command of the Spartan Cheirisophus.

The fact that the convoy was commanded by the Spartan Admiral of the Fleet for that year, Pythagoras, nicknamed 'the Samian', shows that it was an official Spartan response to Cyrus's appeals for help; the Spartans clearly were no longer concerned about offending their eastern ally. Cyrus's Greek corps was also swelled at Issus by 400 mercenaries who had deserted from Abrocomas's army. They were now at full strength: 10,400 hoplites (discounting the 200 lost in the Taurus mountains) and 2,300 peltasts. As well as bringing provisions and troops, the fleet had just one job to do before it left. Not far south of Issus lay the Cilician-Syrian Gates, the only viable way into Syria. In this part of the world, however, spurs of the thickly wooded Nur Dağlari mountains often came close to the coast, and the combination of natural and man-made defences at the Gates threatened a serious obstacle:

> These gates consist of two forts. The one on the nearer side, defending Cilicia, was held by Syennesis and a garrison of Cilicians, while the one on the further side, defending Syria, was reported to be held by the king's garrison. Between these two forts flows a river called the Carsus, a plethron wide [about 30 metres]. The total distance from one fort to the other was three stades [about 540 metres], and it was impossible to force a crossing because the entrance was narrow, with fortifications reaching down to the sea on the one side and sheer rocks above the entrance on the other side. Both forts were also equipped with gates. This defile was the reason Cyrus had sent for the ships. With their help, hoplites could be put ashore between and beyond the gates, and these hoplites could effect a passage by force if there did in fact turn out to be a garrison defending the Syrian side.

Despite this crisp description, the coastline here has been so ravaged by time (there is now an extensive coastal plain, where there was none in Xenophon's day) and by road-building that the precise location of the Gates is uncertain.

Abrocomas, loyal to the king, had mustered an army in Phoenicia, in order to attack rebel Egypt. He was then sent north instead, to defend the Cilician-Syrian Gates just as Cyrus had feared, but he had already withdrawn and Cyrus found the Gates undefended. Artaxerxes had ordered Abrocomas to fall back to Babylonia and join up with the rest of his army in preparation for the decisive battle. After the Gates, Cyrus dismissed the ships and set out south along the coast for Myriandus (now the ugly, polluted city Iskenderun, where it is hard to discern the pleasures of its previous incarnation as French colonial Alexandretta). By then, it was the height of summer; the Cyreans must have wanted to hide from the sun, to bury themselves deep underground, as on sandy beaches there crabs do, only to emerge in their hundreds in the cooler evenings. After Myriandus they would strike inland, so it was here that Xenias and Pasion, who had lost most of their troops to Clearchus, chose to desert: they hired a ship and set off back to Greece. Despite rumours to the contrary, Cyrus did not bother to pursue them.

From Myriandus the army turned east, following Abrocomas's route through the 750-metre high Belen Pass over the Nur Dağlari and into modern Syria. As the quantity of heavy traffic on the road

The bleak, scarcely undulating semi-desert of Syria is occasionally interrupted by wadis such as this one. Along the Royal Road taken by the Cyreans, wadis were bridged, as this one has been, for ease of passage and to evade flash floods.

testifies, for all its height this pass is still the best route across the mountains, saving a long journey south along the coast until the mountains with their impassable ravines peter out. On the other side of the mountains, they descended on to an undulating, fertile plain with low, barren hills, which gradually gave way to a more or less entirely featureless and flat stony desert – or rather, not so much a desert as what in Arabic is called *baddiya*, a semi-desert where the limestone ridges are arid, despite being only a few metres higher than the arable, lower-lying land with its waterways and irrigation systems. In baking heat, they crossed a number of rivers or wadis, none of which was a major impediment. In Xenophon's day, there was plenty of wildlife – as there was until recently, though stories of how guests used to shoot game from the veranda of the renowned Baron Hotel in Aleppo belong a century in the past, and the hotel, in its faded glory, is now close to the centre of the busy city.

The going was harder now, the heat intense: it took the army almost two weeks to travel the 350 or so kilometres to Thapsacus, a prosperous trading town on the Euphrates. Also known in ancient times as Zeugma ('Pontoon'), Thapsacus was one of the most important and commonly used crossing-points of the Euphrates, but its exact location is unknown. It may be as far north as Balkis, 12 kilometres upstream from modern Birecik in southern Turkey, or, more likely, as

Taken from the bridge at Ar Raqqah. If Ar Raqqah is the site of ancient Thapsacus, this is where the Cyreans made the fateful crossing into the Persian heartlands. Cyrus had to bribe them to cross the river and continue from here against his brother.

far south as Ar Raqqah, a Syrian town stained in historical memory as the final concentration point for thousands of Armenians driven by the Turks from their homeland in 1915 and then slaughtered. The Cyreans' first glimpse of the great river as they approached Thapsacus was heart-stopping. The expanse of water, seeming in its shallow stretches as wide as a lake, perfectly reflects the blue of the sky, and provides one of the most intense geographical contrasts imaginable with its surrounding of endless, unforgiving, brown desert. It is not difficult to understand the sacredness of water to the ancient peoples of the Fertile Crescent and of Egypt.

At Thapsacus Cyrus at last revealed his full plans to the Greek commanders. He really had no choice but to do so, since every further step would demonstrate his intention to confront his brother. Crossing the river would be the significant measure, since from then on they would clearly be heading for the Persian heartlands. Meno seized the opportunity to ingratiate himself with Cyrus by crossing before the other generals had made up their minds. Cyrus also had to win the Greeks' backing for a risky decision he had taken. The usual route to Babylonia from Thapsacus involved travelling eastward along one of the Royal Roads, and then striking south down the Tigris. But this was the route Abrocomas had taken with his army just a few days earlier. It was imperative that Cyrus prevent the two armies, that of Abrocomas and that of Artaxerxes, from joining forces. He may also have heard the news that another army was on its way from Susa and Ecbatana, but the threat of Abrocomas's army, which was large enough to have spearheaded an invasion of rebel Egypt, was enough in itself to have justified his decision to travel south along the eastern bank of the Euphrates, despite the fact that this more direct route to Babylonia would take the army through harsh desert – and despite the fact that he would have to increase the pace.

Protest was quickly pacified with the promise of a daily pay increase and of huge rewards once victory was theirs. Abrocomas had destroyed the bridges on his departure, but Cyrus and his troops found the river fordable. In order to flatter Cyrus, the local inhabitants claimed that this was a miracle, though in actual fact the river is often fordable at that time of year. And so they began the last, long phase of their journey, down the Euphrates towards their destiny in Babylonia.

At first, the travel was easy, along the bed of the river valley. After some days, this gave way to completely flat land – as flat as the sea,

Xenophon says, trying to get his Greek audience to understand – where there was less vegetation, but game was plentiful, and a few lucky Greeks, mainly those with horses for hunting, supplemented their usual meagre diet with exotic creatures such as ostrich and bustard, gazelle and onager. They also stocked up at Corsote, a town situated at the junction of the Euphrates and the Mascas (modern Khabur). But south of Corsote the difficulties began, as the tortuous course of the Euphrates took them through true desert, towards the modern border between Syria and north-western Iraq, where bedouin herders still guide their flocks over large distances, in search of scrub vegetation. The river provided enough water, but the yellow-brown, dusty plain, studded with limestone and quartz rocks and distant ranges of low hills, offered no fodder for the animals, and many of them died. On the plus side, this meant that however low their stocks of grain, the men had plenty of meat. It took them two weeks to cross the desert and reach land where the alluvial Euphrates guaranteed fertility and prosperity, and where they could plunder grain stored from the June harvest.

Tempers frayed as a result of the heat and the exertion. It was not uncommon for ancient Greek generals to try to outdo one another, for personal glory, and the rivalry between Clearchus and Meno, who wanted to regain his position as Cyrus's favourite, was a constant, troubling presence. Finally, at Charmande (modern Hit) the situation became explosive. One of Clearchus's soldiers and one of Meno's fell out, and Clearchus, overstepping the bounds of his jurisdiction, judged Meno's man to be in the wrong and punished him. The next day, as he naïvely or provocatively passed through Meno's camp, an axe whistled past his ear, followed by a hail of stones. Clearchus regained the safety of his own camp, ordered his hoplites to stand ready, and while they were arming led his Thracian peltasts and his horsemen against Meno's camp. Proxenus tried to calm the two generals down, but was physically pushed aside. It took a personal appeal from Cyrus to stop the army unravelling. And so, in almost unbearable heat and in an atmosphere that combined determination to succeed with unresolved tensions, they approached the village of Cunaxa.

Logistics

In his account of the journey east from Sardis, Xenophon specifies 178 days: 90 at rest and 88 on the move. If we take Celaenae as the true starting-point of the expedition, the balance alters to 58 days at rest and 81 on the move. But the days on the move always involve unbroken travel; Xenophon fails to tell us how long it took the army to cross rivers and mountain ranges: the narrative tends to end on one side and begin again on the other, with no details. Yet fording difficult rivers or crossing them on rickety pontoon bridges can occupy an army and its train for some days. This means that we cannot pin the length of the journey down with absolute precision. Assuming that Cyrus set off from Sardis in spring (at the beginning of March, say), he arrived at Cunaxa in the early autumn (in the middle of September, perhaps). He and the army had travelled some 2,750 kilometres. Although their pace was leisurely compared to a forced march, their average rate of about 30 kilometres a day on the march was considerably faster than the speed achieved by citizen armies in the rugged terrain of Greece. This was by far the most impressive march before the time of Alexander the Great and his Successors.

Some of the Cyreans' periods of rest were prolonged by unrest among the Greek troops, by Cyrus's diplomacy with local rulers, or by reviews of the army, a practice of which Persian rulers were fond, because the size and diversity of their armies served as a concrete display of their power and overawed potential allies; but many of the rest days were occasioned simply by the logistics of a vast army on the move in the ancient world, and above all by the constant, pressing need for provisions. In what follows, I shall assume, for the sake of simplicity and for want of firm evidence (ancient authors very rarely discussed logistics), that what obtained for the Greek troops also held good for Cyrus's non-Greek troops.

The army consisted, on my conservative estimate, of 30,000 men, of whom almost 13,000 were Greek hoplites (and peltasts and a few horsemen from the margins of the Greek world). The numbers, already considerable, were doubled by non-combatants; at a critical moment during the retreat after Cunaxa, the generals decided to shed as many of the non-combatants and animals as they could, among other reasons because 'they needed to find and carry double the amount of provisions for all those people'.

Better-off hoplites were attended, as Xenophon was, by one or more personal slaves to look after their gear, tend to them, and get them off the battlefield if they were wounded – or retrieve their corpses. Then the train contained women for personal or shared sexual use. More such sexual partners were acquired as prisoners during the journey, including teenage boys: they were valuable booty, as well as satisfying more immediate needs. Cyrus himself brought two concubines, both Greek women from the Asia Minor coast. In a telling aside, Xenophon on one occasion defends himself against a charge of assault on a soldier by dismissing plausible motives for such an assault: 'Was it that I had asked you for something and beat you when you didn't give it to me? Was it a loan you were supposed to return? Were we fighting about a boy we fancied? Was I so drunk that I was spoiling for a fight?' There were not enough sexual partners to go around, and quarrels over whose turn it was were a familiar feature of army life.

There were also many merchants and peddlers in the train: their main job was to provide the troops with a market where goods and food could be purchased. Since the most valuable booty was always civilian and military captives, whose most likely fate was to be sold into slavery, slave-traders accompanied ancient armies as jackals follow herds of vulnerable animals. An army on the move required arti-

A terracotta statuette of a slave baggage-carrier, dating from the end of the fourth century. The coarse physique and features have been exaggerated for comic effect, in much the same way as slave-owners at other times have caricatured their slaves.

sans such as carpenters, bakers and other cooks, weaving-women, blacksmiths, armourers and leather-workers; most of these were slaves, though some were poor free men. A personal slave played some of these roles for his master, and no doubt soldiers often looked after themselves as best they could, but there were also hundreds of others who served larger units of the army. The same jack-of-all-trades principle meant that doctors (if that is the right word) were simply recruited, as the need arose, from existing slaves, but other specialist jobs increased the number of non-combatants: there were diviners (for both official and private consultation), bankers, scribes, musicians and other entertainers, engineers and pontoneers. Finally, there were hundreds more slaves to drive and tend to carts and animals, and as the journey progressed hundreds of prisoners of war joined the rabble.

Cyrus's army was followed by thousands of carts, ranging from two-wheelers to six-wheelers. The wealthy had their own carts, piled high with all or most of the following: unground grain (unground because it spoiled less readily), wine, olive oil, other foodstuffs, cooking utensils, a hand-mill for the grain, money, bedding, clothing and footwear, a medical kit, the hoplite panoply and spare weapons, a sickle for harvesting enemy grain, a mattock for damaging enemy trees and for minor engineering works, an axe for chopping wood, a shovel, a rasp and a file for repairs to weapons, stones for sharpening tools and weapons, plenty of useful leather straps, spare timber and carpentry tools with which to repair the cart, spare parts, firewood, animal hides to act if need be as tent and hammock, booty and other personal possessions. Packing and unpacking the wagon every day was a notoriously tedious aspect of a campaign for those who lacked slaves to do the job, and one of the few ordinary soldiers who has a voice in *The Expedition of Cyrus* puts it top of his list of grievances.

Having a cart to oneself was less common than sharing. The size of the hoplite shield and the weight of the armour meant that, except in cases of immediate danger, all these thousands of panoplies were stacked on special carts, which were called up to the front only for emergencies. Shields were wrapped in protective covers while being transported, to prevent tarnishing, since an array of gleaming shields was held to be more likely to strike fear into the enemy. Hundreds more carts carried provisions, the sick and wounded, and all the rest of the gear. Tents (made out of animal hides) were particularly unwieldy: designed to shelter up to a dozen sleeping soldiers, each of them weighed about 20 kilograms, and even when folded they were bulky and difficult to transport.

If, at a rough estimate, one well-stacked cart could be loaded with the arms, armour, equipment and tents for twenty men, Cyrus's men required 1,500 carts. In fact, though, pack animals and slaves were used as well as ox-carts for transport, and many soldiers also strapped a rucksack on their shoulders. Because of the amount of grain animals consume and the need to find campsites with sufficient fodder, individual human porterage was actually a highly efficient way for ancient armies to transport at least a portion of their equipment.

Apart from the necessity of feeding the team animals, the chief disadvantages of carts were that they lumbered along at a very slow pace (little more than 3 kilometres per hour, compared with an average rate for infantry of 4 kilometres per hour), that ox hooves are ill suited for long journeys (so that at any given time there would have been many lame oxen), that the kind of harness used in Xenophon's day was inefficient (the harder the animal pulled, the more the harness choked it) and that large carts required well-beaten roads; their chief advantage was simply that they could carry so much more than pack animals or porters. One of the main military innovations introduced by Philip II of Macedon and his son Alexander the Great was the almost total abandonment of carts, to increase mobility. Cyrus's army, however, combined carts for the heavy equipment with pack animals and human porters.

The army started with about 3,000 horses, mostly warhorses, and thousands of pack animals (chiefly mules and donkeys) and team animals (chiefly oxen). Since blood sacrifice was a regular feature not just of army life, but of an individual's private worship, they also brought along hundreds of animals, large and small, as future victims. Along the way they stole huge flocks of sheep and goats, sometimes numbering several thousands. On this trip they often had to eat meat, which was a rare treat for Greeks, since at home meat was eaten only after a sacrifice, but otherwise these captured creatures were destined for sale as booty.

An extremely active male requires around 3,800 calories per day, a very active male 3,300, and a moderately active male 2,800. On the way out to Babylonia, we never hear of Cyrus's men being badly short of food, so we may assume that each man was usually getting around 3,500 calories a day. (Compare this to the 6,000 to 7,000 calories regularly taken in daily by many males, even indolent ones, of the prosperous northern hemisphere today.) Standard military rations were 1 litre per man per day of wheat, or 2 litres of barley (which delivers significantly fewer calories, especially if it is ground into coarse flour with the hulls). A litre of wheat supplied 2,800 calories, if eaten as bread, rather than the nutritionally far less satisfying porridge or gruel. Greek fare was plain, but not as boring as just grain products: the rest of each man's calorific needs were made up from other foodstuffs, as available: oil, wine, cheese, fresh or dried fish, fruit, pulses, greens, vegetables – and, under the exceptional circumstances of this march, meat, or even some more exotic item, such as the 'cabbages' of palm trees. This diet also delivered sufficient protein. In order to stay healthy, each man needed, let us say, about 1.25 kilograms of food per day.

As for water, an active adult male requires a minimum of 2 litres a day, rising to 9 litres a day in extreme conditions. The Greeks very often took their water by diluting wine with it: wine was another staple, with a monthly allowance for each soldier on a typical state-financed campaign of about 40 litres. As for the animals: mules, horses and oxen require a minimum of 4.5 kilograms of straw or chaff per day, plus the same amount of grain and over 20 litres of water; donkeys require somewhat less. These quantities rise if the animals are required to put in particularly hard work. But the animals were generally expected to live off the land: fodder was not carried, and its availability was one of the main factors that decided a good spot for camping.

Most of the land the Cyreans passed through on their way to Babylonia was very fertile, and criss-crossed by plenty of rivers. It is easiest to assume that they never had to transport more than a small proportion of their daily water requirements, and to focus on the food. The vast majority of people in the camp were adult males, so we can take their requirements as a kind of average, rounding down to allow for females and youngsters. In easy round figures, there were (let us say, continuing to be conservative) 50,000 men, combatants and non-combatants, on the outward phase of the expedition. If each person received his daily requirement of 1.25 kilograms of food, the total daily requirement was 62,500 kilograms of food (though somewhat more of raw materials, since bread weighs a little less than the unground grain from which it is made). An ancient six-wheeler wagon could carry up to 650 kilograms, so if the army had ever been required to carry all its food, it would have needed about 100 big carts just for this, and 200 for two days' worth of food, and so on. By comparison, a horse can carry about 150 kilograms, a mule about 90, a donkey about 65, and a man about 30.

'We can formulate a general principle,' says historian Donald Engels, after extensive research into the logistics of Alexander the Great's army, 'that is valid for large and small expeditions alike: an army whose supplies are carried by animals and men cannot advance through desert where neither grain, fodder, or water is available for more than four days. If the army were fed full rations, it could not advance for more than two full days without incurring heavy casualties.' Although Engels was studying the logistics of a somewhat different kind of army, the principle holds for the Cyreans with the only qualification being the relatively minor point that the Cyreans were more efficient – in terms of the ratio of weight carried to food consumed by transport animals – because they made greater use of carts and team animals. The principle also holds good for false deserts – that is, regions where the hostility of the inhabitants prevents the army from revictualling. If we assume that the natives could not stop the Cyreans from gaining water, which was more easily available in rivers and lakes, we may double the number of days and reformulate the principle as follows: in regions where climate or hostility means that no supplies other than water are available, the army could carry supplies for no more than four days. By the same token, an army cannot afford to remain long in one place, because it rapidly begins to exhaust the available provisions. The urgency that these considerations imposed on the generals can easily be imagined.

We have no way of knowing in more detail how Cyrus's men coped with their transport requirements – how much was carried on carts, how much by pack animals, and how much by soldiers or their slaves – but the statistics above are enough to show that the movement of such a large army was an enormous logistical exercise, with the major issue always being provisions. Mercenaries were expected to supply themselves with food, or rather they expected their commanders to make sure it was available. Provisions and fodder could be plundered, if they were passing through hostile territory, by slaves or lightly clad soldiers, protected by horsemen, so that the main army could stay in formation. Plundered food was either handed out in lieu of payment, pooled, or sold within the army, with the cash later recycled as pay for the troops.

Plundering was acceptable in hostile regions, but otherwise, with little time spare for hunting, they had to buy food from the traders who accompanied the army or from friendly local villages and towns – in fact, it was more or less the definition of a friendly town that it was prepared to offer the army a market, even if it did so from fear rather than from any true friendly feelings. Of course, for reasons of security, traders set up their stalls outside the town walls, so that the troops would not be tempted to run riot inside. Buying food was essentially what their pay was for, which is why mercenaries found it acceptable to be paid wholly or partly in kind rather than in cash; the two terms 'pay' and 'rations' were often interchangeable. Cyrus's troops could expect to pay about 10 drachmas, not far off two weeks' pay for an ordinary soldier, for one sheep, or for 35 litres of wine, or for 100 litres of grain.

An additional source of food, as long as they were on the main military roads of the Persian empire, was the occasional warehouse, stocked with emergency supplies for the use of passing Persian forces. Up until Thapsacus, when Cyrus made the bold decision to abandon man-made roads for desert tracks, natural trails that followed the lie of the land, he could have plundered these depots, but in any case Persian military roads did not necessarily form straight lines between places, but were deliberately routed through areas with agricultural and water resources sufficient to support large numbers of men and animals.

On the March

As well as being an enormous logistical exercise, the movement of the army was an untidy affair. Ancient armies never marched in step, a drill that had to await well-surfaced roads. The clouds of dust may be imagined, that filled the air, the nostrils and the eyes of the men as they marched, while in wet conditions the men in front churned up the ground for those behind. On the march, the mobile troops – the cavalry and Greek peltasts – preceded the hoplites, then came Cyrus and his household troops, the baggage train and camp followers, and the Asiatic infantry, and finally more cavalry brought up the rear.

Horsemen and peltasts were allowed to break formation, to act as scouts and scavengers. The army did not march in orderly ranks during those stages of the journey when it was under no threat, but threw out stragglers on all sides, partly in order to forage for food and firewood, partly to avoid the worst of the dust and mud. Only at the beginning and end of each day would they properly reassemble into their units. The army on the march occupied about 30 kilometres. If they had to march in single file, as when they bypassed the great trench dug by Artaxerxes close to the Euphrates, the rear of the army would have been even more out of touch with the van.

The Greek corps was structured, essentially, by its division into companies of 100 men – 100 before losses began to take their toll. This meant that, even when marching through friendly territory, they were not a chaotic mob: in friendly territory, they formed an extended column of companies, one behind the other; in hostile territory, several companies marched parallel to one another, terrain permitting, with the rest in the same formation behind. At night, they billeted by company (the word 'company' in fact translates the Greek term *lokhos*, which originally meant a group of men who take their rest together). With the *lokhos* as the basic tactical unit of the army, a clear chain existed by which orders could be passed. The generals each knew their company commanders by name, and the company commanders were personally acquainted with the men in their company. The generals' orders were passed in the first instance to a meeting of the company commanders, who then dispersed and transmitted them to their companies.

The army broke camp at first light and set off without the troops having eaten more than a crust of bread soaked in diluted wine or olive oil. The objective was to reach the next staging-post by the middle of the day, where they would collect water, prepare and eat a meal, arrange themselves, and settle down to rest in the heat of the afternoon, while waiting for foragers to return and for the rest of the column to catch up and settle down. If they felt safe, horsemen such as Xenophon could hunt during the day and still meet up with the main body by midday. There was a late-afternoon meal, and possibly a snack in the evening before retiring. There were no drills or exercises apart from the occasional review, though many of the Greeks continued their athletic training whenever they could. The afternoons or evenings were also times for the officers to meet.

Camps were not constructions, defended by palisades, unless the generals knew in advance that they were going to stay for a while. Normally, they were simply stopping-points, where units of men could protect themselves, find water, fodder, food and firewood, stack their weapons, build a fire and pitch a tent or sling a hammock. The army at rest occupied a huge area. There was no common centre: the Greeks and the non-Greeks occupied distinct areas, and the separate units within each corps carved out their own ground. There were no latrines: people simply moved a little way from the camp, a practice that would anyway serve to make camp-sites temporary. Outlying sentries were posted and replaced during the watches of the night to protect the camp from external enemies, and further guards kept watch over the stacked and stored weapons within the camp. Xenophon's considered opinion, without a hint of irony, was that guards and pickets should be chosen from those who are most inexperienced and fearful, because they are more likely to remain alert.

So Cyrus's army marched and trundled to meet its doom at Cunaxa. The journey there was undertaken in an optimistic and relatively light-hearted fashion, with time for hunting and reviews and an athletic contest. Sometimes, as he gave his horse its head in exotic or glorious countryside, and brought back something for the communal cooking-pot at the campfire, it must have seemed to Xenophon a grand life. The mood was marred only by the tension between rival groups of Greeks, but that could be put down to nervous anticipation. Only once were provisions scarce, and then only the animals suffered badly. Battered later by both physical and metaphorical storms, the men would learn to look back on this phase of the march as a calm sea.

CHAPTER SEVEN

Xenophon Takes Command

By dawn on the day after the battle, the Greek mercenaries had heard the news: Cyrus was dead, the battle was lost, and Cyrus's Asiatic troops had fled or deserted. The Greeks were isolated, strangers in a strange land, 3,000 or so kilometres from home and surrounded by thousands of the very men they had just tried to annihilate. With their baggage train ransacked, they were low on supplies and they would have to enter into an unequal competition with the Persians themselves for scarce resources; they had virtually no horsemen with which to combat the Persian cavalry; in these days before maps and compasses, they had little idea how to get home, or to any other place of safety. They were like a freshly decapitated chicken, poised to skitter aimlessly for a while, haemorrhaging men, before collapsing dead.

Defeat prompted a change in the mercenaries' motivations. Many among them had never had any desire other than to enrich themselves and get back home to their families; but many others, those who had already been uprooted by their commitment to the mercenary life, or by voluntary or enforced exile from their native cities, had been attracted by the possibility of staying in the east, and either continuing in Cyrus's service after he had taken the Persian throne or even founding a colony somewhere. Cyrus himself had dangled these possibilities. When, before the start of the campaign, he appealed to the Spartans for assistance (which led to their sending Cheirisophus and his 700 hoplites), he promised 'that he would give horses to any men who came as foot soldiers, chariots to those who came as horsemen, villages to those who owned farms, and towns to those who owned villages'. Then again, in the pre-battle speech Cyrus delivered to the Greek officers, the prince recognized the two motives that had brought the mercenaries east. He ended by saying: 'If you are men and if my business here goes well, I will make any of you who wants to return home an object of envy to his neighbours; but I think I shall make many of you choose to stay with me rather than return home.'

Now they had no such financial safety net and dreams of a fine future were dispelled by the reality of defeat. Mercenary forces depended entirely on their paymasters, but suddenly the Greeks had no status: they had become a vagabond army of freebooters, no longer mercenaries, with no purpose beyond self-preservation. Cyrus's death brought their worst fears alive and made everything other than survival seem irrelevant, out of focus on the margins of interest. Talk around the campfires was increasingly of home and its comforts, or at least its security.

Their first thought, however, was to continue as king-makers. If they could not place Cyrus on the Persian throne, they would do the same for his uncle, Ariaeus. But Ariaeus, who had fled about 20 kilometres from the battlefield, sensibly pointed out how little support he would receive from the Persian nobility; there were many who had a better claim to the throne than he did, and even if they succeeded in defeating Artaxerxes and his satraps, he could hardly expect to meet with the loyalty that would guarantee his security.

Meanwhile, messengers arrived from Artaxerxes demanding the surrender of the Greeks. The only ray of light was that the king still seemed to consider them a force to be reckoned with, and they refused to lay down their weapons. Cleanor of Orchomenus defiantly echoed the famous and famously laconic reply of Leonidas to Xerxes before the battle of Thermopylae in 480; when the Persian king demanded that the Spartans should surrender their weapons, Leonidas said: 'Come and get them.' But in Cleanor's case it was no more than bravado. They expected to be attacked at any moment; the soldiers' nerves were stretched taut, the camp was filled with rumours and false alarms. Many of the Cyreans felt desperate enough to consider desertion, although in the event only the 40 Thracian horsemen and about 300 peltasts sneaked away during the night, after that first, horrible day.

Under these circumstances, the prudent option was unity, and the Greeks made their way to where wounded Ariaeus had made his camp. The leaders of the two corps swore loyalty to each other with the most solemn and binding oaths, involving the sacrifice of a bull, a boar, a ram and a wolf. Further unity was both possible and desirable, and the Greeks looked less to the individual commanders who had so far led them in separate contingents, and more to Clearchus, who, to Meno's disgust, emerged as the only general with enough experience to win the trust of the men and the unofficial position of commander-in-chief. As professional soldiers, having rejected the idea of surrender, their next thought was to offer themselves to Artaxerxes, to serve as his mercenaries in rebel Egypt. Even though later in his reign he hired Greeks for precisely that task, Artaxerxes could hardly be seen to employ the very troops who had just threatened his throne, and he firmly turned them down.

However much care Clearchus took to paint a positive picture of their situation, the reality was grim. Ariaeus and Artaxerxes had spurned their offers, and their only remaining option was a difficult and dangerous retreat. They could not return by the direct route they had taken, because they had exhausted the limited supplies available there, but they trusted Ariaeus to show them an alternative way home. And so they set out north, marching in battle formation, knowing that substantial numbers of the enemy were close at hand, even though Tissaphernes and Artaxerxes had withdrawn across the Tigris.

But their reputation as a formidable army was still working in their favour. The very next morning they were approached by a Persian delegation, which had been empowered to negotiate a truce. Clearchus agreed to a cessation of hostilities, provided that they were taken somewhere they could satisfy their pressing demand for food. The Persians agreed, and took them to a cluster of mud-brick villages with stores and food sufficient for an extended stay even by such a huge army. Three days later, an even more high-powered delegation appeared, led by Tissaphernes himself. The Cyreans' future depended utterly on the skills their commanding officers could bring to the negotiating table.

Tissaphernes made out to the Greeks that he had been using his time with Artaxerxes to mitigate the king's hostility towards the Greeks. He gave them the impression that he was their only hope of safety, and that he and he alone could restrain the king and the rest of the high-ranking Persians, who wanted simply to annihilate them. The Greeks argued that they had not known until it was too late to turn back that Cyrus had been intending to attack the king, and they resorted to the standard wartime justification: we were only carrying out orders. These feeble excuses would have cut no ice at all with the king if he and Tissaphernes had not already mapped out the immediate future, and a couple of days later Tissaphernes returned, claiming that he now had permission to lead the Greeks back home. Was this Cyrus's old arch-enemy? The Greeks should have been more circumspect.

The Greeks and Tissaphernes entered into an agreement whereby the Persian promised to lead them back to Greece without treachery, and either to sell them provisions or, where no market was available, to allow them to forage. The Greeks, for their part, promised to abide strictly by these conditions – that is, they promised not to treat the land they passed through as hostile territory. The vast majority of the ordinary soldiers had hardly any money left, from what Cyrus had given them weeks earlier in Cayster Field, with which to buy provisions, but their officers had little choice. The alternatives to agreeing to these terms were unthinkable.

Tissaphernes and Artaxerxes then left for Babylon, to consult and to carry out post-battle rewards and punishments. Tissaphernes himself was given one of the king's daughters as his wife and was elevated to the supreme command of Asia Minor – the post left vacant by Cyrus's death. Although Tissaphernes had made out that he was on the Greeks' side, he spent the time plotting their utter destruction. Back at the villages that were supporting the Cyreans, his agents were busy suborning Ariaeus and his officers, promising to pardon them if they turned against the Greeks. Ariaeus would have to betray his oaths of loyalty to the Greeks, but he was in an impossible position. If he remained the Greeks' ally, what would happen to him? The Greeks were planning, as far as anyone knew, to return home and disperse – whereupon Ariaeus would be isolated in a hostile land. Perhaps, since the Greeks had offered him the throne of Persia, he was toying with a lesser idea: to establish himself somewhere with the help of the Greeks. But the king trumped any such idea, and rewarded him afterwards for his treachery with the rich satrapy of Greater Phrygia, when before he had been governor of Hellespontine Phrygia alone.

If we are to believe Ctesias, despite his evident partiality for lurid and melodramatic tales, Parysatis grieved for her favourite Cyrus. She challenged the king to a game of dice, and her reward for winning was the right to do whatever she liked with the man who had cut off her son's limbs. She chose to have him flayed alive and then crucified, with his skin on another stake next to him – but then he was only a slave, a eunuch. The Persians were connoisseurs of savage torture, especially for crimes against the king or a member of the royal family. As a punishment for having lied about his role in the battle, Artaxerxes had one of his noblemen stretched out and tied down, naked but bound loosely in cloth, on the benches of a boat; he was force-fed and his face was smeared with honey; flies, attracted by the honey and in due course by his faeces, laid their eggs. It took seventeen days for the maggots to kill him.

The Capture of the Generals

Days became weeks, and the Greeks grew restless, but Clearchus refused to let them move, in case movement was interpreted as hostile activity. Along with the rest of the Greeks, he was worried about the stream of Persian visitors to Ariaeus's camp, but Tissaphernes had given him his word and bound himself with oaths. One thing every Greek knew about Persians, from hearsay or from reading Herodotus, was that in childhood noble Persians were taught three things above all: archery, horsemanship and honesty. Zoroastrian religion (which, unusually for the times, was based on belief rather than ritual performance) utterly polarized Justice and Falsehood. Pledges, oaths and compacts were especially honoured: a man's word was sacred, and the punishments reserved for oath-breakers were terrible. While this should have led to upright behaviour, kings and even satraps felt that they had been specially chosen by Ahuramazda, which often meant that they interpreted whatever they did as Justice, and what their enemies did as the opposite. The world, the entire universe, was a battlefield involving the struggle between good and evil, and as Ahuramazda's chosen instruments, the royal families could do only good.

During their long wait for Tissaphernes in Babylonia, the Greeks were well supported by the land. This alluvial region was one of the most fertile parts of the great Mesopotamian plain, which extends all the way from the Persian Gulf to the foothills of the Kurdish mountains, and its natural fertility was and still is enhanced by a system of canals exploiting the difference in height between the Euphrates and the lower-lying Tigris. The Greeks ate well and replenished their supplies with barley, dates and garlic, wine, sesame oil and sour cheese. Those with money could have bought linen clothing to replace their worn garments, and the far-sighted may have found a sheepskin and strong footwear to keep them warm during the winter. But the long delay put further pressure on those with little or no money: Tissaphernes was turning the screw.

Tissaphernes returned after three weeks. He and Orontas, the satrap of Armenia, were to escort the Greeks back to Asia Minor, while taking their own troops to their respective satrapies. And so they set out north. Ariaeus no longer maintained even the pretence of being on their side, but marched and camped with Tissaphernes and Orontas. Tissaphernes first had them cross the Tigris to its eastern bank. No doubt the pretext was the presence of an easier road over the level eastern plain, or of well-stocked villages, but the reality was that it would leave the Greeks with two major rivers to cross if they ever decided to turn west and take the more direct route back to Asia Minor. But at this early stage of the northward march through Babylonia and Media, the Greeks still felt that they had no choice but to accept Tissaphernes's lead.

Tension mounted as the two armies proceeded with extreme caution for many days, covering 400 kilometres in a ghastly cat-and-mouse charade. From time to time, the competition for resources such as firewood brought men from the opposing camps to blows, but these incidents never escalated out of control. Meanwhile, Clearchus seized every opportunity to dissuade the Persians from attacking by deploying the Greek army in formidable formations, but for a while he remained unaware that the greatest danger came from closer to hand. Meno had been seduced by Ariaeus, who was now primed to betray the Greeks.

As they marched north up the Tigris and across its tributaries, Meno began spending more and more time with Ariaeus. Sex was the less significant aspect of their relationship. Ariaeus, on Tissaphernes's orders, was working on Meno's intense jealousy of Clearchus. The Phrygian satrap even arranged a meeting between Meno and Tissaphernes: whatever else they talked about, Meno left the meeting with the clear impression that, if Clearchus's position could be undermined, Tissaphernes would raise him to supreme command of the Greek mercenaries and find them employment.

Meno's next move was to bring Proxenus over to his side, with the offer of senior command under his leadership. Proxenus was one of those people whose ambitions outstrip their abilities, and he was easily won over. From there, Meno proceeded less surreptitiously, and gained the allegiance of other contingents in the army with the argument that he had the support of Ariaeus and Tissaphernes, while Clearchus was still hostile to the Persians. With Clearchus as their leader, Meno argued, open warfare with Tissaphernes was sooner or later inevitable; under his leadership, however, danger could be averted and they would

The ruins of Nimrud. Xenophon passed by the ruins not long after he had taken command of a division of the army, but had no time to explore since he had a Persian army on his tail. He wrongly identified the Assyrian site as Median.

be gainfully employed. By this stage Clearchus was of course aware of Meno's manoeuvring, and although his own men remained loyal to him, he took steps to counteract Meno's growing influence and open rivalry.

When the armies halted at the junction of the Tigris with the Greater Zab river (the ancient Zapatas, not far south of the ruined Assyrian city of Nimrud), Clearchus arranged a meeting with Tissaphernes. The pretext for the meeting was an attempt to defuse the potentially explosive tension between the two armies, but Clearchus used the opportunity to try to thwart Meno: he insisted to Tissaphernes that he and he alone could control the Greeks, and at the same time he offered them again as employable mercenaries. He also insinuated the suggestion that the Greeks would be available to help, if Tissaphernes himself had kingly ambitions. Tissaphernes let Clearchus believe that this idea was pleasing to him, with a reference to an arcane aspect of Persian court protocol: 'Only the king,' he said, 'may wear the royal tiara upright on his head, but perhaps, with your support, someone else too might easily so wear the tiara that is in his heart.'

Clearchus followed the slippery trail of Tissaphernes's words. Spartans were famously god-fearing and superstitious, and Tissaphernes had eloquently affirmed his adherence to their mutual oaths. Clearchus was convinced, and Tissaphernes was able to move rapidly on to the end game. He suggested a further meeting, attended this time not by Clearchus alone, but by all the senior Greek officers. At this meeting, Tissaphernes said, he would tell Clearchus who the trouble-makers were (that is, he would confirm Clearchus's suspicions about Meno and Proxenus), and Clearchus reciprocated by promising to tell Tissaphernes which Greek officers were still refusing to trust the Persians. Tissaphernes knew that Clearchus would do his best to persuade even those Greek officers who were reluctant to attend, in order to demonstrate that he was in charge; he also knew that he could count on Clearchus's gaining the enthusiastic support of Meno and Proxenus, who expected Tissaphernes to use the meeting to raise them to overall command of the mercenaries.

In the event, five out of the eight generals went to the meeting, and they were accompanied by twenty company commanders, out of 120. While the company commanders waited outside, Clearchus, Meno, Proxenus, Agias and Socrates entered Tissaphernes's spacious pavilion. Before the meeting had gone on for very long, both Meno and Clearchus realized their foolishness: personal rivalry had blinded them to Tissaphernes's trickery.

A short while later, at a single signal, those who were inside were seized and those who were outside were murdered. Then some of the barbarian horsemen rode across the plain, killing every Greek they came across, whether free man or slave. The Greeks in their camp were surprised to see all this riding about, but they did not know what the Persians were doing, until Nicarchus of Arcadia managed to escape. He reached the Greek camp, holding his entrails in his hands from a wound to the guts, and told them all that had happened. The Greeks were terrified, and they ran to get their weapons, thinking that an attack on the camp was imminent.

The Greek generals were not killed immediately. They were taken in chains to Babylon, where they were displayed before the curiosity of courtiers and citizens. Parysatis tried to persuade the king to spare the life of Clearchus, at least, but Stateira demanded his death and won. Before many days had passed, Clearchus had been put to death along with Socrates, Agias and Proxenus. It was said that whereas birds and dogs tore at the bodies of the rest of the generals, a miraculous gust of wind covered Clearchus's body with dust and earth, and that in later years date palms flourished on this tomb, improvised by nature. Meanwhile, the traitor Meno was spared for a while and kept as the king's adviser, until he was no longer useful: within a year he too was dead. His supposed lover, Ariaeus, made not the slightest effort to save him.

Was all this simple treachery on Tissaphernes's part, or were there legalistic grounds that could exculpate him in the eyes of the gods before whom he had sworn to do the Greeks no harm, unless they initiated hostilities? The Greeks had sworn to buy their food from the market provided by the Persians, but not all the Greeks had money with which they could keep this promise. Cheirisophus and his 700 hoplites, for instance, had joined the army after the payment at Cayster Field, so they had only whatever money they had brought with them from Sparta. At the time of the fateful meeting in Tissaphernes's tent, in fact, Cheirisophus and his men were out foraging, and so were a number of other Greeks. But Tissaphernes was still providing them with goods for sale, and another 200 soldiers had accompanied the generals and the company commanders to the Persian camp in order to visit the market, which was located there. In other words, Cheirisophus and the rest were not supposed to be out foraging. By the terms of the truce, they were allowed to forage only when Tissaphernes gave them permission and could not provide them with a market – as, a few days earlier, he had let them plunder some Median villages belonging to Parysatis, who had loved Cyrus and who loathed Tissaphernes.

This was a purely technical transgression of the truce – but it was enough for Tissaphernes's conscience. Of course, he had intended all along to kill the generals, or at any rate to find some way to destroy the Ten Thousand (perhaps just by abandoning them to the pitiless cold and the savage tribesmen of the northern mountains), but now he could also justify his action to the Greeks by accusing the generals he had captured of being oath-breakers, a terrible crime in both Greek and Persian eyes. Tissaphernes had behaved throughout with consummate cunning. He had manipulated the situation so that the Greeks had no choice but to enter into an unfavourable truce with him, he had sown discord among the generals, and he had enticed most of the senior officers into a trap. The only mistake he made was assuming that, without leadership, the army would fall apart. He had not reckoned on Xenophon.

Xenophon to the Rescue

The treacherous arrest of the generals – the Greeks saw it as treacherous, anyway – and slaughter of their comrades was the turning-point for Xenophon, and when he came to write up his account of the expedition he indicated as much by introducing himself for the first time into the narrative. After recapitulating his reasons for joining the army, he returned to the present, and to a significant dream. The night after the arrest, when he finally fell into a restless sleep, he dreamt that his father's house was struck by lightning and burst into flames. Ever the optimist, he was inclined to interpret this as hopeful – as a sign that Zeus would illuminate his household. At any rate, he woke up, convened the company commanders of the contingent formerly led by his friend Proxenus, and delivered a speech that blended encouragement with a bid for generalship. The company commanders were happy to take Xenophon up on his offer to take over as their general. The decision was unanimous, once they had scapegoated and evicted from their number the only dissenter, a Boeotian called Apollonides, who had lived abroad long enough to attract ridicule from his conservative comrades for the habit he had gained in Lydia of wearing earrings.

Why would they elect Xenophon a general, when by his own account he had not joined the expedition as a soldier? Not just because he impressed them with good ideas. Although there was a trend towards increasing professionalism, in many Greek cities, including Athens, generalship was still a political as much as a military post, and the first requirement was membership of the right class. A little later that night, when Xenophon was addressing all the surviving company commanders and generals, he came up with what was obviously expected to be an irrefutable argument: 'In peacetime,' he told them, 'you had more money and standing than your men; in a time of war like this, you should insist on being better than the rank and file.' As in Europe until recently, social rank and military rank were inseparable. It was assumed that a gentleman's upbringing would equip him for command, and not least by triggering his inbred assumption that he should rule. In any case, it is also likely that Xenophon had experienced battle and possibly some degree of command in the last decade of the Peloponnesian War. On the first day of his new command, Xenophon exposed some of his men to unnecessary risk, but he learnt from his mistake and one of the themes in the rest of the narrative is his personal brilliance as a commander and how everyone, from the lowest ranks to the highest, came to depend on his advice.

It was still the middle of the night, but in their desperation Xenophon and his company commanders did not hesitate to convene the surviving officers of other contingents. They too elected generals to replace those they had lost. As a glorious dawn rose over the table-flat plain and made the water of the Zab sparkle with new hope, they called a general assembly of all the troops, to win them over to their view that there was no longer any point in negotiation, principally because they could not realistically adhere to the terms of any treaty. But war would at least bring the advantage that they could plunder the countryside with clear consciences. In any case, they expected to be attacked by the Persians at any moment, and Xenophon even wore his most ornate and costly armour to the assembly, since he wanted to greet death with glory.

The decision to make open war on the Persians, rather than try to treat with them or hope for their protection during the retreat, was one of the critical moments of the expedition, in terms of the effect it had on welding the army into a whole. They still operated in separate contingents under different commanders, but we hear of surprisingly few desertions, and nothing of the fragmenting of the army, until they reached the relative safety of the Black Sea. Their sole purpose was survival, and they worked well together to achieve it. In an odd sense, Tissaphernes had done them a favour by lancing the boil of Clearchus's and Meno's personal animosity.

At the assembly, Xenophon reminded them how their grandfathers had defeated the Persians and pointed out that they could reasonably hope that the gods would abandon the treacherous Persians. As if in confirmation, just as Xenophon mentioned the possibility of their salvation, one of the men sneezed. A sudden sneeze, being outside one's conscious control, was god-given, and all the Greeks agreed that this was a good omen from Zeus the Saviour.

At Xenophon's insistence, the men took drastic steps to prepare for the journey. They burnt the carts, so that their pace was not dictated by the slow movement of the teams of oxen; they discarded their cumbersome tents, and they shed all non-essential baggage. The tactic of purging the army of superfluous equipment was incredibly risky, given that they did not know what conditions they might face in the future and what equipment might then be needed. But in addition to the obvious practical purpose, lightening a load often brings emotional rewards in terms of commitment to a new future, as people find when moving house. There is said to be an Amazonian tribe that conducts a week-long ritual involving the destruction, every night, of more of their property (little enough in the first place), until they have nothing. They have to disburden themselves, they say, in order to be able to return to their birthplace, their beginning. Xenophon's men were also headed home, back to the lands of their birth.

At first, the Greeks were constantly harried by Persian skirmishers, but Xenophon again optimistically saw the bright side, and argued that they had gained a cheap lesson. He organized effective defences against such harassment by raising a small troop of fifty horsemen (some horses were being used as transport animals) under his friend Lycius, who proved surprisingly effective even against far larger numbers of Persian cavalry. At the same time, he drew on the expertise of the Rhodians in the army as slingers. They foraged for lead to make bullets, which could travel further than the stones used by the Persians; they could travel further, in fact, than javelins (a maximum of 75 metres with a run-up, less from horseback) and arrows (about 150 metres). Slings were made out of two strips of leather, linen or plaited horsehair, about a metre long, with a pouch to hold the shot, which was cast in strings in clay moulds and then broken off for use. The sling was whirled around the head and then one end of it was released, so that the shot flew off. With an average weight of between 30 and 40 grams, such bullets could be fatal, or a fatal nuisance. The chance discovery of a lead slingshot in Lydia, inscribed with the name of Tissaphernes, shows that he learnt from his experience of the Cyreans: on his return to Asia Minor, he began to have his troops make their own lead bullets and marked them with his name.

The Greeks gained a couple of days of untroubled but slow marching, during which they passed the ruins of Assyrian Nimrud and Nineveh (destroyed by the Medes towards the end of the seventh century). At Nimrud, the terrified inhabitants of the local villages had taken refuge on the stepped sides of the towering ziggurat. They had no great love for the Persians, who had bankrupted many of them and forced them into selling their labour for hire rather than managing their own smallholdings; but they had even less love for a marauding army of pillagers.

After Nineveh (near modern Mosul), the Greeks left the Tigris and continued more directly north. For days they dragged themselves slowly onward, worrying less about rapid progress and more about finding villages where they could halt, treat the wounded and stock up on provisions. They rested when they could in secure villages in hills where the Persian cavalry could not easily reach them, but otherwise they marched in whatever defensive formation suited the terrain, which varied from level plain to rugged cliffs pierced by valleys. Cheirisophus, as an experienced Spartan, commanded the van, while Xenophon and Timasion (who had taken up the life of a mercenary commander when he had been exiled from Dardanus, his native town in the Troad), were in charge of the rear. On a couple of occasions, the Greeks were involved in a deadly race to occupy crucial high ground before the enemy; almost every day Tissaphernes or his subordinates did their best to slow them down, by threat of attack or actual assault, and almost every day the Greeks lost a few more men. Every moment of carelessness, such as leaving foragers undefended, cost them dearly. Although Tissaphernes gradually brought ever larger forces to bear against the Greeks, he was content to skirmish: he had no need to risk an all-out battle, because if his first objective was the destruction of the Greek army, his second was just to see them out of Persian territory.

The impassability of the Zagros mountains of north-eastern Iraq forced them to turn north-west, keeping to the foothills to dissuade attacks by the Persian cavalry. Close to modern Zakhü (not far from the junction of the borders of modern Iraq, Syria and Turkey), they forded the last of the serious tributaries of the Tigris. A few days of further travel, in landscape so rugged that the Persian forces might disappear for a whole day, only to reappear unnervingly on a ridge above them, brought them back to the Tigris, near modern Cizre in Turkey.

Cizre is on a major crossroads, and the Greeks had to make a decision there. The Tigris was still too deep to ford, and they were hemmed between the river and awesome mountains. The prisoners they were using as guides told them what lay roughly to the north, south, east and west, but the generals had already made up their

Typical highlands near Cizre. For a sense of scale, see the pylon in the bottom right corner. The Cyreans had to cross these high hills and deep valleys to reach the Carduchian mountains.

minds. They had come from the south; both the east and the west were securely held by the Persians (a troop of Persian horsemen was even visible on the western bank of the river, which put paid to a wild plan to float the army across on inflated skins); they had to go north, into the mountainous domain of the Carduchians, wild tribesmen who had never been tamed even by the might of the Persians.

The Greek Sea

It was Xenophon's intention to lead his men 'home', or to rejoin 'the Greeks'. Under any circumstances, but especially theirs, the word 'home' carries a potent charge. But the army consisted of men from all over the Greek world: the majority were from the Peloponnese; others originated in central and northern Greece, in Crete and Sicily and the Aegean islands, and in Asia Minor. Many had formed attachments with places or people in the east itself. Where, then, was 'home'?

In about 2000 BCE, a people speaking proto-Greek made their way into the Greek peninsula. The poverty of the land and increasing awareness of opportunities abroad prompted a wave of emigration, between about 1050 and 950, until the Greek world consisted of numerous independent communities on the peninsula, the islands and Asia Minor. From 750 to 550, population pressures and ever-present poverty initiated another wave of colonization, as flourishing cities sent out groups to settle around the shores of the western Mediterranean, and east around the Black Sea.

Men took a founding band with them and went in search of richer lands, either because they had been exiled, or out of a sense of adventure and to secure a strategic location along a trade route for the good of their native city and their own pockets. Metals and timber were in especially high demand, but wheat and other foodstuffs such as salted fish came a close third, to supplement what Greek soil and sea could provide. Sometimes the new colonies owed ties of allegiance to their mother city; more often they were independent foundations, with the right to refer back to the mother city in later years if it became politically expedient. Typically, only 100 or so able-bodied men went out on these colonizing expeditions with their slaves, and they took local women as their wives to perpetuate the new community. There were no issues about purity of lineage, because women were commonly held to be no more than receptacles for children, who gained all their characteristics from their fathers.

By the time this stream had slowed to a trickle, there were around 1,500 Greek communities and the Greek world extended all over the Mediterranean and the Black Sea; the traditional phrase was 'from the Phasis river to the Pillars of Heracles', the Phasis being in modern Georgia and the Pillars of Heracles being what we call the Straits of Gibraltar. In Plato's memorable image the Greeks were scattered around the coastlines of the known world 'like frogs or ants around a pond'. The Greek world had no clear centre: what stood duty for the centre was the sea.

Through trade and colonization they had made the coastlines their own: everywhere they went, they could expect to be able to communicate with fellow Greeks, with only minor local variations in accent and dialect. They were always wary about travelling too far inland from the sea. Even on the Greek peninsula, the mountainous inland separated rather than united communities, and turned eyes away from the land and towards the sea. Every visitor to Greece recognizes the limpid beauty and the emotional power of the sea: the jolt of delight at the sight of turquoise shallows and purple depths, half-glimpsed rocks and patches of weed. When Xenophon told his men that they were going 'home', then, he meant that they were going to find the sea. That was where they would rejoin the Greek world.

Only some, including Xenophon, still wanted to settle in the east. Not far into their cat-and-mouse journey north with Tissaphernes, while the first batch of generals was still alive, there was speculation in the camp that the Persians were afraid that the Greeks might try to carve out a piece of defensible territory and make it their own. The idea was not entertained as a serious possibility: it would be far too risky to settle in the Persian heartland. Nevertheless, Xenophon attempted to address the inevitable slump in morale after the murder of the generals by mentioning the possibility of settling there, as a way of encouraging his men by claiming that the Persians were more afraid of them than they need be of the Persians.

More realistically, he suggested that they should first get home to Greece, and then send out a colonizing expedition. It was only after the retreating army reached the Black Sea coast that their own colony became a more realistic and contentious possibility. The dream took hold of Xenophon's mind at Cotyora:

> Meanwhile, Xenophon had been looking at how many Greeks there were there, counting not just the hoplites, but also the peltasts, archers, slingers and horsemen; their experiences seemed to him to have given them a high degree of proficiency and there they were on the coast of the Black Sea, where it would have taken a great deal of money to organize such a large army. As a result of these reflections, it occurred to him that it would be a fine achievement to found a city and acquire extra land and resources for Greece. It would be a sizeable city, he thought, when their numbers were added to the local inhabitants of the Black Sea coast.

At the time, the idea caused Xenophon nothing but trouble: those who wanted to get back home spread the rumour that Xenophon was making plans without consulting the troops, in order to gain power and fame for himself, while two unscrupulous officers seized the opportunity to blackmail the nearest Greek cities. If you don't send us ships and money, they said, we won't be able to stop Xenophon founding a settlement which would act as a base for plundering raids on your lands. Xenophon found a clever way to simultaneously save his face, keep the army together, and allow the Greek cities to send the ships they had already promised without succumbing to unscrupulous blackmail. But the plan was put on the back burner only for a short while. Further along the coast, he dreamt of founding a colony at Calpe Harbour, which seemed the perfect spot: there was a good natural harbour, fresh water, a defensible headland, plenty of timber, and rich, arable land. Before long both Greeks and natives living near by were so convinced that the mercenaries were there to stay that they began sending delegations to Xenophon, as the prime mover of the settlement. Once again, however, the project did not prove popular: more of the men just wanted to take the money they had accumulated by then and get back home. The battle cast a long shadow over the motivations that prevailed in the army.

For all Xenophon's rhetoric about getting 'home' to wives and children (or 'children and wives', to use the usual, telling Greek order), and for all the men's expressed desire to do just that, the irony is that in the end extremely few of them made it home. First, it turned out that the Greek cities they encountered on the Black Sea coast had intermingled too much with the local populations to count as Greek – at any rate, Xenophon describes Byzantium as the first truly Greek city they reached – and they were certainly not as welcoming as home is meant to be (though that was largely the Cyreans' fault). Second, by the time the army reached Byzantium, there were fewer than 7,000 men left: the army had almost been halved. Then the vast majority of the remaining men re-enlisted, first under the Odrysian warlord Seuthes, and subsequently to help the Spartans in their war against the Persians. Within the time-frame covered by Xenophon in *The Expedition of Cyrus*, only a few hundred men trickled away from Byzantium and returned to their native lands. And this small group of men included none of the protagonists, who died, disappeared, or re-enlisted in the east to fight against Tissaphernes again, back where they had started. Xenophon's dream of fire was after all about the loss of his family home, not about its glorification.

What went wrong? Was talk of 'home' mere rhetoric? Whatever happened on the expedition itself, by the time Xenophon wrote *The Expedition of Cyrus*, it was subtle rhetoric indeed. By making 'home' the Pole Star of the retreat from Cunaxa, he draws our attention to the fact that we cannot give a precise answer to the question of that home's whereabouts: it might have been the sea, but the communities on the Black Sea let them down; it might have been wherever the men came from, but they came from all over the Mediterranean. This openness turned the tale Xenophon wrote into an archetypal search: like Homer's *Odyssey*, it is the story of a journey 'home' against terrifying obstacles; like the *Odyssey* it resonates with any journey home and with every reader's deep desire for security. As such it has been used as the basis for both fictional and non-fictional treatments of the theme, from Walter Hill's 1979 film *The Warriors* to accounts of similar treks in World War II and the 2003 invasion of Iraq.

The focus on home, when they failed to create a new home for themselves in the east, and when the good and the bad alike failed to reach home, also serves to highlight the appalling uncertainty the Cyreans faced. Home was an ideal, but was unrealizable; the only thing that kept them going was unrealizable. The desire to go home thwarted the ability to reach any kind of home, because they had to remain on the move, fluid, with no fixed identity such as a colony would have forged. They were lost, often in bewilderingly difficult landscapes, in a geography of obstacles and fighting, of impassable mountains and uncrossable rivers, flooded canals, places so wild that an entire Persian army could vanish without trace, as was rumoured to have happened in the Carduchian mountains.

This was what led Clearchus to put his trust in Tissaphernes: 'I believe,' he told the Persian satrap, 'that at the moment we have no greater benefactor than you. With you, we easily travel every road, cross every river, and keep ourselves supplied with provisions. Without you, every road is shrouded in the darkness of our ignorance, every river is hard to cross, and every crowd is frightening – and yet there is nothing more frightening than solitude, which teems with uncertainties.' The uncertainties were so overwhelming that Clearchus felt forced to trust an enemy – who killed him. Even when they reached the sea, they were again faced with obstacles, and again the geographical obstacles were compounded by mistrust, and by difficulties in interacting even with fellow Greeks, culminating in the behaviour of the Spartans based in Byzantium, who proved almost as duplicitous and hard to read as the Persians earlier. Selfish behaviour created mistrust within the army, just as it had done before and immediately after Cunaxa, and led to the uncertainties created by a weakening of discipline. Even the gods were not always on their side, and communicated ambiguously.

The Cyreans had no clear identity: they were not a regular army, nor even a normal mercenary army, having no paymaster; they were not an Athenian-style community, nor a Spartan-style community, nor really any kind of political entity at all, because they were on the move and they failed to settle anywhere, even though demographically, as a group of able-bodied men, they resembled an unusually large colonizing expedition. But they were constantly trying to assert their identity, or to discover it: by scapegoating and expelling Apollonides as foreign, the Other; by toying with the idea of forming a colony; by contrasting themselves with the barbarian tribesmen they encountered; by the rhetoric of Xenophon's speeches, in which he reminded them of the glorious past of their ancestors in an attempt to forge their Greekness in a foreign land and to stiffen their resolve, lest they be seduced, he said, by the beautiful women and the luxurious living there. But in trying to establish or maintain an identity in the face of overwhelming uncertainty, they themselves became the Other, constantly rejected and kept homeless by foreigners and Greeks alike, finding communication difficult wherever they went.

And so when the army reached the crossroads on the Tigris, their choice to head north into the mountains came as no surprise. Turning east or south would take them back towards the heartlands of the Persian empire; the direct route home lay west, across the Tigris and then the Euphrates, but the plain there was perfect for the Persian cavalry, and in any case Tissaphernes forced the issue by destroying the villages on the plain and whatever stocks of supplies they had that his own army did not need. To the west, east and south, then, lay the certainties of civilization, indicated by proper roads – but in those directions lay also the certainty of death. The Greeks chose uncertainty; they chose to enter the chasm of the mountains. They were already more or less lost, but they had to get more lost in order to stand a chance of finding themselves safe.

CHAPTER EIGHT

Fearful Odds

By the time they reached the foothills of the Carduchian mountains, the Greeks had reasons for pride and cautious optimism. True, there were bound to be dangers and unknown terrors ahead, but, with the help of flexible tactics and co-operation between the various units of the army, they had escaped from Tissaphernes's clutches. The Persian satrap stopped pursuing them, not just because he was in a hurry to return to Asia Minor, to take up his command there and to keep the Greek cities in the Persian fold, nor just because he had achieved his objective of seeing the Greeks out of secure Persian territory, but because he could reasonably expect that few of them would emerge from the winter mountains. He thought he had seen the last of them.

Their grounds for optimism were even more shaky. Since the Persians had never subdued the Carduchians, the certainty of Tissaphernes's hostility would be replaced by the possibility of a truce with the mountain tribes, on the principle that 'the enemy of my enemy is my friend'. Furthermore, although the mountains were already covered with snow, and the higher they climbed the more savage the weather became, they could expect to find the rivers more easily fordable the closer they got to their sources in the vast mountain ranges. A true reflection, in fact, of the huge size and ruggedness of the eastern Turkish highlands is the fact that they give birth to two of the world's great rivers, the Euphrates and the Tigris, with a combined length of 4,500 kilometres and a combined annual volume of over 100 billion cubic metres of water, almost three-quarters of which originates in this area of the Turkish mountains, which was formerly known simply as 'Thousand Lakes'. It is some of the most difficult terrain in the world.

Once the council of Greek officers had chosen the northern route, the Greeks set out at dawn the next day, armed and wary. They crossed successive waves of hills, each range higher than the one before, with fertile highland valleys in between. As soon as they entered the mountains, the tribesmen abandoned their villages and sought the safety of the high ground, taking with them not just their families, but also the Greeks' hopes of a neutral or even friendly reception. The Greeks had no way to communicate with the Carduchians and hunger left them no choice but to plunder the villages for supplies, which was bound to commit them to hostilities. And so by the end of the first day they found themselves being harassed by expert mountain fighters armed with slings, stones and bows. Their arrows were so long that the Greeks recycled them as javelins, and their bows were powerful enough to penetrate Greek armour. The mountain men picked off Greeks one by one, and at night camped high in the mountains, with their campfires visible to the Greeks and their incomprehensible cries echoing down the frigid canyons.

The next morning the generals ordered another purge. They were about to enter snow-covered mountains, where fodder would be scarce, and so all lame transport animals were to be abandoned. This was a hard choice, because they had always been able to rest some animals while others worked. From then on they would have no fallback: every mule that died or became too lame to carry on would mean the abandonment of further baggage, or its division among already overburdened men and animals.

The knowledge that conditions were going to get worse forced the officers also to order the abandonment of all the men, women and children who had been captured for future sale. There were simply too many mouths to feed, and the army did not need to be slowed down by their inevitable reluctance. This too was a hard decision, not just for the mercenaries, who had to give up a ready source of good profit, but for the prisoners themselves, who begged pitifully not to be abandoned in the freezing mountains, with no means of defending themselves against the Carduchians.

In making such a decision, the officers weighed in the balance only its tactical soundness against its likely effect on the morale of their men. There were no Geneva Conventions in the ancient world, and the abandonment of unwanted prisoners to fend for themselves, or to die by the roadside, was not uncommon. The ancient Greek word for a prisoner of war was ungendered: they were regarded as objects, literally 'man-footed creatures' (*andrapoda*), not human beings, and even while captive, prisoners of war could expect to meet with physical and sexual abuse. Not unnaturally, then, prisoners tended to be obsequious to their captors, and if given the opportunity tried to make themselves useful, as servants or sexual partners, or by offering military information. The most important kind of information for the Cyreans was guidance.

Familiar as we are with maps, it is hard for us to project our minds back to an era when local knowledge was the only reliable resource – and when without it whole armies could get lost, pass close by sources of food without knowing it, or suffer the morale-draining terrors of uncertainty. Every day of the retreat, the Greeks sent out scouts to brave the hazards of assessing what the land was like, where they might stop for the night, and whether there were any signs of hostile activity. This information was so important, Xenophon believed, that the commanding officer himself should reconnoitre, whenever it was feasible to do so, and he reserved some of his highest praise for a good scout. But they also needed local guides, and preferably more than one at a time, so that they could cross-check, even when the guides had been required to give them sacred pledges of their honesty and sometimes hostages too. The critical importance of accurate information helps to explain the most horrifying act of cruelty Xenophon records – a barbaric act carried out not by barbarians, but by the Greeks themselves.

After three days of picking their way through the Carduchian highlands, threatened and harassed at every turn by the enemy, and with the weather rapidly deteriorating, the Greeks were close to breaking. The rearguard, commanded by Xenophon and Timasion, was especially plagued by Carduchian attacks. Whenever Xenophon saw the Carduchians massing on the ridges above the passes, he sent a message up to the front to get Cheirisophus to halt, so that his troops would be able to stay in touch even while defending themselves. On one occasion, Cheirisophus failed to stop, and Xenophon lost some good men in the course of their chaotic attempt to catch up. When the two generals met later in the day, Xenophon stormed up to Cheirisophus and asked him what had happened. Cheirisophus explained that he had pressed on in order to try to prevent the Carduchians from occupying the only visible way ahead, a road – more like a steep mountain track – through a narrow canyon. But the Carduchians had got there first and the guides in Cheirisophus's contingent were unaware of any other way. The Greeks appeared to have reached a dead end, or to be faced with a costly assault on an easily defensible position.

Xenophon, however, had taken two prisoners during the Carduchians' most recent forays against the rearguard. As locals, they could be assumed to know the region.

> They lost no time in having the prisoners brought before them, and they questioned them one at a time, to see if they knew of any road other than the obvious one. However often and however fiercely they tried to intimidate the first man, he denied knowing of any other road, so since he had no useful information for them they cut his throat in front of the second man. The remaining man then said that the first man had denied knowledge of an alternative route because he had a married daughter living there, but that he would show them a route which even the yoke-animals could manage.

Xenophon's dead-pan style, which permits no editorial comment, leaves his readers not just to imagine the details, but to appreciate the gap that too often exists between military necessity and moral virtue.

The Greeks extricated themselves from this predicament by sending about 400 hoplites and peltasts, four companies volunteered by their captains, along the alternative route revealed by the prisoner, to chase off any Carduchians they might find, and to find a way over the mountains the next morning to come at the Carduchians occupying the pass from the side while the rest of the army made a direct assault. In order to distract attention while the volunteers set out, Xenophon led an attack on the pass in freezing rain, but failed even to get close, because the Carduchians adopted the simple tactic of rolling boulders at them, which bounded down the steep slopes and ricocheted in unpredictable directions. I have seen mountain slopes in the region littered with an astonishing profusion of rocks, as if some insane deity had hurled oversized gravel from the sky. The Carduchians would never run short of this ammunition, and they continued sending boulders down the gorge even at night, to dissuade any foolhardy attempt to sneak along the track under cover of darkness.

In the mist of the following morning, the Greek pincer movement successfully cleared the pass. Cheirisophus took the majority of the men through the canyon, while Xenophon and his men escorted the baggage train along the circuitous route, which was more suitable for animals, as the prisoner had told them. The way had not been cleared by the volunteers, however, and Xenophon had to drive Carduchian fighters off a series of hills, and then occupy the hills himself to stop the enemy regrouping there and falling on the baggage train. It was an extremely difficult and dangerous operation, and it cost Xenophon dozens of his men. The reunited army endured another two days of fierce fighting, with Carduchian guerrillas waiting to ambush them at every opportunity, before finally reaching the end of these mountains, the Kayaönü Dağı, and overlooking the plain of the Centrites river, the modern Botan Çay, not far from the town of Siirt. In five days among the Carduchians they had lost as many men as they had lost in three months in Persian territory, and the prospect of leaving the Carduchian mountains behind filled them with false hope – false because beyond the river was Armenia, which was a securely held Persian satrapy, and further mountain ranges.

Winter in Armenia

Wiser minds were hardly surprised when the men woke up the next morning to find the river held against them by Orontas, the satrap of Armenia. Orontas had not had time to summon his main army, but he had under his command a force that was strong enough, in combination with the river's slippery bottom and chest-high, swiftly flowing current of freezing water, to put paid to the Greeks' first attempt to cross the river at a place where a road on the far side seemed to indicate a usable ford. By the time they had pulled back and camped on the south bank of the river, to their dismay they could see a horde of armed Carduchians behind them, in the foothills where they themselves had spent the previous night. They were caught in a trap.

The gods had not abandoned them, however, and they granted Xenophon an optimistic dream, which suggested that they would succeed in crossing the river, and then a favourable sacrifice. These omens began to be realized when two soldiers told Xenophon (who proudly informs us that he was always available to receive military information, at any time of the day or night) that they had discovered a shallower stretch of river not far upstream, where the far bank was unsuitable for Orontas's horsemen. What followed is worth quoting at length, not just because it was a thrilling engagement, but as a model of how far the Greeks had come, in a short space of time, from relying merely on traditional hoplite battle tactics, and as a piece of exemplary co-operation between the various units of the army.

When everything was in place, they set out with the two young men showing them the way, keeping the river on their left. It was about four stades to the ford and, as they marched along, the cavalry squadrons on the other side took a parallel course. When they reached the crossing and the river bank, they halted with their weapons at the ready. Cheirisophus was the first to act: he put a wreath on his head, took off his cloak, and was handed his weapons. He ordered everyone else to do the same, and told the company commanders to form their companies into columns to the right and left of him. The diviners let the blood from the throats of their victims pour into the river. The enemy kept shooting arrows and hurling sling-shot at them, but they were still out of range. When the omens were favourable, all the soldiers struck up the paean and raised the war-cry, while the women (there were a lot of kept women in the army) all joined in with the ritual cry.

Then Cheirisophus and his men entered the river, while Xenophon took the fastest men from the rearguard and sprinted back to the ford opposite the road up to the Armenian mountains, in a feint designed to make the horsemen by the river think that he was going to cross there and trap them. When the enemy troops saw Cheirisophus and his men easily wading through the water, and Xenophon and his men running back, they were terrified of being cut off; they galloped back towards the road which led up into the mountains from the river and once they reached it, they raced for the mountains. When Lycius, the cavalry commander, and Aeschines, the officer in charge of the peltasts who were attached to Cheirisophus, saw that the enemy troops were in full flight, they set out after them, with their troops calling to the others in an attempt to get them to keep up and join them as they made for the mountain. As soon as Cheirisophus had crossed, rather than pursuing the horsemen, he made his way over to the banks that abutted the river to attack the enemy soldiers who were up there. At the sight of their own cavalry in flight, and of hoplites advancing on them, the barbarians abandoned the ridges overlooking the river.

Once Xenophon saw that everything was going well on the far side of the river, he retraced his steps as quickly as possible back to where the army was crossing, because by then the Carduchians could be seen coming down to the plain to attack the tail-enders.

The high ground was in Cheirisophus's hands, and the attempt of Lycius and his small cavalry squadron to hunt down the fugitives had resulted in their capturing the remnants of the baggage train, including some beautiful clothing and goblets. The Greek baggage train and camp followers were just in the process of crossing, when Xenophon wheeled his men around to face the Carduchians and halted them with their weapons at the ready. He ordered the company commanders to divide their companies into sections and to form up for battle section by section, starting on the left, until the company and the section commanders faced the Carduchians and the last man in each line stood with his back to the river.

Without the camp followers, the rearguard looked very thin and low on numbers, and the Carduchians picked up speed and struck up their martial songs. But once Cheirisophus was sure that everything was secure on his side of the river, he detailed the peltasts, slingers and archers to go to Xenophon and put themselves entirely under his command. When Xenophon saw them starting across, he sent a man with their instructions: they were to stay put by the river, without crossing, but when his men started to cross, they – the men on the other side – were to enter the water to either side of his men, as though they were going to cross, the javelin-men with their fingers already through the loops of their javelins and the bowmen with arrows notched; but they were not to advance far into the river.

The instructions he gave his own men were that as soon as they were within range of the enemy slingers and could hear the sling-shot hitting shields, they were to strike up the paean and charge at the enemy; when the enemy turned, the trumpeter by the river would give the signal for battle – but that would be the signal for them to turn right and about-face, so that the last man in each file was at the front, and then everyone was to race across the river as fast as he could while maintaining his place in the formation, so that they would not obstruct one another; and whoever got to the other side first would be considered the best man among them.

By now, there were only a few men remaining, because quite a lot even of those who had been ordered to stay had already left, to look after the yoke-animals or the baggage or the women, so the Carduchians approached full of confidence and began to fire sling-shot and arrows. The Greeks struck up their paean and charged at them. The Carduchians did not stand their ground, because although their equipment was perfect for swift strikes and hasty retreats in the mountains, it was inadequate for hand-to-hand combat. At that point the trumpeter gave the signal, and while the Carduchians hugely increased the speed of their flight, the Greeks turned around and started to cross the river as fast as they could. Some of the enemy noticed what was going on, rushed back towards the river, and managed to wound a few men with their arrows, but most of them could be seen to be still in flight even when the Greeks were on the other side of the river. As for the reinforcements, their courage got the better of them and they advanced further into the river than they were supposed to, which meant that they crossed back again after Xenophon's men, and a few of them too were wounded.

Admirable tactics, admirably carried out – though the Greeks were fortunate that long enmity between the Armenians and Carduchians made it impossible for them to co-ordinate their attacks.

The plain to the west of Lake Van. The Ten Thousand marched across the plain in biting cold (the altitude is about 1,700 metres) and turned the corner around the end of the hills. All the while, they were shadowed by Tiribazus's scouts.

Six days of travel, first north and then north-east towards Lake Van, brought them a much-needed respite from hostilities and the chance to stock up on provisions. After the Centrites plain, they crossed only occasionally troublesome highlands, until they reached the broad, high-altitude plain that starts not far west of Lake Van and extends beyond Muş. The wind cut through their inadequate clothing, but they had made it across the mountains and into what was then Western Armenia. They set out in a north-westerly direction across the fertile plain, which now grows fruit, grain, sugar beet and tobacco, while in the surrounding mountains plentiful streams and rich pastures support not only the inevitable sheep, but also cows and horses, in a landscape reminiscent of the meadowed slopes of the European Alps. It is odd that Xenophon does not mention the spectacular lake, which is some 3,750 square kilometres in size and at 1,700 metres is one of the highest lakes in the world. Though their route did not take them directly by its shores, some outriders must have seen it, but no report reached Xenophon's ears – or none that he remembered later, when he came to write up his experiences.

There, on the plain, they met Tiribazus, the Persian sub-satrap of Western Armenia, at the Teleboas river (the Murat, or one of its tributaries), and at his request came to an agreement whereby if they promised not to destroy any housing, they could have free passage and could take whatever provisions they needed from his land. Although the two sides parted in peace, Tiribazus's army shadowed the Greeks as they continued across the plain, heading north-west before turning north again (to avoid the worst of the once-volcanic Nemrut range that spreads out from the north-west corner of Lake Van), and then east and north-east, roughly parallel to the northern shore of the lake, following the winding course of the Murat. There is something odd about their roundabout route here: it should have been possible for them to head more or less directly north, towards the ancient citadel town of Erzerum and then on to the Black Sea. Rivers would have supplied them with water, and the mountains, though high, are not impassable. Probably there was just too much snow, or the lower route was better supplied – but perhaps their guides had ulterior motives for taking them on a more circuitous route.

For, as it turned out, Tiribazus was planning to attack them after they had turned north again at modern Malazgirt. Their route up the Murat valley, towards modern Tutak and Ağri (marked on some maps

The worst weather endured by the Cyreans fell on them as they travelled beside the Murat a little north of this beautiful stretch of the river.

as Karaköse) – one has to orient oneself by modern landmarks, because this was barren land, with no ancient settlements large enough to have left an impression – would take them through a narrow valley between two peaks, a perfect spot for an ambush. Just as Tissaphernes had before him, Tiribazus had legalistic grounds for this 'treachery': once again, the undisciplined Greeks had broken a treaty. They had specifically promised not to damage any housing, but some soldiers had burnt houses in the villages where they had bivouacked. Perhaps it was an attempt to keep warm – they were, after all, faced with bitter cold and extraordinarily heavy falls of snow – but it directly contravened the terms of the truce. The Greeks learnt of Tiribazus's plans from a captured Persian, however, and on the principle that attack is the best form of defence most of the army marched on Tiribazus's mountain camp. The Persians scattered before them, and the Greeks passed through the valley in safety.

On the plain beyond the hills they were exposed to a relentless, savage, strength-sapping north wind. They were so desperate that at one point they sacrificed to the howling wind and managed to convince themselves that it became less bitter. It took them four days to travel

north beside the Murat to the relative safety of some villages beyond
Ağri, and during those four days about a hundred soldiers and camp
followers died of cold, their weakness exacerbated by lack of food,
which was virtually impossible to find under these conditions, and by
the difficulty of trudging through snow that lay up to 170 centimetres
deep in some places. Others watched frostbite blister, swell, blacken
and rot their extremities, or lost their sight, temporarily or perma-
nently, to snow-blindness, though some learnt to keep wiggling their
toes and fingers, even when at rest, and to wear something dark over
their eyes. They learnt to take their shoes off at night, because otherwise 'the straps sank into their flesh and their shoes froze on to their
feet'.

Despite the appalling weather, small bands of the enemy still dogged
their heels and preyed on those who fell behind, killing the men and
stealing the animals. Under these conditions, the army lost formation
and men straggled along in small groups; the rearguard fell about half
a day's march behind the van, and suffered more from the raids of the
enemy. We are inevitably reminded of the British retreat to La Coruña
across the Galician mountains in the winter of 1808–9, or of
Washington's retreat from New York in the winter months of 1776:
in all three cases, the men were inadequately equipped for harsh
weather, and Sir John Moore's British troops suffered as badly as
Xenophon's men from shortage of food. The differences are also
instructive: the Greek army did not experience the mutinous indisci-
pline of the British or the desertions that plagued Washington.
Xenophon's men had to stay together; there was nowhere to run to.

Once they gained the safety of the villages, they devoted nine days
to rest and recuperation. They were not molested by Orontas's troops,
who had finally been deterred by the terrible conditions. The soldiers
looked after themselves, while they or their slaves cleaned and
repaired weaponry and armour. They ate well and enjoyed the plentiful barley wine, and were kindly treated by the villagers, with whom
they communicated largely by gestures, though the headman spoke
some Persian. The location of these villages, and the route taken by the
army for the next five weeks, remain uncertain; the terrain is incredibly tortuous and featureless (especially in the snow), and Xenophon's
descriptions are understandably imprecise.

The houses in these villages were built underground – 'low hovels,
mere holes in the hillside', as the nineteenth-century archaeologist

Austen Layard described them. They were shaped like bottles, with narrow, sloping entrances, opening up underground with enough space to accommodate animals as well as humans. All over the world peasants have lived like this to escape extremes of weather – the searing heat of Baluchistan, for instance, or the cold of Armenia and Romania. John Macdonald Kinneir has left us a vivid impression of such a village and the surrounding countryside, early in the nineteenth century:

> The climate here is so severe, that the people are compelled to live under ground; fruits do not reach perfection, and the wretched crops of barley on the steeps of the mountains, scarcely repay the labour of the husbandman. ... Nothing was to be seen but bleak and barren mountains tipped with snow, intersected with hollow glens and frightful precipices. The villages were hid from the view; the roofs of the cottages being on a level with the ground and covered with earth, so that the path led not unfrequently over the tops of the houses.

Abandoned underground dwellings overlooking the Tigris at Hasankeyf, south-west of Lake Van, give an impression of the hovels in which Xenophon's men found comfort further north.

The Greeks left the warmth of the underground villages, and their abundant supplies of wine and food, with some reluctance, but took the headman as a guide, and his son as a hostage, as they continued north through Armenia. The going was no easier, and tempers flared as exhaustion undermined restraint. Nine days and about 225 kilometres later, they reached a mountain range with a pass that was held against them by a combined force of Chalybians, Phasians and Taochians. Rather than risk battle in the narrow pass, they followed Xenophon's suggestion and sent a force out by night to occupy another part of the mountain. At daybreak the next day, they engaged the enemy from the front and the flank simultaneously, and soon routed them. As they had against the Carduchians, they were using the terrain to their advantage.

Five days later they were again held up, this time by a Taochian stronghold, probably somewhere in the Kargapazarı mountains northeast of Erzerum. Xenophon came up with a clever scheme for exhausting the enemies' missiles, which were no more than stones and rocks hurled down from a crude wall perched on top of a cliff, by tempting them with apparently easy targets. It then took little effort for the Greeks to break into the fortress. The Taochian men were protecting their women and children, who were huddled together on the edge of the defensive wall. To the Greeks' horror, as they approached, the women began to push their children over the cliff. When all the children were dead, the women jumped, and were followed by the men. What panic or presentiment impelled the Taochians over the edge? Were the Greeks so fearsome? One Greek officer tried to prevent a particularly well-dressed man from hurling himself over the edge, less for humanitarian reasons than for the prospect of some valuable clothes and jewellery, but fell to his death along with his intended victim. The desperate Greeks soon overcame their shock and restocked their provisions from the undefended stronghold.

Xenophon on Leadership

The winter journey north from the crossroads of Cizre was by far the most arduous stage of Xenophon's retreat. The twists and turns of the Cyreans' route were dictated not just by the exigencies of the formidable terrain, but by the fact that they were sometimes more or less lost, or being misled by one of their guides, or found their preferred route blocked by snow or hostile tribesmen. They lost large numbers of fighting men, not just to enemy missiles, against which they could at least take steps to defend themselves, but to the savage weather, which must have taken an even heavier toll on the non-combatants, always the first to suffer in such conditions. Some 350 years later, in 36 BCE, when a far better equipped Roman army was starving and being harassed by the Parthians in much the same part of the world, their general, Mark Antony, paid tribute to the endurance of the Ten Thousand. I have driven much of the route in the comfort of a modern Land Rover, in autumn rather than winter, and even then the going was hard as soon as I left the made-up roads. Xenophon's men were tough.

By sheer chance, the mercenary army was exactly the right size: a smaller force might have been overcome by one of the many opponents they faced; a larger force would have been less mobile, and harder put to find sufficient provisions. Rather than picking on endurance or chance, however, Xenophon attributes their success to good leadership and, relatedly, the ability to work together. One of several ways in which his account of the expedition is nuanced – more, or less, than a straight-forward, objective historical narrative – is the prominence he gives to his own leadership skills, which are contrasted, usually implicitly, with those of other generals. These implications dovetail perfectly with more theoretical remarks about leadership elsewhere in Xenophon's extensive corpus of writings, and so we can begin to see that *The Expedition of Cyrus* is a subtly layered text – 'pretentiously simple', to borrow the oxymoron perceptively coined by Lawrence of Arabia.

From the time of the capture of the generals, Xenophon is ever in the foreground, encouraging the troops individually or en masse, taking the lead in the officers' councils, and generally proving himself to be a capable leader. Leadership is a recurrent topic in Xenophon's works and was a live issue for debate in the fourth century at the time he was writing. In a number of his books, Xenophon developed one of his most important insights, that there are parallels between any form of social organization – a state, an army, a workforce, a household – and similarities in the qualities required to manage them. In *The Expedition of Cyrus* he digresses to give us character sketches of leaders such as Cyrus or Clearchus, especially as obituaries. The sketches cumulatively reveal Xenophon's reflections on leadership: each of the leaders, himself included, gains a portrait, or at least a cameo role, which is supposed to help us triangulate on to the qualities of the ideal leader, or recognize the qualities of poor leaders.

Xenophon saw the essential ingredient of successful rule as knowledge:

Socrates said [with Xenophon's approval] that it was not those who held the sceptre who were kings and rulers, nor those who were chosen by unauthorized persons, nor those who were appointed by lot, nor those who had gained their position by force or fraud, but those who knew how to rule.

The required knowledge was of how to recognize and work for the common good. Successful rulers, in Xenophon's opinion, know how to care for the interests of their subjects better than the subjects themselves do; they lead by example – aristocratic self-confidence is a huge advantage here – and they show that they are flexible and imaginative, even inspired, enough to devise various means of attaining the common good and the safety of their subjects, and strong enough to stand up to aggression and wrongdoing. Such a leader is immediately attractive to his subjects, who, as a result, respect and honour him, and willingly obey him. Willing obedience is best, but in emergencies it may also be generated by compulsion or emulation or a sense of shame or of duty. However it comes about, the vertical virtue of obedience to a superior is chiefly a means of instilling in his subordinates discipline, the horizontal virtue of being able to work with others. This in turn raises morale, the value of which, especially in military success, Xenophon recognized with exceptional clarity.

A good leader needs more specific characteristics, though: courage, intelligence, tactical and strategic skill, self-discipline and piety; the ability to act slyly; accessibility to his men, and knowledge of their strengths and weaknesses; the ability to negotiate with foreigners. Of these qualities, self-discipline is the most critical, because as a good Socratic Xenophon saw self-discipline as the foundation of all moral virtue, including the ability to do good to others, or to inculcate self-discipline in them. Deficient leaders, on the other hand, lack the determination and strength of moral certainty. They fail to find the correct balance between coercion and the instilling of willing loyalty; they are too swayed by personal motivations; they do not tell men off when they are making mistakes, but buy them off instead with rash promises; they cause divisions in the army; and they ignore the omens sent by the gods.

It was a sign of the disillusionment of the fourth century that there were more and stronger arguments in favour of single leaders than there were champions of democracy. Political theory was largely a fourth-century development, born out of the attempt to denigrate Athenian democracy. Xenophon's reflections on leadership arose out of his experiences during the retreat, and one of the main subtleties of his account is that the retreat from Babylonia simultaneously represents a withdrawal from the high ideals of the fifth century, when political issues had been black and white, to a recognition – not without a hint of nostalgia – of the vulnerability and drawbacks of all forms of constitution, and of the necessity of strong but flexible leadership as a means of compensating for these weaknesses. And so, quite remarkably, we find Xenophon in *The Expedition of Cyrus* reflecting on all the major forms of constitution recognized by his contemporaries, and even suggesting that, while one political system might best suit normal, day-to-day administration, in emergencies others may fit the bill better

Ever since the Greeks first began to theorize about political systems, they had recognized a fundamental threefold division of constitutions into monarchy, oligarchy and democracy. The division was regarded not just, in linear terms, as reflecting what proportion of the citizen body held political power – one or a few or the majority – but often also as two radical extremes, monarchy and democracy, with a compromise or balance in the middle. And so some form of oligarchy was often seen as an ideal 'mixed' constitution, at any rate by the leisured theorists whose written works are all that remain.

This threefold division had a long history. Its origin is lost in the mists of traditional lore, around the end of the sixth century BCE, but it is still being reflected 400 years later in the work of, for instance, the historian Polybius or in Stoic political theorists of the same era. We first find it implicit in some lines written by Pindar in the late 470s: 'Under every kind of administration,' the poet says, 'a man of straight speech stands out for his excellence, whether he is in the court of a tyrant, or whether political power is in the hands of the impetuous host or of the wise.' Government by the wise, Pindar implies, strikes a balance between tyranny and reckless impetuosity.

Then there is the extraordinary constitutional debate in Herodotus's *Histories*, written in the early 430s. Herodotus has three sixth-century Persians anachronistically and implausibly debate the three forms of government, each championing one of them. Otanes, the champion of democracy, criticizes monarchy for giving power to just one man, on the grounds that he is bound to be corrupted, and praises democracy because it is equitable and its officers are accountable to the people. Megabyzus praises oligarchy as the government of the best men, and condemns both the extremes as brutal and hard to control. Darius, the future Darius I, King of Kings, thinks that an enlightened monarch is obviously the best kind of ruler, while both democracy and oligarchy lead to factional feuding, and history, he claims, has shown that it takes a good monarch to sort out the mess left by feuding oligarchs or democrats.

Herodotus's recognition that there were arguments for and against each form of constitution led, in the fourth century, Xenophon's era, to the division by philosophers such as Plato and Aristotle of the three constitutions into six, a good and a bad version of each. So Plato divided the rule of one man into kingship and dictatorship, the rule of the few into aristocracy (literally, the 'rule of the best') and oligarchy, and the rule of the people into democracy and ochlocracy (mob rule). But it also led to world-weary relativism: perhaps no one constitution was better than another. Xenophon is only a degree less cynical, or more flexible, in suggesting that each of the constitutions could be useful under different circumstances.

It has often been remarked that the Cyreans behaved like a *polis*, a citizen body, on the move. There were assemblies at which every soldier, however humble, could have his say; there was the advisory council of generals and company commanders. They were a sovereign and autonomous body, of roughly the same size as an average Greek state, and the structures they assumed for deliberation, legislation and decision-making reflected the typical political structures of a Greek state. But to say that the Cyreans behaved like a *polis* on the move is not to say very much, and more can be said by paying attention to the subtleties of Xenophon's text. In his account, the army acted on different occasions in ways that reflected all three forms of political constitution.

It would not have astonished an ancient Greek to find Xenophon using an account of a military expedition lightly and whimsically to develop a little political theory: soldiering and politics were always intimately related in the Greek mind. The fulfilment of one's obligations as a citizen included, above all, being called on, at any time between the ages of eighteen and sixty, to serve in the branch of the army appropriate to one's social status. In the ode of Pindar from which I quoted above, the term used for the masses is *stratos*, which means 'army host'; opponents of Athenian democracy frequently referred to it as the rule of the navy oarsmen; and Aristotle describes his ideal, balanced, moderate constitution as 'consisting of those who serve as hoplites'. From a political perspective, citizens could be regarded simply as troops, so it is not surprising to find Xenophon treating his troops as quasi-citizens.

Oligarchy is what one would expect. Oligarchy is normal in an army: the few, the officers, issue orders and the many obey them. So the generals naturally formed themselves into a kind of board, with the power to command on their own, to entertain ambassadors from cities or other armies, to draw up the agendas for general assemblies, and to convene assemblies. Some such board was especially inevitable given that in the first instance the mercenary corps consisted of separate units, each owing allegiance to a separate general. Sometimes the eight or ten generals met on their own; occasionally they included the 120 or so company commanders. Either way, they were still an oligarchy, with more or fewer men in power. This board of officers was the norm in the army, and they met on a daily basis. It was only when there was a danger of such high-handed methods encountering a degree of real refusal from the troops that they felt compelled to call an assembly to win the troops' approval. Otherwise, the oligarchic system worked well.

As far as democracy is concerned, from time to time in the earlier stages of the journey, and then commonly once the army reached the Black Sea, we hear of general assemblies at which the whole army was consulted by the officers. On a few occasions, the men even assembled of their own accord and took on the power of telling their officers what to do and of fining them for past mistakes. This is quite remarkable, of course, close to mutiny from a normal army perspective: soldiers usually assemble only to be addressed or harangued by their officers. In *The Expedition of Cyrus*, the rank-and-file soldiers actually had a say, from time to time, in what went on, even though Xenophon was aware of how easy it is to manipulate mass meetings, as Clearchus did at Tarsus, and even though, in actual practice, it was the company commanders who did most of the talking on behalf of their men. But all these meetings were crisis meetings. They occurred when the soldiers were in danger of mutinying, or of splintering into factions, or of committing some crime, or of losing confidence. They occurred when the officers were contemplating such a risky action that it made sense to try to gain the troops' agreement before carrying on; as in many city-states, the assembled people owned the right to declare war. They occurred when the men needed the comfort of being reminded of familiar political structures. They did not occur when army discipline and coherence were such that the officers could run things smoothly on their own.

Even after the death of the autocratic Cyrus, Xenophon provides insights into monarchy. At Sinope, for instance, on the Black Sea, the men were again restless, on this occasion because they were getting closer to home, but felt that they had not yet accumulated enough booty and profit. And so they decided to choose a single commander-in-chief, as distinct from the board of generals that had largely governed them up until then. Their first choice was Xenophon, but geopolitics made a Spartan the better choice, and Cheirisophus got the job. As it happened, the army fell apart only a few days later, and then Cheirisophus died, but these facts are by the by. What is important about this passage is that Xenophon tells us why the men wanted a single leader: because the members of a board or committee can disagree with one another, and this slows down both the decision-making process and the enactment of decisions. The sole leader, we understand, is supposed to work wisely for the good of his subjects – to enrich them, in this case – and elsewhere in *The Expedition of Cyrus* Xenophon makes it clear that the difference between good and bad autocracy is precisely that the aims of a bad autocrat, a tyrant, are purely selfish.

Xenophon displays, then, his functional insights into the three basic constitutions. His narrative applies in the first instance to the Ten Thousand, but his conclusions are meant to be more widely applicable and to make a minor contribution to current political theory. It is typical of Xenophon not to trumpet a message, but to leave a trail of clues. And the first clue is the number of overtly political terms littered throughout the text – as when a breakaway company commander is described as a tyrant, or when Xenophon himself is called a demagogue, because of his overriding concern for the common good.

For Xenophon, the good of the army dictates the form of political system. Monarchy is good for quick reactions in emergencies; oligarchy for normal, everyday administration; democracy for appeasement and the averting of popular uprisings. Oligarchy, he clearly thinks, is the most serviceable constitution, but in the face of an emergency, whether generated by internal or external factors, one of the two extremes might become the better way to maintain discipline and to bring about the people's best interests. It remains the case, however, that this is a compromise. To put it in modern terms, you cannot simultaneously vote for collectivism and individualism, for left and right. It might seem no more than common sense to argue that both sides have policies to approve of, but in fact the inability to commit oneself is always a sign of disillusionment. Xenophon never shed his oligarchic proclivities, but the retreat from Babylonia taught him that there were no magic bullets in politics, and that safety lay in substituting a degree of irresolution for certainty and depended almost entirely on the quality of the leaders. Whether they were democrats, oligarchs or monarchs, they had to be able to combine a strong moral foundation with intelligent flexibility. And he thought that he himself had come close to this ideal.

The main trouble with a political ideal based on strong leadership is that it is open to abuse. Every dictator begins by assuming that he knows better than other people what is good for them. Periods, such as Xenophon's (and ours), that are characterized by moral uncertainty are easily exploited. The strong leadership that arrived in Greece was not moral, but the imperialism of Macedonian conquerors. Our world too continues to demonstrate the narrow dividing line between the assertion of moral values and the mere imposition of power.

CHAPTER NINE

'The Sea! The Sea!'

The nightmare continued over the next seven days of marching through the Chalybian highlands. Danger was ever present and weary stragglers were likely to have their throats cut. The Chalybians had the gruesome custom of cutting off the heads of those they killed and taunting their enemies by waving at them these relics of their former comrades. But the Greeks had taken enough supplies from the Taochians to avoid having to break formation and forage, and they made it across the Harpasus river (probably the Kara Su, as the northern stretch of the Euphrates is called) to the relative safety of the land of the Scythenians, where they were able to replenish their supplies. Four days and 100 kilometres later, after travelling across a final plain 1,800 metres above sea level and criss-crossed with rivers, they arrived at the town of Gymnias (modern Bayburt), in the foothills of the truly enormous Doğu Karadeniz mountain range that fringes the south-east coast of the Black Sea.

By this time marching had become staggering, as cold and hunger had sapped all their energy. Days that stretched into unrelenting weeks of marching at full readiness, nerves stretched taut, had also taken their toll. But at Gymnias the local ruler promised them a guide who would take them in five days to a place from where they could see the sea. With a jolt of anticipation, the Greeks looked ahead to an end to their trials. Their notion of their value as mercenaries adapted to circumstances, and in order to secure no more than a good guide they agreed to the chieftain's terms: they would ravage the land of some of his enemies, even though this would turn a day's journey north into five days of travel east and then back west again. We cannot know what local dispute the Ten Thousand helped to resolve. But then, in the words of one of the most famous passages in western literature:

On the fifth day they did in fact reach the mountain, which was called Theches. When the first men got there, a huge cry went up. This made Xenophon and the rearguard think that the van too was under attack from another enemy force, as in the rear they were being followed by men from the land they were burning ... . But the cry kept getting louder and nearer, as each successive rank that came up began to sprint towards the ever-increasing numbers of those who were already shouting out. The more men who reached the front, the louder the cry became, until it was apparent to Xenophon that something of special significance was happening. He mounted a horse, took Lycius and the cavalry, and rode up to lend assistance; and before long they could make out that the soldiers were shouting 'The sea! The sea!' – that this was the word they were passing along. Then all the men in the rear began running too, and the pack animals and the horses broke into a gallop. When everyone reached the top of the mountain, they immediately fell into one another's arms, even the generals and the company commanders, with tears in their eyes. Suddenly, at someone's suggestion, the soldiers began to bring stones and to make a great cairn.

The mountains there are so wild and remote, occupied, if at all, by just a few transhumant shepherds, that only recently have scholars identified the site: Theches is modern Deveboynu Tepe, and the identification was aided by finding near by the vestiges of the very cairn Xenophon and his men built. The grassland around the cairn is still remarkably free of the stones that litter all these mountains: Xenophon's men used them all. Long passion for ancient history has driven me to visit countless sites, but the experience of finding and then standing on the remains of the cairn delivered the greatest historical thrill of my life. A lammergeier carved huge spirals overhead as if to confirm that this was indeed the place.

Thálatta! Thálatta! The cry sent up by Xenophon's men when they saw the sea was not the cry that echoed frequently in nineteenth- and twentieth-century literature, in which the sea became infused with self-conscious eroticism, religion, patriotism or nostalgia, or with some subliminal desire for redemption or loss. Just as sailors after a storm shout 'Land!', so the cry of the Ten Thousand was a cry of sheer joy – joy multiplied a thousandfold by the dangers they had survived, the distance they had travelled and the uncertainty they had overcome, and spiced by the prospect of soon finding Greek settlements. The poet Louis MacNeice spoke of Xenophon as 'crusted with parasangs' (a parasang being the ancient

The remains of the cairn built by the Cyreans, which still forms a roughly circular mound. The blanket of clouds in the distance obscured the sea, so I could not cry 'Thálatta! Thálatta!' The height is over 2,500 metres above sea level.

Persian unit of distance, over 5 kilometres long, that Xenophon employed in his book), but he was not also burdened with Freudian or Romantic images of the sea. The power of the scene derives from nothing more complex than our innate, human longing for home. This is not the only time in *The Expedition of Cyrus* that Xenophon touches on something archetypal.

Snow and Mad Honey

There can be no doubt in the mind of anyone who has visited this spot that the Cyreans were moved not just by their first sight of the sea, but also by the sheer natural beauty of the place, where you feel the glory of being on top of the world. These mountains are popularly called the Pontic Alps, and though they are geologically older, more rounded than the upstart European Alps, the comparison is apt for the beauty of the countryside and its mixture of high pastureland, well above the tree line, and mountain peaks. The Greeks were standing on a good, grassy platform, about 2,500 metres above sea level. The platform is broad enough to allow many men at one time to look out over the sea. They were lucky: on the day I was there all I could see was a bank of cloud, typical for the region, hundreds of metres below me, which extended far out over the sea. There are few days in a year when the sea is visible from there.

It became absolutely clear to me while I was there that the usual dating of Xenophon's journey is wrong. Scholars have usually dated Xenophon's sight of the Black Sea to early March at the latest. I was there in the middle of October, and in deliberately taking one of the high 'scenic' routes across the mountains from Bayburt to Trabzon, along unmetalled tracks, I coincided with the first snowfall of winter. Returning the next day with a Turkish-speaker to try to locate the cairn, I was lucky that the clouds of the previous day had lifted and, at this altitude, had made way for dazzling weather with occasional drifts of light mist. The ground was sprinkled with the previous day's snow. The snow would then increase for several months (there is a ski centre just a couple of peaks away) and would finally leave only in June. Gullies become clear of snow only in July. Xenophon makes no mention of snow; his men built a cairn. Even granting some leeway, the earliest he was there was the middle or end of May.

Another factor points securely to the same conclusion. A few days later, as they were picking and fighting their way down the mountains towards the coast, Xenophon tells an astonishing story:

> There were a lot of swarms of bees, and all the men who ate honeycomb became deranged, suffered from vomiting and diarrhoea, and were too weak to stand up. Those who had eaten a little behaved as though they were drunk, while those who had eaten a lot behaved like madmen, or even like people on the point of death. The ground was so thickly covered with supine men that it looked like the aftermath of a defeat, and morale plummeted. On the next day, however, no one died, and they began to recover their senses at about the same time of day that they had eaten the honeycomb. Two or three days later, they were back on their feet, as if they had been treated with medicine.

For those of us whose honey generally comes in jars from a supermarket shelf, the story sounds unbelievable, on a par with medieval travellers' tales of sciapods and the unattainable kingdom of Prester John. But it is absolutely right: honey derived from a few species of rhododendron in the world is toxic; the active ingredient is acetylandromedol, a powerful drug whose effects include dizziness, hallucinations, impaired speech, respiratory difficulty and a very low pulse rate. The local tribes of these mountains are said to have left out quantities of this honey, 350 years later, as a trap for Pompey's troops. But the point is this: the fragrant yellow flowers of *Rhododendron luteum*, the species native to this area which produces 'mad honey', bloom only from the middle of May to the middle of June. Xenophon's men found fresh honey, so they were there around the end of May. By the same token, they found fresh grain among the Mossynoecians, further along the Black Sea coast, a few weeks later than this episode: they were there in July, when the harvest begins.

But then we are confronted by a puzzle. All the way up to the Cyreans' arrival at the Black Sea coast, Xenophon has taken pains to appear quite precise, within only a small margin of error, about the distances travelled and the time taken. Every stage of the journey is prefaced with sentences such as 'the next leg, a two-day march of seven parasangs, brought them to such-and-such a place'; in addition there are clues provided by what Xenophon tells us about the climate and the vegetation of the places he passed through. Naturally, scholars have used these indications as the best way of timing the Cyreans' journey. Assuming (as everyone does) that the army started from Sardis in the early spring of 401, Xenophon's clues bring them to Trapezus in February, or at the latest in March, of 400. But this is out of the question: they could not have found the honey then, and the snow would still have been lying impossibly thick on the ground. There appears to be a gap of as much as three months in the text.

We could have fun speculating as to what went on during these three months. What was it that Xenophon chose to omit altogether from his narrative? Was he embarrassed at having got lost, and perhaps at losing large numbers of men to the harsh winter? Did the army do something so discreditable and shocking that it suited Xenophon to pass over it in silence? Why is there no mention of the famous mineral mines (gold, silver and copper), which used to be located near the modern town of Ispir? The Cyreans certainly passed by them. In all probability, the truth is rather more banal. Though Xenophon is quite precise about the time taken under normal conditions, he is considerably less exact about how long it took for the army to cross rivers and mountain ranges. We get only phrases such as 'Once they had crossed the river ...' or 'On the other side of the mountains ...'. Stopovers too are not always precisely measured. 'When the guide arrived,' Xenophon says, they set out from Gymnias – but how long had they been waiting around Gymnias for him? All these imprecisions over the course of the entire journey are probably enough to account for the 'snow lacuna'.

At Trapezus

And so they came down, through the territory of the Macronians and the Colchians, to Trapezus. Trouble with the Macronians was averted by the fortunate coincidence that one of the peltasts in the army, a former slave in Athens, was originally from there and was able to negotiate a peaceful passage. How many times must Xenophon have wished that there were other such useful linguists among the camp followers or in the army? Almost everywhere they went, they met with hostility – the inevitable reaction to the sudden appearance of an enormous vagabond army of toughened strangers. And so, as usual, they had to fight their way past the Colchians. Once they left behind the high, sloped meadows, they followed the route of mountain torrents, which have carved the slopes into mist-filled gorges. Beautiful woods of both evergreen and deciduous trees, with a profusion of multi-coloured flowers, now make this famous walking country for spring and summer visitors.

Trapezus (modern Trabzon and Byzantine Trebizond) was built on ridges between deep ravines that run down to the sea. For 250 years, the city was the capital of a splinter Byzantine empire, founded by exiles after the sack of Constantinople in 1204, which at its fullest extended along the coastline from west of Sinope to Georgia, and quite a way inland, and grew to be enormously wealthy from trade and mining. With its position on the coast and on one of the main Silk Roads east, Trabzon remained an important trading centre until the opening of the Suez Canal in 1869. The Greek presence lingered long: even in the 1920s, before the exchange of populations between Greece and Turkey, three-quarters of those living around Trabzon spoke Greek.

The magnificent Pontic Alps through which Xenophon and his men trekked to reach Mount Theches, from where they could see the sea.

The southern coastline of the Black Sea in Xenophon's day, however, consisted of a few Greek settlements, some of a respectable age, separated by extensive tracts of uncertain and dangerous lands. The first Greek colonists to the area had been attracted by the astonishing profusion of fish in the sea. Until recently, it was so rich in fish, especially anchovies, that you could catch them with just your bare hands or a bucket. And so the Greek settlers' main business was the curing, packing and exporting of fish, and they became the main source of cheap fish for their western cousins on the fish-poor Mediterranean. Though other trade went on too (for instance, in hazelnuts, iron and timber), we should imagine Xenophon being greeted on his arrival in Trapezus with the stench of smoke-houses and fish, and with a hybrid of Greek and native cultures.

The Greek colonies of the Black Sea had of course reached a modus vivendi with many native tribes, but there were still long stretches of the coastline where a Greek army could expect to meet with hostility rather than help. The Cyreans' best hope would be to leapfrog from settlement to settlement by sea, in order to avoid the hazards of a land journey. This was their plan when they arrived in Trapezus: as one of the soldiers put it, with a reference to Odysseus's legendary arrival back home by boat, in a miraculously deep sleep, 'I'm fed up with packing my baggage, walking and running, carrying my arms and armour, marching in formation, standing guard and fighting ... I'd like to arrive in Greece flat on my back, like Odysseus.'

The provincial townsfolk must have been astonished and terrified at the sight of this band of fearsome men, weathered and stained by travel and hardship, appearing out of the hinterland. In typically Greek fashion, the Cyreans celebrated their arrival at the coast with a rough-and-ready athletic competition, in which many of the contestants made fools of themselves as they struggled over inappropriate terrain, to the amusement of their colleagues, who now felt safe enough to laugh again. While waiting for their ships to arrive, they settled in and around the nearby villages and supplemented their stores by plundering villages further afield, which were inhabited by tribes who had never adapted to the presence of the colonizing Greeks.

Their main hopes for finding ships on which to sail out of the Black Sea rested with Cheirisophus, the only general whose background would make him acceptable to the Spartan officials who controlled the passage to and from the sea. He set out for Byzantium, the headquarters of the regional Spartan military command, to talk to his friend, the Spartan Admiral of the Fleet for that year, Anaxibius. He did not have an easy job: before trying to persuade the Spartan authorities to lend them ships, he had to convince them that the army was no threat to the stability of the region. This meant promising, without yet having gained the men's agreement, that those who did not disperse to their homes would be available for employment by the Spartans. Anaxibius and his colleague Cleander, the 'harmost' or governor of Byzantium, did not want a maverick army roaming around their territory.

Xenophon, for one, did not believe that Cheirisophus would make the slightest impression on the Spartans, and while the Spartan was gone, he put an alternative plan into motion. They commandeered the Trapezuntians' only warship, with the intention of using it to hijack any passing vessels, until they had enough to accommodate the entire army and sail away (or to dismiss them with thanks and recompense, if Cheirisophus was successful); since some of the passing vessels might be grain ships, this would also be a way to keep the army in food without too much trouble. Xenophon's piratical plan was foiled, however, when the man they put in charge of the warship, a Laconian mercenary commander called Dexippus, simply sailed away to safety on it.

The longer the Greeks stayed near Trapezus, the more difficult their situation became, as they had to roam further afield to steal their supplies, and the further they left behind the town's zone of influence, the more hostile were the tribes they came up against. Finally, a plundering raid that came very close to ending in complete disaster made them realize they had to move on. After thirty days, however, they had managed to gather enough ships only for the sick and the wounded, the women and children, the older men and some baggage; but they could wait no longer for Cheirisophus, and they sent the ships on ahead to Cerasus, their next stop. The rest set out by land, and soon lost sight of Trapezus behind successive escarpments.

The Dangers of Greed

It took them three days to reach Cerasus, travelling right by the coast. The weight of traffic affirms that this is still the only feasible route, as thickly wooded hills come pretty much right down to the sea. They crossed rivers, medium-sized and small, but none too deep at their outlets into the sea; they passed coves and headlands, and occasional islets. Ancient Cerasus was located at the now-insignificant spot called Kireşon Dere, Cherry Valley (cherries, the 'fruit of Cerasus', were first imported from there into Europe in Roman times). At Cerasus, the Greeks sold their prisoners and other booty, such as the silver-footed couches and the goblets taken from Tiribazus in Western Armenia. Xenophon made so much that he was able to handsomely fulfil his thanksgiving vows to Artemis and Apollo, by making a dedication at Delphi and by the extravagant gesture of building a temple to Artemis on a specially purchased country estate. They also counted the survivors and found that they were 8,600. 'These were the men left alive, while the rest had been killed by their enemies, by the snow, and some by illness.' Another few thousand slaves and baggage-handlers must have died too, though in the manner typical of ancient historians, Xenophon leaves us guessing about their fate.

The Cyreans stayed at Cerasus for ten days and ended by disgracing themselves. The day before they left (with the same division of land and sea travel as before), one of the company commanders, called Clearetus, set out to plunder an undefended village that had already proved its friendliness by selling the Greeks provisions. His intention was to attack the village under cover of darkness, but he miscalculated and arrived after daybreak. The villagers were able to defend themselves, and they killed Clearetus himself and many of the men he had persuaded to go along with him. The survivors returned to Cerasus and hoped to keep their secret, but the villagers sent a delegation to Cerasus to complain. By the time the delegates arrived, the bulk of the Greek army had left, but some remained, including members of Clearetus's misjudged expedition. Mollified by the Cerasuntians' explanation that the action had certainly not been officially sanctioned, the villagers were prepared to catch up with the Greek army by boat and invite them to carry out their sacred obligation to bury their fallen comrades. The remnants of Clearetus's gang, however, ambushed the delegates and stoned them to death.

This was a quadruple crime, a severe offence against the gods. They had broken the sacred bond of friendship by attacking the village in the first place, and now they had not only denied their fellow Greeks a proper burial, but had killed delegates, whose persons were considered more or less sacrosanct. Finally, they had wronged the army, which, like any Greek community, needed to know when it had to make expiation to the gods, to keep in their favour. A short while later, further along the coast, the chaos worsened when another group of Greeks also picked up stones and were prepared to stone a market official, a weigh-master whose regulations they resented. To escape the angry mob, the official himself and a number of others took to their boats or plunged into the sea, where some drowned. By a fateful coincidence, this was witnessed by Cerasuntian messengers who had arrived to tell the generals about the Clearetus episode. The Trapezuntians regarded them as robbers of their one and only warship; the Cerasuntians now severed relations with the Cyreans. Xenophon's men were not proving adept as diplomats.

These stories introduce one of the major themes of Xenophon's book. It is one of a number told by Xenophon of the Greeks' journey along the Black Sea that suggest how a community falls apart, and that underline Xenophon's own personal disillusionment, as one by one his dreams fail. Their arrival at the sea was meant to change the focus of the army. Their worst dangers seemed to be past; there was no longer the unrelenting psychological pressure on each man of fearing imminent death. They expected to be safe, and as a result unity no longer seemed as essential as before. Their arrival at the sea was supposed to be an end, not a continuation of the uncertainties of the retreat; they were supposed to have come home, and not still to be outsiders.

A little further on from Cerasus, some of the Greek soldiers, greedy for plunder, broke away from the main army to attack a Mossynoecian settlement and suffered a severe setback; further along the coast, selfish motivations split the board of generals; a short while later, the desire for booty broke up the army into three separate divisions, the direct result of which was that in Bithynia they suffered their worst losses of the entire expedition. As at the start of the expedition, the men were once again more loyal to their individual commanders and their ethnic group than to the whole, and more liable to be influenced by bad apples such as Dexippus and Clearetus, or like Boïscus, a ruffian who was a professional boxer in civilian life and a professional robber of civilians in army life. Finally, the army fell apart more or less totally in Byzantium and became little more than a band of brigands. One is inevitably reminded of how irregular troops often consist of men and women with different agendas, as in the Greek resistance to the occupying forces in World War II. It takes a strong and sometimes unscrupulous hand to forge them into unity.

The first principles of organization, as far as Xenophon was concerned, were that the ordinary soldier should be obedient and should meet with good leadership. As long as the majority was functioning according to role, as long as the objectives of the army as a whole could be attained, minor aberrations could be accommodated. But now neither the officers nor the rank-and-file troops were playing their part. This was no longer the army that had earned Xenophon's praise for its flexible collaboration in the face of danger, and it is a sign of his desperation that he pushed through a proposal that the army should be purified, in a ritual that normally happened only after a mutiny. Eventually, his speeches began to be coloured by allusions not as earlier to the Persian Wars, when the Greeks had united (in his whimsical version) against the barbarians, but to the bloodbath of the Peloponnesian War, when Greeks had fought Greeks – when, in all probability, men who now were supposed to fight and vote and sleep alongside one another in Xenophon's army had been the bitterest of enemies.

Initially, the army consisted of more or less separate units, under their own commanders. Despite minimal desertion and some rumblings of discontent, they were capable of functional unity (as at the battle of Cunaxa, or on parade before Epyaxa), but there was no true homogeneity. The men were looking ahead to an easy victory, and to the profit that would follow whether they stayed in the east with Cyrus or returned home. Following the capture of the generals, however, preservation replaced profit as the motivator, and it became clear to everyone that unity was essential if they were to get home safely. Thanks largely to wise leadership, the men were forged into a whole that was capable of acting flexibly and effectively, and Xenophon portrays the army as a band of heroic warriors and suppresses any disagreements that might have arisen. The scene on Mount Theches, with soldiers of all ranks embracing one another at the sight of the sea, is the high point of the army's unity, as well as being the book's climax. Once the army reached the Black Sea, it began to disintegrate under the influence of greed. It is easy to see why Xenophon's mind entertained dreams of colonization: those who chose to stay would necessarily be unified by their common purpose.

Xenophon was always the kind of historian whose choice of events to present and manner of presentation were nuanced by underlying themes. He wanted his readers to be aware not only of the external events that befell the army, but also of its inner life. In his narrative, the army is portrayed as a living gestalt organism, reacting with anger or dismay to its circumstances, descending on the hapless villages and towns in its path like a swarm of locusts, excreting corpses and unwanted baggage, adapting to external conditions, losing many members but struggling on, until it is so maimed by greed that it is barely capable of effective action.

Further Trouble on the Black Sea

With its long stretches of barbarian-infested wilderness, interrupted by pockets of quasi-Greek civilization, the Black Sea was the ancient Greek equivalent of the Wild West, and the Greeks located many of their mythical and legendary monsters in the wilder and more remote parts of its coastline. This was where the Other lived, in the form of the Amazons (women warriors who were the exact opposite of the ancient Greek feminine ideal); where the barbaric witch Medea hailed from (Xenophon remarked on a place called 'Jason's Point', where the hero was supposed to have landed on his way to Medea's Colchis and the Golden Fleece); where Heracles was supposed to have descended into Hades in order to capture Cerberus, the three-headed, half-snake, half-dog guardian of the underworld (Xenophon visited the spot: 'They show the marks of his descent, to a depth of more than two stades [about 350 metres]'); where for his crimes against the gods Prometheus was pegged out on a rock while a vulture every day gorged itself on his liver, which miraculously grew again each night; where Iphigeneia sacrificed unlucky travellers to Artemis, her goddess.

Xenophon is, on the whole, remarkably free of prejudice: he writes as a curious traveller and an objective witness. But in his description of the Mossynoecians, the next tribe the army encountered as they travelled west along the coast, he does pander somewhat to Greek expectations that this region would throw up an alien people. The easternmost Mossynoecians (the word is Greek, meaning just 'dwellers in wooden towers'), posed enough of a threat for the Greeks to decide to form a temporary alliance with another group of Mossynoecians. Xenophon's description of the arrival of the friendly western Mossynoecians is tinged with more than a hint of disdainful humour: we are prepared for their ineffectiveness in battle. Then we learn that this people too had the unpleasant habit of cutting off the heads of their vanquished foes and using them as visual taunts; that they used stinking dolphin blubber for all the many purposes for which the Greeks used olive oil (including oiling the body); that they could call out to one another across distances of up to 14 kilometres (the travel writer John Freely came across a similar phenomenon in the region, late in the twentieth century). The climax comes in Xenophon's final remarks, after they had defeated the hostile Mossynoecians and burnt their ruler alive in one of the wooden towers:

> The people of the friendly towns to which their journey brought
> them showed them the sons of the well-off members of their society.
> These boys, who had been fattened up on a diet of boiled nuts,
> were soft and extremely pale, and almost as wide as they were tall.

They had complex and colourful flower designs tattooed all over their backs and fronts. The Mossynoecians also wanted to have sex in the open with the kept women the Greeks had brought, because that was their custom there. All the Mossynoecians, men and women, were pale. The soldiers who took part in this expedition agreed that, of all those whose lands they passed through, the Mossynoecians were the most alien and the most remote from Greeks in their customs. They used to do in public what others did when no one was looking, and when they were alone they did the kinds of things that others did in company; they used to talk to themselves and laugh by themselves, and they would start dancing, wherever they happened to be, just as if they were putting on a display for others.

After passing with considerably less difficulty through the territory of the Tibarenians, the Cyreans reached another Greek outpost, Cotyora (modern Ordu). Preceded by their reputation as a dangerous band of thugs, the first problem they faced during their 45-day stay there was the overt hostility of the inhabitants, who would not sell or give them supplies, and even refused to accommodate their sick and wounded in comfortable quarters in the town. Then there arrived a delegation from Sinope, further along the coast (modern Sinop), since Cotyora, like Cerasus, was a colony of Sinope. The envoys threatened to ally themselves with the Paphlagonian king and turn against the Cyreans if they damaged Cotyoran territory. In response, Xenophon assured them that the Cotyorans would come to no harm as long as they behaved in a friendly fashion, instead of shutting their gates – and he trumped the Sinopeans' threat by suggesting that the Paphlagonian king would be more open to an approach from the Cyreans, since he could then drive the Sinopeans from his territory, where they had carved out their Greek niche. The Sinopeans' bluster collapsed.

As if it were not bad enough that Xenophon's Greeks were not trusted by fellow Greeks, treachery next split the board of generals. The Sinopeans warned them of the extreme difficulties they would face if they continued by land: they would be liable to ambush in the Paphlagonian mountains, and there were deep rivers to cross. The only sensible option was to sail from Cotyora to Sinope, and then from Sinope to Heraclea, and they set about once more begging for vessels from all the Greek settlements along the coast, and commandeering others. This took time and while they waited Xenophon began to dream about turning the army into colonists and founding a city somewhere on the southern Black Sea coastline. Xenophon's dream was not automatically doomed to failure: the prospect of owning property abroad could have appeared attractive to anyone, especially the poorer members of the army, and there were enough men to make up the core voting citizen body of a good-sized community. As for women – well, wives were little more than breeding stock anyway, and there was plenty of that available in the nearby villages.

The story now gets sordid. Xenophon's democratic plan was foiled because there were those among or close to the senior officers who had profited from the expedition and were anxious to get back home as soon as possible with their wealth intact. His chief opponent was Silanus, the most senior diviner in the army, the one who had been so massively rewarded by Cyrus: he wanted to get home with his 3,000 darics. Silanus and others spread the rumour that Xenophon was contemplating a colony only for personal aggrandizement, and they seized the opportunity to frighten the people of Sinope and Heraclea with the threat that this freebooting army might stay in the region. The anxious Sinopeans and Heracleots told some of Xenophon's colleagues that they would pay the men's daily wage for as long as it took to get them out of the region, and they sweetened the offer with personal bribes.

For the sake of unity, Xenophon backed down – but then the Sinopeans and Heracleots went back on their word, and provided only ships, not the army's wages. Those who had trusted the original offer and had promised the men pay were now terrified of the consequences when the men learnt that they would get nothing. They came to Xenophon and suggested instead that they would support him if he wanted to lead the army back east, beyond Trapezus, and seize some land around the Phasis river in what is now Georgia. When the men got wind of this plan, they came closer to mutiny than ever before, and Neon, who had replaced the still-absent Cheirisophus as commander of the Peloponnesian contingent, continued to stir them up against Xenophon. With a long and impassioned speech, Xenophon managed to mollify the men and restore a semblance of unity. This was the moment when the army needed ritual purification, and the generals were also called upon by the men to account for some of their past actions. Heavy fines were imposed upon three of them, but Xenophon was acquitted on a charge of assault.

And so the troubled Greeks sailed in summer sunshine along the Paphlagonian coastline to Sinope, where they were welcomed with gifts of barley and wine. Cheirisophus, who had been delayed in Byzantium by illness and protracted negotiations, at last returned to them there, but he came empty-handed, except for the assurances he carried from Anaxibius that they would be gainfully employed – once they had left the Black Sea – and the news that Cleander would come in person to assess the situation. Not surprisingly, no one trusted the Ten Thousand. The Spartans, now busy constructing their own empire, had promised the Black Sea communities security after years of warfare and uncertainty, and, as the Cyreans' own behaviour had demonstrated, it was essential to that promise that the Cyreans were removed from the picture. Xenophon's dreams of colonization automatically made him suspect to the Spartans, and his cause was not helped by the fact that his old *bête noire*, Dexippus, had turned up in Byzantium and was filling receptive ears with slanted versions of Xenophon's intentions.

The men were still restless, however, and this was the point at which they wanted to elect Xenophon as their sole commander. Xenophon resisted temptation: given the importance of not offending the Spartans, he recommended that they choose Cheirisophus instead. After only a few days at Sinope, then, the Cyreans set sail west under Cheirisophus's command. At the cape called Baba Burnu, they turned south down the coast to Heraclea, now modern Ereğli (Karadeniz Ereğli, 'Black Sea' Ereğli, to distinguish it from other identically named towns), a nightmare of sulphurous pollution. The people of Heraclea were just as anxious as their Sinopean friends to keep the Cyreans happy, and they too provided food and drink, enough for three days. But the majority of the Greeks were still in piratical mood, and they used threats to try to extract a large amount of money from the Heracleots as well. The Heracleots responded, not unnaturally, by closing their gates to their increasingly unpredictable guests.

The Cyreans had angered and alienated every single Greek community they had reached so far. Troublemakers in the army, however, blamed the generals for not doing enough to guarantee their daily provisions, let alone their enrichment, and all Xenophon's attempts to maintain unity came to nothing as the army fragmented into three pieces. The Arcadians and Achaeans, some 4,500 hoplites, banded together and chose their own board of ten generals. They extracted ships from the Heracleots and sailed off to Calpe Harbour, a sheltered bay about halfway between Heraclea and Byzantium, with the intention of using it as a base from which they could raid Bithynian territory inland and enrich themselves.

Cheirisophus, who was by now very ill and tending to rely more and more on the advice of Neon, retained his command over only about 1,400 hoplites and 700 Thracian peltasts, and set out for Calpe Harbour by the winding coastal route, where ravines sliced deep into magnificent cliffs. Finally, Xenophon, with 1,700 hoplites, 300 peltasts and 40 horsemen, persuaded the Heracleots to take his contingent at least some of the way. He was dropped at the border between Thracian and Heracleot territory, and then set out overland for Calpe Harbour. It looked as though it was the end of the army: they had become three distinct groups of marauders. Xenophon was so disheartened that he wanted just to leave and make his own way home to Athens, but the gods had indicated that he should stay and lead his men.

The gods were right, as usual: Xenophon still had important work to do. As he was marching towards Calpe Harbour, he received information that the Arcadians had lost several hundred men to the warlike Bithynian Thracians, with the remainder under siege on a hill. Still convinced that their best hope for deliverance lay in unity, he persuaded his men, and himself, that reconciliation should win out over rancour, and that they should go to their comrades' help. The Bithynians fled at just the news of their approach, and the Arcadians seized the opportunity to escape and make their way back to Calpe Harbour. Xenophon followed them. By the time they got there, Cheirisophus and his men had arrived too, and in a display of unity the three contingents greeted one another like brothers. Cheirisophus's death a day or two later, however, left Neon in command of his contingent, and Neon was always hostile to Xenophon. The army's internal troubles were not over.

Not long after Ereğli, south-west down the coast, the cliffs give way to lush, low hills, and tame hazelnut orchards replace wild forests. (The fairly extensive sandy plain, dotted today with summer apartments for holidaymakers from Istanbul, is largely a more recent geological development.) Xenophon's dreams of colonization were reawoken by the fertile countryside and the reunification of the army, and when, years later, he came to write up his memory of Calpe

Harbour, his tone became wistful and he made sure that his description highlighted all the features his immediate readers might have dreamt of in a colony. It was defensible and self-sustaining (the countryside just inland is indeed a slice of agricultural heaven), and could thrive by supplying navies with timber:

> Calpe Harbour is situated at the halfway point of the voyage from Byzantium to Heraclea or vice versa. It is a headland on the coast, and the bit which actually runs out into the sea is a sheer cliff, which at its lowest point is at least twenty fathoms high, while the neck, which connects the cape to the mainland, is about four plethra [90 metres] wide. The headland itself, beyond the neck, is large enough to accommodate ten thousand people. There is a harbour right under the cliff, with a west-facing beach and a freshwater spring which flows in generous quantities right by the sea and falls within the confines of the place. There is a great deal of timber of various kinds, with good-quality ship-building timber especially abundant and growing right by the sea. A hilly ridge extends about twenty stades back into the mainland; the ridge itself is well covered with stone-free soil, while the land by the coast is thickly wooded for a distance of more than twenty stades with tall trees of all kinds. The rest of the region is fertile and plentiful, and there are a number of inhabited villages there, because the soil produces barley, wheat, all kinds of legumes, millet, sesame, a good number of figs, plenty of grapes which make a sweet wine, and so on and so forth – everything except olives.

Today, Kerpe Limani is a recently developed holiday resort, quieter and more tasteful than many in the region. It is odd that its development had to wait so many centuries, when Xenophon clearly saw the place as a perfect site for the foundation of a colony. But in Xenophon's account the dream was tinged with a specific sadness. Calpe was to be a haven not just against marauding Bithynian tribes, but against time and change themselves. Calpe was where the army had reunified, and Xenophon dreamt that there his army could avoid not just physical disintegration, but the disintegration of values, the onset of amorality inspired by personal greed that Dexippus, Clearetus and Boïscus typified. The clash was between collective values, in which the individual supports the community by ruling or obeying as best he can, and selfish values, in which an individual is

The headland of Calpe Harbour, where Xenophon once dreamt of founding a colony with the Cyreans. A holiday resort has turned out to be the height of the place's development.

simply out for all he can get for himself. Calpe, in Xenophon's dream, was to be a haven of virtue.

There are few roads along the coast from Kerpe Limani to Byzantium (Istanbul) and back towards my Greek home, so my tracking of Xenophon ended there, where Xenophon would have liked his journey to have ended with the foundation of a timeless city. Although I spent no more than an afternoon there in the warm autumn sun, I too was affected by the charm of the spot. Leaving it felt like a return to everyday reality.

Encounters with Spartans and Thracians

The rumour spread through the army that Cleander would arrive with enough ships to carry them to Byzantium, so once they had gone out to bury the Arcadian dead before the corpses rotted too badly in the late-summer heat, they chose to wait rather than attempt a potentially dangerous overland march. For a while, Calpe was not so much the haven that Xenophon wanted to see there as a fortress. Enemy guerrillas lurked in the thick woods near by and even the gods seemed to have turned against them. Time after time they sacrificed with a view to going out and gathering provisions, and time after time the omens were unfavourable.

When Neon, under pressure from the famished troops, ignored the omens and took a large body of men out, he lost a quarter of his force, fully 500 men. The Bithynian Thracians had been joined by Pharnabazus's cavalry, who cut Neon's men down on the gently rolling hills, while the Bithynians slaughtered them in the woods. The rest were trapped, and once again Xenophon had to go and rescue them. They had barely got back to the camp when the Bithynians fell on their sentries, but penetrated no further into the stronghold of the Calpe headland. The Greeks had lost close to a thousand men in a single week, and the losses had been caused by greed and by turning a deaf ear to the gods' advice. But the omens at last proved favourable, and the Greeks made a sortie. Again, they first had to bury their dead, or those they could find. While they were gathering supplies, a Persian force drew near and engaged them, but after a close-fought battle the Greeks routed them so thoroughly that for the next few days they could go out and rob the rich farmland with little fear.

Cleander arrived with Dexippus in attendance and the Greeks continued to demonstrate an extraordinary ability to undermine their own best interests. Cleander was there to see whether the Cyreans could be trusted, whether they might even be useful to the Spartans themselves. But another near riot happened, prompted again by greed: by their own regulations, booty gained during a common sortie was to be pooled, but some of the troops tried to keep for themselves some sheep and goats they had captured under just such circumstances, and they enlisted Dexippus to help them. Others protested vociferously and even manhandled the wrongdoers; the riot was about to spread, and Cleander and the sailors who had brought him there fled in fear to their ships.

Some of Xenophon's men were prominent in protesting the illegality of the thieves' actions, and Dexippus used the opportunity to further denigrate Xenophon to Cleander. The Spartan governor was poised to sail back to Byzantium and not only close the city against the Cyreans, but order the governors of all the other cities in the region to outlaw the Cyreans. It took all of Xenophon's and the other generals' diplomatic skills to persuade Cleander of the truth of the case. Within a few days Xenophon and Cleander were getting on so well that they took the solemn oaths of guest-friendship. Cleander even wanted to engage the Cyreans and lead them back to Greece himself, but the omens from repeated sacrifices were unfavourable and he sailed back to Byzantium. The gods would not yet rid them of their status as free-booters.

All else appeared to be well, and the Cyreans eventually set out from Calpe Harbour by land, abandoning their dead in unmarked mass graves. Five days later, they arrived in Chrysopolis, directly opposite Byzantium on the Asian side of the Bosporus, where they sold the live-stock they had taken over the previous couple of weeks. (Now, of course, the site of ancient Chrysopolis is no more than a small part of the modern city of Istanbul, which sprawls on both sides of the Bosporus.) Everyone profited from the sale, and they looked forward to employment by the Spartans. But this goal was not to be reached by a short or straightforward path.

The Spartans and the Persians were clinging to the notion that their alliance, dating from the end of the Peloponnesian War, still meant something, even though within a year they would be at war. The Phrygian satrap Pharnabazus promised Anaxibius a lot of money if he could get the Cyreans out of Asia, so Anaxibius promised Xenophon's men wages and employment, and they were ferried across the Bosporus. Xenophon still wanted to go home straight away on his own, but Anaxibius asked him not to do so until the army had reached Byzantium. But when they arrived, Anaxibius convened the officers and ordered them to get their men out of town; he informed them that he was just going to count them, and then dismiss them, without employment and therefore without pay. Xenophon washed his hands of the whole treacherous business and made plans to leave the army as soon as they were outside the city walls. One of the subtle ironies built into *The Expedition of Cyrus* is that, since both Tissaphernes and Tiribazus at least had legalistic grounds for turning on the Greeks, Xenophon and his men faced more treachery from Spartans and from within their own ranks than they did from any Persian opponent.

Even after the sale of booty in Chrysopolis, the men did not have enough money to make the prospect of the journey home attractive. The rumour spread, as they were still streaming out of the city gates, that they were to be sent packing, and resentment immediately exploded into violence. They turned back and stormed the city, the first truly Greek city they had come across, and the Spartan senior command fled, leaving the Cyreans in effective control. In a perversion of Xenophon's dreams, they suggested that he could make himself tyrant of Byzantium and found his 'colony' there. There were already a number of dissidents among the powerful citizens of Byzantium, who wanted to drive the Spartans out of their city, and he would have the support of the enraged Cyreans too. But Xenophon assembled the men and pointed out the hopelessness of their situation: the Spartans were the rulers of the Greek world, and the entire Greek world would therefore be hostile to them. Relentless war would come to them at Byzantium, and none of them would ever be allowed to go home. They would be outcasts, branded as murderers of fellow Greeks.

The troops calmed down, and a delegation was sent to reassure Anaxibius and persuade him to treat them better. Anaxibius's and Cleander's year of command was drawing to an end, and Anaxibius said that he would report back to the authorities at home in Sparta and leave it up to them to decide the Cyreans' future. The troops left the city, and Anaxibius promptly barred the gates against them and said that any Cyrean caught inside would be sold as a slave: he could not afford to allow the anti-Spartan faction within the city the slightest potential support.

The situation was still tense, but peace had been restored. Xenophon therefore resigned his command and booked passage on the ship that would carry Anaxibius back to Gytheum, the port of Sparta. Cleander had to be brought in to reconcile the two enemies. Meanwhile, the army was uncertain what to do next, and the senior officers were divided. Their best hope was either to take up an offer of employment from Seuthes, an Odrysian warlord who was trying to extend his power base in southern Thrace, or to work for the Spartans in their campaign against other Thracian tribes on the Chersonese. As the days passed, about 500 men, mostly peltasts, sold their weapons and trickled away back home or made a new life for themselves somewhere in the region. The fragmentation of the army was increasing, and its motivation had once again changed. Now that those who wanted to go home had done so, the rest were looking for employment. Many of them were long-term mercenaries, or had been converted to mercenary service over the past two years; others were still hoping for enrichment before going home.

Anaxibius and Xenophon eventually set sail, but they had not gone far when they were met by Cleander's replacement, a man called Aristarchus, and by the news that Anaxibius's successor, Polus, was only a day or so away. No sooner had Aristarchus arrived in Byzantium than he sold 400 of the Cyreans into slavery, in accordance with the emergency measure put in place by Anaxibius. In Anaxibius's absence, Cleander had connived at the return of some of the Cyreans to the city to find better quarters. Those who had waited outside remained mindful of Xenophon's warnings about the consequences of antagonizing the Spartans and avoided serious protest.

The imminent arrival of Polus made Pharnabazus realize that he no longer had any reason to deal with Anaxibius, and he reneged on his promised bribe. Furious, Anaxibius persuaded Xenophon to return to Byzantium, to resume command of his troops and take them back to Asia, where they could act as irregulars against the Persians. Maybe he promised to argue, once he got back home, in favour of their official employment. Xenophon was welcomed back by his men, and he led them to a new camp at Perinthus, from where they planned to embark for Asia. But the Spartans and the Persians were still allies, and Aristarchus countermanded Anaxibius's orders and threatened to sink any ship that ferried the Cyreans across the Propontis. Neon, anxious not to displease his Spartan masters, took 800 of the Peloponnesian troops who were most loyal to Sparta and made a separate camp a couple of kilometres away from Xenophon. The core army, commanded by Xenophon, now consisted of about 6,000 men.

Seuthes, the Odrysian Thracian, was still soliciting the Cyreans' help, and his terms of employment were in line with standard mercenary wages. The men needed the certainty of regular employment and of easy access to winter provisions. Aristarchus repeated the counteroffer, that the Cyreans should march to the Chersonese and work for the Spartans there, but, given Anaxibius's earlier treachery, no one was sure whether to trust Aristarchus's promise of pay some time in the future, and the men unanimously chose to work for Seuthes. Besides, there was a rumour that Aristarchus wanted to have Xenophon assassinated. And so – mercenaries once more, for the first time since Cyrus's death – they spent the winter of 400 to 399 campaigning hard and successfully in Thrace. The Odrysians already controlled much of modern Bulgaria, but Seuthes wanted to control southern Thrace and set himself up as a rival to the main Odrysian ruler, Medocus, in the north.

The winter campaign ended in accusations of bribery and embezzlement, and without the Greeks having received all the pay Seuthes had promised, but they were better off than they would otherwise have been. By the time the campaign was over, early in 399, the Spartans and the Persians were at war. The conflict had long been inevitable, and was ignited when Tissaphernes returned to Asia Minor and resumed his long-lost satrapy. He still resented the fact that the Asiatic Greeks had sided with Cyrus, and he went about in a heavy-handed and threatening fashion demanding that they resume paying him. The cities appealed to the Spartans, while Tamos, Cyrus's loyal lieutenant, fled to his native Egypt to help the rebellion there, and took with him the cream of the Persian fleet in the Aegean.

Tissaphernes ignored Spartan warnings and attacked Cyme. The Spartans took this as an act of war and sent Thibron to Asia with only 4,000 men, but with the knowledge that he could find willing recruits from the Greeks in Asia Minor and could hire at least some of the remaining Cyreans with Xenophon as their general. To whom else should Thibron turn than those who had already proved their loyalty to Cyrus's cause? At first, the enemy was not Persia in general, but Tissaphernes in particular, and the Cyreans had bitter experience of Tissaphernes. Time had given the Spartans the opportunity to regret their bad treatment of Xenophon in Byzantium, and they paved the way for Thibron's arrival by sending agents with the offer of employment – an offer that was gladly accepted, not least because it made up for the shortfall in the pay they had received from Seuthes. Xenophon's book ends at this point, with him and his men marching south through Lydia to join Thibron. He and the remaining Cyreans were to stay in Spartan employ for several years, as a succession of commanders first tried to keep the Asia Minor cities out of Tissaphernes's control and then escalated the war to a full-scale but ill-planned invasion of the western satrapies.

CHAPTER TEN

Xenophon's Retreat

At the end of *The Expedition of Cyrus* we find Xenophon and his men trekking south through western Asia Minor to join up with the Spartan general Thibron and help him protect the cities of the Asiatic Greeks. The enemy was Tissaphernes, now restored to his satrapy of Sparda, but also with overall command of the Persian land forces in Asia Minor. On the way Xenophon paused for a raid that had far more to do with profiteering than with Greek–Persian hostility. Asidates was a Persian grandee with a vast estate near Pergamum, one of those Persian colonists who, or whose ancestors, had been sent into the area with a substantial body of troops, a kind of baronial army, to keep the peace. At first, Xenophon planned to enrich just himself and the men of the companies whose commanders had become his friends, but word leaked out and in the end a force of about 1,000 Greeks made off with all Asidates's flocks and cattle and slaves, and the next day even managed to capture the man himself, along with his wife and children, for ransom.

As commander, Xenophon was granted the lion's share of the spoils; it was enough to set him up handsomely for the foreseeable future. Similarly, as recently as the early nineteenth century, British naval officers could retire on their share of the proceeds from captured enemy shipping. As well as resolving his financial situation, Xenophon was also more certain that his immediate future was bound up with the Cyreans and Spartans. It was good to have the security of protection by the most powerful state in Greece.

Thibron's year of command in Asia Minor was not extended. He had not proved particularly effective, and above all he had not been able to control the Cyreans. He foolishly chose to winter in friendly territory and at the same time lacked the funds to pay Xenophon's men so that they could buy their food; they promptly demonstrated their tenuous loyalty to the Spartan cause by plundering and alienating Spartan allies. Xenophon did not disapprove: after the traumas of Byzantium and Thrace, he had no love for paymasters who did not pay his men, and he was certainly prepared to stand up to Spartans. In 397 the Spartan authorities officially pardoned the Cyreans for their behaviour under Thibron, and 'the man who had been in charge of the Cyreans', as Xenophon describes himself on the unique occasion when he appears in his *Hellenica*, replied with the haughty independence of someone who knows he has the loyalty of his men that if the mercenaries had become less unruly it was due to the change of Spartan commander, not any difference in the mercenaries. The threat was that, unless the Spartans kept sending men like Dercyllidas, who had replaced Thibron in 398, Xenophon would let his troops enjoy a greater degree of freedom than the Spartans would find comfortable.

Dercyllidas had come not only with the cash and the courtesy to calm Xenophon's men, but also with a mandate to extend the war. He began well. He made a truce with Tissaphernes, targeted Pharnabazus and successfully secured the Troad; the following year, with his command extended, he made a truce with Pharnabazus as well, left the Cyreans to guard Asia, and finally completed the long-promised project of walling off the Chersonese against Thracian incursions. On his return to Asia, he was instructed by the Spartan authorities to take the war to Tissaphernes, whom the Asiatic Greeks still perceived as a threat to their full independence: they did not particularly care who they paid tribute to, but they insisted on the right to choose their own governments. A major battle was averted only at the last minute by the commanders' preference for conciliation rather than confrontation. They met and exchanged terms: Tissaphernes, who had been joined by Pharnabazus, demanded the withdrawal of the Greek forces from Asia, and Dercyllidas demanded the independence of the Asiatic Greeks.

It was the same old stalemate, but they went through the motions. They agreed on an armistice to give them time to consult their respective governments – and in the Persians' case, to accelerate their ship-building programme. The previous year, at Pharnabazus's recommendation, the Persians had hired Conon, a brilliant Athenian admiral who had long been in exile on Cyprus, and he was supervising the reconstruction and modernization of the Persian fleet. The news of the rapid growth of the Persian fleet galvanized the dithering Spartans. King Agesilaus was at last dispatched in 396 with a realistic force of about 8,000 men, and with orders to emulate the achievement of the Cyreans: the idea was no longer just to defend the Asiatic Greek cities, but to invade the Persian empire. Agesilaus joined forces with Dercyllidas's troops (including the Cyreans, whose loyalty such that they were briefly known as the 'Dercyllideans') and repeated the demand for the guaranteed independence of the Greek cities. Tissaphernes, his confidence bolstered by the arrival of reinforcements, replied with an ultimatum: leave Asia now, or we will drive you out.

Over the next year, Agesilaus waged a two-pronged campaign, against both Pharnabazus in the north and Tissaphernes in Lydia. His strategy, especially his use of large-scale ruses, was brilliant, and his successes included victory in a major battle against Tissaphernes outside Sardis. Tissaphernes fell from grace: his clumsy and harsh treatment of the Asiatic Greeks had contributed to the outbreak of a futile and costly war, which he then failed to prosecute wholeheartedly. Tithraustes, the king's Grand Vizier, was sent out not just to replace him, but to see to his death. Tissaphernes's enemies at court had seized the opportunity to convince the king that he was planning to rebel and set up an independent kingdom, perhaps with the help of the Greeks.

Tissaphernes's execution was carried out in a particularly underhand fashion. Tithraustes came with two letters from the king. One confirmed Tissaphernes in his supreme command of Asia Minor, and the other gave Ariaeus, now ensconced in Greater Phrygia, his instructions. Ariaeus invited Tissaphernes to Colossae for an urgent conference. When he arrived, unsuspecting, he undressed for a bath – and Ariaeus's men pounced. Even great satraps are vulnerable when naked. Bound and gagged, Tissaphernes was bundled on to a wagon and taken to Celaenae. Here Tithraustes had his head cut off and sent to the king in Persia, a gruesome and stinking burden to those entrusted with the task. Parysatis exulted at the fate of her old enemy; Xenophon and the Cyreans no doubt felt a bitter pleasure.

Tithraustes offered Agesilaus a compromise: the Asiatic Greeks would once again be Persian tributaries, but they would be ungarrisoned and would otherwise retain their autonomy. Although this was close to Dercyllidas's original position, for a number of reasons the Spartan response was a resounding rejection: they still wanted the Asiatic Greek cities to form part of their own empire, they were under pressure from hostile elements within Greece to make good on their promise to be the new champions of all Greeks against barbarian aggression, and they thought they stood a good chance of further

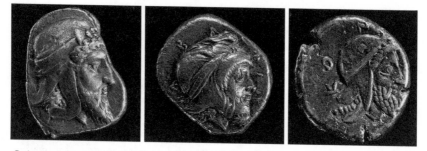

Coin portraits of, from left to right, Tissaphernes, Pharnabazus and Tiribazus. Satraps minted coins mainly to bribe Greek politicians or pay Greek mercenaries.

weakening the Persians and reducing their threat in the future. So they gave Agesilaus a unique double command, of the navy as well as the land army, and told him to get on with the war. His first task was to neutralize Conon.

Tithraustes was dispatched to attempt to put down the ongoing Egyptian rebellion, and Pharnabazus was left in command of Asia Minor. Like a nepotistic Persian, Agesilaus put his brother-in-law Peisander in charge of the navy and waged war indecisively in Phrygia, but any hopes he still had of major success in Asia had been dashed by Tithraustes's judicious distribution of cash on the Greek mainland, where resentment of the Spartans was running high. Politicians were bribed, recruitment financed, and a coalition of Greek states, led by Argos, Athens, Boeotia and Corinth, went to war against Sparta. The success of the ploy is nicely encapsulated in an implausible story from Xenophon's *Agesilaus*. On hearing the news of a Spartan victory against the combined forces of the other Greek cities – a battle in which thousands of Greeks fell – Agesilaus is alleged to have said: 'Alas for Greece! Had they lived, the men who have just died would have been enough to have defeated the entire Persian army.' Meanwhile, the Spartan fleet under the scarcely competent Peisander was heavily defeated by Pharnabazus and Conon off Cnidus. The Spartan situation in Asia Minor was now untenable, and in 394 Agesilaus and his men were recalled from Asia to meet the more urgent threat at home.

The Spartan invasion of Persian territory had given Xenophon the opportunity to transfer his hero-worship from dead Cyrus to

Agesilaus – strong leaders played a big part in his life as well as in his theories – and he accompanied the Spartan king back to the Greek mainland to prosecute what came to be known as the Corinthian War. Some of the Cyreans went with him; others had deep roots by now in Asia Minor. Seven years of fighting in the east had ended with little gained beyond a formidable reputation and the death of their old enemy Tissaphernes. Agesilaus had been forced to abandon Asia Minor and leave the Asiatic Greeks in a tense limbo, Spartan supremacy in Greece was threatened, and Pharnabazus even achieved the symbolic coup of temporarily occupying the strategic island of Cythera, just off the coast of Laconia, the Spartan heartland.

This was Pharnabazus's finest hour and before long he was recalled to Artaxerxes's court, to be one of his chief advisers and his son-in-law. Overall command of the land forces in Asia Minor was transferred to Tiribazus, the former governor of Western Armenia. He was immediately approached by a Spartan ambassador called Antalcidas, who offered peace on much the same terms as in 412: the Persians could have the Asiatic Greek cities, but the islands were to remain free. A climb-down such as this deserved to be taken seriously, and Tiribazus went east to consult Artaxerxes, while the Spartans unsuccessfully argued in favour of the terms at a conference of the major Greek powers.

After several years of inconclusive warfare on the periphery of the empire, and of patient negotiation, Antalcidas persuaded the Persians of the wisdom of an alliance. The combined threat of Sparta and Persia immediately cowed Sparta's enemies on the mainland into accepting the terms of what became known as the Peace of Antalcidas or the King's Peace, which came into force in 386. It was a 'common peace', because the oaths were sworn in the name of all Greeks everywhere (even though few of them were actually consulted) and judged on these flimsy grounds to be universally binding. If they made war on one another, they would risk war with Persia, the broker of peace in Greece.

Rather then quelling the always-belligerent Greeks, the main impact of the peace was to leave the Spartans utterly in control of the Greek mainland. The treaty assigned Persia the Asiatic Greek cities and Cyprus, and the Greek states, united or separately, were not to interfere. There were moments of tension later (for instance, when Persia protested about Athenian help in rebel Egypt, or when Sparta and

Athens backed the rebel satraps who came close to fragmenting the empire in the 360s), but each time warfare was averted. Persia had gained what successive Great Kings had wanted for the last hundred years: Persia had won.

Xenophon at Scillus

On the Greek mainland, the warring states had ground one another into exhaustion and bankruptcy, and they were relieved to see the Corinthian War brought to an end. Xenophon had notoriously fought on the Spartan side against fellow Athenians at the battle of Coronea in 394. His personal experience, and the knowledge that it was his final battle, resulted not just in the vivid description he included in two of his published works, but also in a touch of overenthusiastic exaggeration: he described it as 'the most remarkable battle of modern times', although in terms of both the numbers involved and its effects, it was equalled or eclipsed by others within his lifetime. Coronea did not resolve anything.

Returning to Greece had reawoken in Xenophon the desire for a more normal life and, now over thirty-five years old, he wanted to marry and settle down. It was time for him to retreat not just from the east, but from military life. In thanks for his years of loyal service, the Spartans granted Xenophon the freedom of the city of Sparta, and settled him on a large estate outside the town of Scillus, a little south of Olympia in the western Peloponnese (in the region bounded by modern Krestena, Makrisia and – a renamed village, not a trace of antiquity - Skillountia). The Selinus river is now little more than a sluggish irrigation ditch, but the surrounding countryside is still as beautiful as it was in Xenophon's day, with lush, well-watered vegetation, wooded hills dappled with sunshine, and rivers fringed with bamboo, bulrushes and bullfrogs. Here Xenophon spent the next twenty years.

The Spartan authorities sold him the land cheap, and even supplied him with the slaves he would need. It is going too far to liken his acceptance of this favour to Judas's of the thirty pieces of silver – after all, it was Athens that had given up on him, not the other way round – but it is true that he was still working for the Spartans. Scillus was part of a new federation of towns and villages in the coastline and plain south of Olympia, which was created by Sparta in 400 after a brief war in which the Spartan army crushed Elis. Xenophon's home was on politically sensitive land, close to the border between this Triphylian federation and Elis: as well as rewarding his friend, Agesilaus used him to displace Elean residents and remind Elis of Spartan power, somewhat as Israeli settlers do in disputed Palestinian territory.

Some time after moving to Scillus, Xenophon recovered the money he had made from the sale of booty at Cerasus; temples were often used to safeguard valuables, and he had entrusted the money to the temple of Artemis at Ephesus, where the bank was run by a man known only by his cult title, Megabyzus (a Greek distortion of a Persian word meaning 'servant of the deity'). In his book, Xenophon fast-forwards about ten years from the expedition in 400 BCE to tell us what he did with some of the money, and simultaneously to provide us with a delightful vignette of a slice of rural life, painted in the autumn colours of nostalgia:

> After Xenophon became an exile, when he was living near Olympia in Scillus, where he had been settled by the Spartans, Megabyzus came to Olympia as a spectator and returned the deposit. Xenophon used it to buy land for the goddess, after consulting the god [Apollo] about where precisely this land should be. It so happened that there was a river Selinus running through the land he bought, and there is also a river Selinus in Ephesus, which flows past the temple of Artemis. Both rivers contain fish and shellfish, but the land at Scillus is also good for hunting every species of wild animal that is normally hunted. Xenophon also built an altar and a temple from the sacred money, and afterwards he always set aside a tenth of the produce of the estate and performed a sacrifice to the goddess; and all his fellow citizens and neighbours, men and women, joined in the feast. The goddess would supply the diners with barley meal, loaves, wine, dried fruit, and a portion not only of the sacrificial victims from the sacred herd, but also of any animals which had been hunted down by Xenophon's sons and the sons of the other townspeople, who used to go out hunting for the festival, along with any other man who wanted to join them. The animals – boars, roe deer and stags – were caught partly on the actual sacred land and partly on Mount Pholoë.
> The spot is about twenty stades [3.5 kilometres] from the temple of Zeus at Olympia, on the Olympia-Sparta road. The sacred land

also contains meadows and tree-covered hills with good fodder for pigs, goats, oxen and horses, and so even the yoke-animals belonging to the people who come to the festival eat well. Immediately around the temple there has been planted an orchard containing every kind of tree which produces edible fruit season by season. The temple was constructed as a small version of the one at Ephesus, and the image of the goddess, though made out of cypress wood, resembles the golden one in Ephesus. Beside the temple stands a stele with the following inscription: THIS PLACE IS SACRED TO ARTEMIS. HE WHO OWNS IT AND HARVESTS ITS FRUITS MUST EVERY YEAR OFFER A TENTH OF THE PRODUCE TO THE GODDESS, AND MUST USE SOME OF THE REMAINDER TO KEEP THE TEMPLE IN GOOD REPAIR. NEGLECT OF THESE DUTIES WILL NOT GO UNNOTICED BY THE GODDESS.

The army had chosen Ephesian Artemis and Apollo as the recipients of their thanksgiving tithe because she was the Greek deity most favoured by the Persians, so they needed her on their side, and he was an emblem of Greek culture. At the same time, the significance of the fact that they were the twin deities of hunting was not lost on these men, who lived by fighting and foraging. During his prolonged stay in Asia Minor, Xenophon had visited Ephesus a number of times and had been impressed by the quasi-eastern cult of Artemis there, in which she was assimilated to the Persian water goddess Anahita, as mother of all species; he was pleased to be the one to introduce the cult into mainland Greece. He intended to make Artemis the protector of the community, even though a sizeable temple of Athena had recently been built on a nearby hilltop. Little remains of this Athena temple now, apart from the foundation and footings, and outstanding views of the sea and quiet countryside, with the Arcadian mountains in the distance.

No remains at all of Xenophon's temple have ever been discovered. It is impossible now to estimate the cost of the huge project: there are just too many unknown variables, such as the amount and quality of the booty sold, what price slaves and so on would have fetched at Cerasus, the cost of land around Scillus. Nevertheless, such projects did not come cheap and were usually funded by entire communities rather than single individuals. It is also impossible to tell exactly when Xenophon undertook it. Megabyzus came for one of the Olympic festivals, but we have no way of knowing which one: they

The remains of the temple of Athena, on a hilltop near where Xenophon lived for twenty years.

took place, as now, at four-yearly intervals. Perhaps he came soon after Xenophon moved to Scillus, for the games of 392.

Xenophon killed more than one bird with this stone temple. In the first place, Agesilaus was particularly fond of Ephesus, so Xenophon was pleasing his patron; in the second place, and above all, Xenophon planned to put Scillus on the map with a somewhat pretentious temple, and a lavish annual festival that remembered Artemis as an earth goddess, as mistress of animals and patroness of hunting, and as educator of young men. For a new community such as Triphylia, the introduction of a new deity was appropriate and sent a signal of permanence to the outside world. The fact that it also helped to establish Xenophon as a prominent citizen was not irrelevant.

There was a somewhat pretentious side to Xenophon's character; he was, after all, the one who chose to make his first major speech to the ruffian mercenary army, after the capture of the generals, in his finest armour, the metalwork chased in gold, the helmet mightily plumed, the shield beautifully engraved. This makes it less surprising that he chose to copy the world-famous, iconic Artemisium in Ephesus, one of the seven wonders of the ancient world. With an area of 60 by 103 metres, and with a colonnaded peristyle containing no fewer than 106 twenty-metre columns, the Ephesian temple was enormous; it was also elaborately decorated, with even pillars bearing life-size relief sculptures. It would have been silly for Xenophon simply to have built an exact copy on a smaller scale, so he surely altered the design: there must have been fewer columns, for instance, and less ornamentation, though the cult statue may well have been a more exact reduced-scale copy. Even so, it was a major undertaking.

This new estate, which may not have been exactly adjacent to Xenophon's home in Scillus, was owned by Artemis, and Xenophon presents himself as a kind of tenant. But he also made a little money off it himself: 10 per cent of the land's produce went towards the annual festival, and further money had to be spent on the shrine's officials, on occasional rites other than the festival and on maintenance, but Xenophon himself kept the rest. With his savings, and his income from two estates, Xenophon lived comfortably.

Home Life

In the excerpt translated above, Xenophon mentions his sons. The twins Gryllus (named, in the typical Greek fashion, after his paternal grandfather) and Diodorus (named after his maternal grandfather) must have been born around 390, because their father sent them to join in at least part of the famous Spartan *agōgē*, the military acculturation and training undergone by all full-blooded Spartan youths, and extended to Xenophon's sons out of gratitude for his past and ongoing assistance. Perhaps this was when they came to be nicknamed the Dioscuri, the Heavenly Twins, after the legendary Spartan twins Castor and Polydeuces. Spartan power was broken once and for all by the Thebans in 371, and one of the many consequences was that Triphylia was lost: some of it was taken over by Arcadia, and some, including Scillus, reclaimed by Elis. By then, though, Xenophon and his family had packed and left. The twins' stay in Sparta must therefore have happened before 371, while the Spartans were still Xenophon's protectors.

Placing their birth around 392 gives the boys just enough time for a few years of the kind of hunting Xenophon fondly mentions in the excerpt. It also follows that Xenophon must have come to Scillus already accompanied by his young Athenian wife Philesia, though we have no way of knowing how or where they met. Perhaps she was sent out to him while he was still campaigning in Asia Minor – before his exile in 394, while he was still well enough respected in Athens for an Athenian father or guardian to agree to the marriage.

Ischomachus in Xenophon's *On the Management of an Estate* is so transparently a mouthpiece of the author that we can sketch a few more aspects of Xenophon's life and character. He liked a plain and functional house, in which there was a place for everything and everything was in its place. He thought that marble should be reserved for public buildings, and scorned the colourful wall paintings of mythological scenes originally made fashionable by Alcibiades. By the same token, he expected that his wife would be as demure and proper as ancient Greek wives were generally supposed or imagined to be: she would mind her business (which consisted almost entirely of domestic duties, with a smattering of religious functions to attend outside) and preserve the separation of the sexes; she would not draw attention to herself by wearing cosmetics or talking in public. Xenophon recognized the value of a woman's contribution to the household, but offset this hesitant step towards equality by making plain his view that, fundamentally, men are superior to women in all things, and that women should therefore be ruled by men. Even though he expected his wife to manage the household, she was his delegate and he had told her, in broad terms, what was expected from her.

A man's 'estate' consisted not just of his land and its produce, the house and the animals, but also of his household – his wife, children and slaves. Xenophon believed that they could all be managed best by applying the same theory of leadership that he developed during the retreat from Babylonia: by means of his wisdom and morality, the estate-owner encouraged all his subordinates to respect and work for him. Xenophon treated the best and most responsible of his slaves as fairly intelligent and receptive human beings, but above all he saw them as walking tools, to help his young wife in her domestic chores, to work the land, prepare and serve food, look after the animals, bring up the children, and be available for his and his friends' sexual needs.

So Xenophon managed his estate, went out in the early years on one or two brief expeditions with Agesilaus, received visitors (especially during the Olympic festivals, which were attended by tens of thousands from all over the Greek world) and raised his family – but above all, he wrote. The protection of the Spartans could not change Xenophon's Athenian nature; the Spartans had long forsworn literary pursuits in favour of an extraordinary militaristic culture, yet Xenophon felt compelled to put pen to paper. And the pen was impelled by a creative mind: Xenophon's output was impressive, and his ever-restless intellect enabled him to invent or contribute to a wide variety of different genres.

Xenophon as Writer and Philosopher

At his best, Xenophon is an outstanding writer and a great storyteller – graceful, lucid, urbane and witty. He speaks about events plainly and impassively, though with flashes of humour, and lets them tell their own tales. But he is not artless: those who think him so cannot have read with open minds *The Expedition of Cyrus* or *Symposium* (the best of the six books posing as memoirs of Socrates). *The Expedition of Cyrus* is nuanced and thematized, beautifully paced and dramatically broken up with anecdotes, speeches, vignettes, contrasts and digressions. It is always readable, holds the attention and has the inimitable presence of an eyewitness narrative. Xenophon felt no need to exaggerate, and the most terrible events are recounted without resorting to purple prose. Above all, the book has the quality, so highly prized by the ancient Greeks, of vividness, of finding just the right words to bring events immediately before the mind's eye. It was this that led the Italian postmodernist fabulist Italo Calvino to compare the experience of reading the book to that of watching an old war documentary on television.

Although it is impossible now to date Xenophon's works with much confidence, either absolutely or relatively, many of them (though not *The Expedition of Cyrus*, as it happens) were written during his twenty years of leisure at Scillus. His dozen or so books range from history (not just *The Expedition of Cyrus*, but especially *Hellenica*, which completed Thucydides's unfinished account of the Peloponnesian War and followed Greek affairs down to 362) to specialist treatises (on Athenian economics, Spartan society, horsemanship, hunting and cavalry command), a eulogistic biography of Agesilaus, a fictional account of the life and leadership of Cyrus the Great, a short dialogue on tyranny, six volumes of largely moral tales featuring Socrates

(*Recollections of Socrates* in four volumes, *Symposium* and *On the Management of an Estate*), and a version of the defence speeches Socrates delivered at his trial.

Those eras and generations that are suspicious of moral earnestness do not find Xenophon to their tastes, and many people reading these words will have been brought up to think that Xenophon's writings reflect the concerns of a well-to-do landowner, and that he was a moral conservative and even, occasionally, a ponderous fool. Xenophon's detractors picture him as a blimpish retired general, dictating his memoirs from a comfortable armchair on his grand estate. There is a great deal of exaggeration in this. Several of his books started sub-genres of literature. Is this the mark of a plodder, or of a versatile and original writer and thinker, whom numerous others wanted to imitate? Chief among these was *The Expedition of Cyrus*, the first eyewitness campaign narrative, later emulated by, among others, several of Alexander the Great's generals, Julius Caesar and the Duke of Wellington. His treatise on the management of an estate, which is couched as a dialogue between an Athenian estate-owner and Socrates, spawned several more pedestrian imitations and was translated by the Roman orator and philosopher Cicero. His moralistic biography of Agesilaus and pseudo-biography of Cyrus the Great have earned him the description 'a pioneer experimenter in biographical forms'. *The Education of Cyrus the Great* was particularly influential: among many who could be mentioned, Machiavelli plundered it, and as the first didactic novel it was the model for Voltaire's *Candide* and Christoph Martin Wieland's *Agathon*.

Biography was not yet meant to uncover the 'truth' about its subject, and readers of Xenophon's books that feature Socrates as their protagonist should not imagine that they are hearing the authentic voice of Socrates. After Socrates's death, a number of his followers began to write dialogues or homilies featuring Socrates; apart from those from Xenophon's pen, we also have the complete set of those written by his contemporary, Plato – but, sadly, only a few fragments from other Socratics. The purpose of all these works was not to reproduce Socrates's exact words, but to give an idea of what Socrates might have said, had he addressed the philosophical concerns of Plato, for instance, or the more down-to-earth interests of Xenophon. So we find Xenophon's Socrates conversing about topics such as farming, horsemanship and statesmanship, rather than metaphysics and pure mathematics.

Thoughtful reflection on morality with a practical and prudential emphasis: this is Xenophon's signature. Self-discipline is important not just for itself, but because it enables a person not to be distracted by his appetites from doing his duty. Education is desirable provided it stops short of useless theoretical studies and idle speculation. You do good to your friends so that they stick by you, defend you from your enemies and otherwise repay you. The purposes of the management of an estate are to create wealth and to train a man to administer his country. Hunting too is ideal training for future defenders of the state.

But these external and prudential aims should not distract us from the internal emphasis that underlies them. Self-discipline is the foundation of true goodness: you cannot achieve any other moral virtue without it. You cannot manage your estate, let alone your country, if you cannot manage yourself; you cannot do good to your friends unless you can restrain your appetites; you cannot be a true leader, in control of others, unless you are in control of yourself. Self-sufficiency is also the foundation of happiness: I am more likely to be happy if I adapt my needs until they are more easy to satisfy. This is a truly Socratic conception of how to attain happiness.

One of the difficulties with appreciating the profundity of this notion is that, once stated, it is strikingly obvious. Of course we would all be happier if we did not succumb to illusory desires, did not want more than we could have. This obviousness disguises the fact that the theory is incredibly difficult to put into practice, and indeed lies at the heart of lifelong practices such as Buddhism. Consider, then, what kind of person Xenophon is portraying Socrates (and, to a lesser extent, his other heroes) as being. He is someone who can *consistently* live in this adaptive fashion, free from temptation and in full control of his desires, wishes and expectations. It is no wonder that it was Xenophon's Socrates who became the model sage for the Stoics.

Xenophon may have upheld traditional values, but he did not do so in an unthinking way. He had concluded that external activity requires certain internal conditions if it is to be genuine morality, rather than merely imitative action. A truly good person, one who deserves Xenophon's honorific epithet 'beautiful and good' (a single, compound word in Greek), has certain identifiable qualities, underlying all of which is the ability to be self-sufficient – to be free rather than in servile dependence on others for one's livelihood, self-esteem, actions, feelings and opinions. If Xenophon had merely been superficially putting his weight behind the traditional Greek virtues, as he is accused of doing by countless scholars, there would have been no need for him to stress self-sufficiency to this extent; it did not occupy this central a place in the life of a traditional Athenian gentleman, who, if asked whether he was free, would assume that the question referred to his social status rather than to any internal state. Xenophon learnt from Socrates, thought things through by himself, and tweaked the traditional conception of goodness.

Xenophon's moral concerns to a certain extent informed even his historical works: he wrote what has been called 'paradigmatic' or 'exemplary' history, focusing especially on the actions of past leaders, who were to stand as paradigms for current and future leaders. He structured his presentation of events and people (and even occasionally suppressed events, or selected among alternative versions) in order to communicate various subtextual messages, such as the inevitable downfall, engineered by the gods, of arrogant leaders. Philosophy for Xenophon, as for many of his contemporaries, was not an academic exercise, but a practical, if arduous, way to try to attain moral virtue as a steady state. Since examples of virtuous people can help an aspirant philosopher, even history-writing could serve a moral purpose. Whatever he was writing, Xenophon always had moral and educational agendas; ancient authors were right to classify him more as a philosopher than as a historian.

A Nuanced Text

It should come as no surprise, then, that *The Expedition of Cyrus* is a far more nuanced text than a superficial reading reveals – however much this was missed by the generations of schoolchildren, from Roman times onward, who learnt ancient Greek by wading laboriously through portions of the text. The earliest the book could have been written, or at least completed, is the late 370s, by which time Xenophon's sons would have been old enough to warrant mention as hunters. More likely, it was written in the 360s, after Xenophon had left Scillus, if the past tenses and nostalgic tone of his sketch of life there are anything to go by. At any rate, the book was not written in haste. Xenophon had time to reflect and to insert subtextual themes, and it has been one of my purposes to suggest how clever a book it is. I have scattered examples of themes and subtleties throughout recent chapters, but one deserves brief mention here because it reveals an aspect of Xenophon's character, albeit one that will by now be obvious.

A book that focuses so much on episodes in which the author shone carries more than a hint of self-aggrandizement and self-defence. Ctesias had by then published his own account of the battle, but mainly Xenophon was responding to rumours and pamphlets. The Ten Thousand were instant celebrities, in much the same way that the survivors of the 1934 Long March of Chinese communists were, and many stories circulated about the expedition. Xenophon wanted to make sure that everyone knew what an important part he himself had played, and perhaps to make his Athenian readers regret having exiled him. So he lets us know not just how important his actions were in preserving the army, but also how close he came to the model leader of his imagination. To borrow Italo Calvino's image, Xenophon sometimes comes across as a comic-book superhero. But if Xenophon has exaggerated his role, it is hard to feel anything more critical than a degree of generous amusement. His character was formed on the march more than anywhere else, and he could look back with pride upon his achievements.

Xenophon's defence was improved by one of the most intriguing aspects of *The Expedition of Cyrus*. Not only does he himself appear throughout in the third person (not 'I did such-and-such', but 'Xenophon did such-and-such'), but when in another work he had reason to refer to the book, he attributed it to somebody else altogether, called Themistogenes of Syracuse. Who was this Themistogenes? Was he the first known western ghost writer? No, he was either simply Xenophon's *nom de plume* or one of Xenophon's friends – perhaps the one who first suggested that Xenophon should write up his memories of Cyrus's expedition. Twenty-five years later, on this whimsical speculation of mine, Xenophon found a way to express gratitude to his friend, as well as a graceful way to set the record straight, perhaps even straighter than it really was, without appearing to boast.

In writing the book, Xenophon supplemented his memory with personal notes jotted down at the time and over the years, official army notes, conversation with other survivors who came to visit, and by reading others' accounts of the relevant events and regions. These accounts, such as Ctesias of Cnidus's *Persian Tales* and Hecataeus of

Miletus's lost ethnographical and geographical book on Asia, gave him details such as the basic layout of the ruined Assyrian cities of Nimrud and Nineveh, which Xenophon certainly did not have time to survey himself, since at the time the army was being shadowed by Persian troops. Old comrades from the campaign described to him episodes at which he was not present.

But he relied above all on his memory. It is hard for us today to put ourselves in the position of people who had fewer books (which in any case, as scrolls, were hard to use as research tools), and no access to libraries or the Web. Their memories were naturally better and better trained than ours. Besides, Xenophon was a young man at the time, and *The Expedition of Cyrus* covers the two most intense years of his life: events would inevitably have impressed themselves upon him. Not that his memory and note-keeping were perfect: it is notorious, for instance, that he omits two tributaries of the Tigris in Iraq that the army must have crossed, including the Lesser Zab, which at the time of year when he was there was certainly full enough to deserve a mention. Nevertheless, memory was his chief tool – and reliance on memory gives a writer the opportunity to structure his memories in certain ways. It is not surprising that *The Expedition of Cyrus* displays plenty of craft.

The End of the Golden Age

The dark side of *The Expedition of Cyrus* – its subtle stress on deceit, the difficulty of communication, disappointment, and the army's dis-integration under the influence of greed – helps to give it depth; it is not just a *Boy's Own* tale of derring-do. By the time he wrote the book, Xenophon was utterly disillusioned with world affairs and pes-simistic about the future. At the end of *The Education of Cyrus the Great*, after portraying at occasionally tedious length a model society, a fictional version of Persia from almost two centuries previously, he painted a bleak picture of reality under the current king. All the old virtues had vanished or were fast disappearing; society was immoral from top to bottom, Persians were no longer honourable and god-fearing, but effeminate, over-indulgent and cowardly. The end of *Spartan Society* contains a similar account of deterioration from the time of Sparta's legendary founder, Lycurgus.

The collapse of the old Spartan virtues must have struck Xenophon particularly hard, since he had been a (somewhat naïve) admirer and affiliate of Sparta for all his adult life (though he has some harsh words to say in *Hellenica* about certain Spartans' conduct during their hegemony of Greece). But disappointment had begun to set in not long after the Peloponnesian War. Sparta had been the leading city of Greece and claimed to be the liberator of Greece and protector of the most cherished Greek values, but had proved the hollowness of the claim with alarming speed. The Spartans ignored the justified demands of the Persians and set about pushing their former allies out of Asia Minor and bringing the Greek cities there into their own empire. So far from granting the former Athenian subject states of Ionia and the Aegean their autonomy, they treated them with even greater harshness. They imposed pro-Spartan oligarchies or Spartan governors and tried to extend their empire, or at least their sphere of influence, into northern Greece, Sicily, and even Egypt. Money was flooding into Sparta for the first time in history, and corruption, inevitably, was spreading.

Nor was it just Sparta and Persia that fed Xenophon's despondency. He could look back on almost half a century in which desire for dominance had torn all the major Greek states to pieces, in which interstate relations had been marred not only by warfare but by cynicism, treachery and self-interest, and in which Persian cash had continued to play an important role. In short, the same themes that give *The Expedition of Cyrus* its depth were also written large in the world around him. This, of course, is no coincidence: what Xenophon did was project the troubles of his present world back on to the expedition. The course of the expedition is made to encapsulate or reflect recent Greek history. The army as a whole, and Xenophon in particular, started off with 'soaring expectations', but in the crucible of hardship and treachery, optimism withered into disenchantment.

This was sheer projection, but that is what writers do: they inform their material with an architecture of their own devising. We should not read *The Expedition of Cyrus* as straightforward, objective history; if we had an alternative, independent version of the expedition, we would more easily spot the biases in Xenophon's account. If the retreat contains resonances with the transition, the retreat from a golden age of optimism to an era of realistic disenchantment, this is because the writer, Xenophon himself, was a transitional figure, conditioned by the values and standards of the Greek world before the Peloponnesian War, but propelled by the uncertainties of the post-war fourth century.

The legacy Xenophon gained from Socrates, to confirm moral standards by reflection and experience, gave his works a degree of poignant nostalgia. This too was a reflection of the prevalent mood when he was writing, rather than of the times he was writing about. The fifth century had been a time of moral certainty; the harsh realities of the Peloponnesian War, combined with the subversive theories of the intellectuals known as the Sophists, undermined this foundation, and the fourth century was characterized by the search for meaning and stability, and often by attempts to turn back the clock.

Sophists no longer found rich and ready audiences for their teaching, as fathers reclaimed the right to indoctrinate their sons in society's traditional standards. Many Greek states were involved in the attempt to stabilize their constitutions by having them written down for the first time; this was often cast grandiosely as a search for 'our ancestral constitution'. Writers pandered to popular adulation of the past with a spate of local histories, at the same time that Xenophon and his fellow Socratics were attempting to pin down Socrates, the man for whom philosophy was interaction and the living word. Deliberate archaizing characterized art, literature and rhetoric, while others turned their backs on the present so thoroughly that they wrote fanciful utopias, such as Xenophon's *The Education of Cyrus the Great* or Plato's *Republic*, where good order prevails under the rule of reason and law, where concord is guaranteed because everyone knows his place in society and sticks to it. Nostalgia features in *The Expedition of Cyrus* in a typically nuanced fashion: nostalgia is literally the pain caused by the desire for home, which was where Xenophon's men claimed to want to go, but in the event very few of them did so. Most of them either died or stayed homeless soldiers of fortune, so that Xenophon leaves his readers with the impression that one cannot go home, cannot turn back the clock.

Greed too, the vice that destroyed the army, in Xenophon's account, was more prevalent, as an inevitable degree of economic instability after the Peloponnesian War resulted in the illusory belief that security depended on wealth. In Athens, it had always been the way that, in lieu of taxation, the rich were expected to contribute towards society, especially by financing religious occasions such as the dramatic festivals, and by fitting out warships. This 'liturgy', as it was called, had once been a source of pride for the individual concerned, a way to enhance his and his family's prestige; but now people increasingly tried to wriggle out of their obligations.

Business practices in general began to change. Before the Peloponnesian War, as is common in pre-market societies, business relationships were embedded in the structure of society; in the fourth century they began to become disembedded, and the price or value of goods came to be dictated by market forces rather than by social factors such as reciprocity, ritualized barter and neighbourliness. Again, production began to change from being production for use (with the householding ideal of self-sufficiency) to production for gain. Commerce, rather than industry and agriculture, was beginning to be the basis of economic life. Increasing urbanization uprooted peasants from the land and made them buy goods in the market, rather than produce them themselves.

The disembedding of business relationships from the household was part of a more general fourth-century phenomenon, the detachment of large numbers of people from allegiance to any city, even the city they lived in. Following the example of the Thirty Tyrants of Athens, mass exiling of dissidents became common enough for there to be up to 20,000 exiles in the Greek world at any one time around the middle of the century. Then there were other vagabonds, including pirates, peddlers and mercenaries for hire, who either had no permanent residence within a city and therefore were not registered as citizens anywhere, or, if they were more respectable and successful businessmen, occupied the limbo state that resident aliens had, which fell well short of full citizenship. Once again, this phenomenon aroused strong emotions: with good reason, fourth-century orators tended to classify all travellers and people who lived outside their native cities as shady characters, and Aristotle, having defined human beings as essentially creatures who lived collectively, called those who lived outside the city-state system either criminals or, *per impossibile*, gods.

Again, *The Expedition of Cyrus* reflects the state of affairs current at the time of its composition: Xenophon himself, and all the Cyreans who stayed with him, despite their original intention 'to get back home', were in a similar limbo. Even though Xenophon's exile fell outside the time period covered by the book, he inserted two references to it. The device of attributing the book to Themistogenes was in part Xenophon's unconscious recognition that he had been uprooted by the expedition, that he no longer was who he had been. He chose to end the book at precisely the point when his personal uncertainties had been resolved because he did not write the book with the intention of stressing security and stability.

Later Life

We have less than a trickle of information about the last decades of Xenophon's life, but there were two significant moments. First, at some point, most likely in the early 360s, the decree of exile from Athens was repealed; this is proved by the fact that his sons served in the Athenian cavalry, for which they had to be citizens. Several of his written works focused on Athenian concerns, and it is tempting to see this as an expression of gratitude. At any rate, he still felt something for the land of his birth. Above all, probably the last thing he wrote, in the mid-350s, was a treatise called *Ways and Means*, in which he recommended bold policies for the stabilization of Athens's economic situation.

Perhaps, in writing *On Cavalry Command* also for an Athenian audience, he dreamt that one or both of his sons might one day be chosen for the command of the Athenian cavalry. This was not to be: we know nothing of Diodorus's life, and all we know of Gryllus is his death. He died, fighting for the Athenians, in a skirmish before the battle of Mantinea in 362. The biographer Diogenes Laertius, writing some 600 years later, seized the opportunity to present a typical sketch: 'We are told that Xenophon was offering a sacrifice, with a garland on his head, when the news came of his son's death. On hearing the news, he took the garland off, but when he was told that his son had died nobly, he put it back on again.'

Gryllus died trying to protect unarmed peasants from a Theban army, and he was not just celebrated by memorial poems and by a eulogy from the pen of the eminent orator Isocrates, but also figured prominently in a painting of the battle by Euphranor of Corinth, considered to be the best artist of his day, in a public stoa in the Athenian agora. There is even nowadays a village called 'Gryllos' in his honour in the region of ancient Scillus. But the bitterness of Xenophon's personal loss was compounded by his awareness that the indecisive battle that followed this skirmish did nothing to resolve the struggles that continued to tear Greece apart. The battle was meant to be the end of an era, to mark the transition from instability to peace, but it failed to fulfil this promise.

The second major change came when political circumstances and shifting borders forced him to leave Scillus. Despite the repeal of his banishment, he chose never to return to Athens, except for odd visits: his family estates had been confiscated when he was first exiled and had long been under new ownership; he had few friends there now. But it is not at all clear where he ended his life, in or around 354 BCE. Pausanias, the travel writer of the second century CE, tells us that guides at Scillus used to show visitors a tomb that they claimed was Xenophon's; but Pausanias was too busy with Olympia to visit Scillus in person, and reported no more than hearsay. The most persistent rumours name Corinth as the place where Xenophon lived out his old age, and this is the story I choose to believe, because it gives him yet another temporary home. He was still a bit of a restless mercenary, not fully at home anywhere. Even in this respect he reflects the uncertainties of his time.

CHAPTER ELEVEN

The Legacy of the Battle

Some battles change the world for ever. Cunaxa cannot claim such lofty status, but the expedition, taken as a whole, did become a major tributary of a flood that swept away one era and irrigated another. It had to build up energy, however, and intermediaries were required to spin it on its way.

The starting point was the celebrity status of Xenophon and his men. Xenophon's heroism – the unlikely heroism of a scholar and a philosopher – showed that the Persians were vulnerable: after all, as many Greeks saw it, the Cyreans had marched some 2,750 kilometres more or less unopposed into the heartland of the Persian empire and had defeated a large Persian army in a battle, only to have true victory snatched from them by Cyrus's pointless death. For much of the fifth century, Greeks had been accustomed to think of the Persians as easy prey. By the end of the fifth century, however, Greece had been shattered by twenty-five years of warfare, while the Persian empire was intact and in the ascendant. However ambiguous the success of the expedition from Xenophon's point of view, many saw it as the convincing demonstration of Greek military superiority for which they had been hoping. The epoch needed heroes, men of the stature of the Persia-fighters of a hundred years earlier, men such as Miltiades and his son Cimon, Themistocles and Leonidas; the Cyreans would have to do.

First, within five years, Agesilaus of Sparta, inspired by the Cyreans' expedition (or so Xenophon tells us, and he did at least have the advantage of being by Agesilaus's side), set out to invade the Persian empire; then the generalissimo Jason of Pherae, who before his timely assassination in 370 had spent a decade establishing himself as the ruler of Thessaly and was casting covetous eyes southward, used the example of the Ten Thousand to argue for Persian vulnerability; finally, Philip II of Macedon took on this Hellenic crusade and was preparing to invade Persia when he died in 336 (another assassination), bequeathing the task to his son Alexander the Great.

Sometimes the pen and the sword work together: these men of action were encouraged in their eastern ambitions by a series of orators, pamphleteers and politicians whose supremacist invective classified Persians as the polar opposite of robust Greeks. They saw the achievement of the Ten Thousand as proof of Persian weakness (even if really it was only proof of the Cyreans' incredible toughness), and argued, with various agendas, that the Greeks should unite against this common foe. They were the intermediaries who put the spin on Cunaxa and, ultimately, enabled it to contribute to world-changing events.

The Invention of the Barbarian

These fourth-century orators' stock themes had been around for a hundred years, ever since the first major confrontation between Greece and Persia, in the invasions of the early fifth century. Before the Persian Wars, the Greeks had spelled out their vague sense of kinship with one another in stories and complex genealogies. After the Persian Wars, however, they began to define themselves more exclusively, and especially by contrast with barbarian antitypes.

Scholars have a useful term, 'panhellenism', which covers, among other things, the ancient view that there were certain qualities essential to Greeks, and certain others, their opposites, essential to non-Greeks. Despite the centuries-long history of hostility and mistrust among the Greek states, panhellenists claimed that Greeks were somehow similar and related, and they did so above all by defining barbarians as 'other'. The Greeks started the assumption that there is something intrinsically alien about easterners – an assumption that has been and unfortunately still continues to be hugely influential in world affairs as well as in literature – and started the western trend of self-definition by contrast with easterners. Orientalism, as described by Edward Said, is the child of panhellenism. Greek propaganda about easterners remained undiluted throughout the Hellenistic and Roman periods (though, in a lovely piece of irony, the Greeks were themselves orientalized by the Romans), and from there passed into the general European cultural stock.

Prejudice is easy to define. You prejudge someone by subsuming him or her under a generalization or a set of generalizations, by talking about 'them' rather than individuals. Orientalism works simultaneously on the macro and the micro levels: at the macro level it collapses differences between members of different eastern peoples; at the micro level it manifests as the equally monolithic tendency to identify people by a single facet of their constitution, especially nowadays by their religion (not by the jobs they do, nor by the poetry and music they write, nor by the kinds of people they befriend, love and hate, nor by their feelings, nor by all the other things that make people individual and fascinating). The Greeks came to regard easterners as arrogant, decadent, soft, irrational and servile. It is easy to see the continuity between this nest of terms and others prominent in western discourse today or in the recent past: lazy, dirty, cunning, lying, childlike, gullible, irrational and vague, fanatical, cruel. The Greeks saw the east as a place of excess, and so in another stream Europeans fantasized about the east as a place of exotic or erotic adventure. But polar oppositions based on essentialist notions about easterners and westerners are no more than crude, blunt instruments wielded by politicians, and never tell the full, the human story.

The distinction between Greeks and 'barbarians' (any and all non-Greeks, whose languages sounded to Greek ears like nonsense, like *bar-bar-bar*) became fundamental not only to Greek foreign policy, as east and west were polarized as natural enemies, but also to their sense of identity, their ethnicity. The earliest and most famous clash between east and west was the legendary attack on Troy by a Greek alliance, as sung by Homer in his *Iliad*. Although in Homer's verses there are more similarities than differences between the two sides, and although his rare comments on different peoples smack more of curiosity than racism, to Greeks of the fifth and subsequent centuries the Trojan War became the archetypal confrontation of brave, well-disciplined Greeks against unruly and effeminate easterners.

Despite Homer's lack of prejudice (*his* overriding contrast was between mortal men, doomed to die, and immortal gods), both sides exploited the legend in a series of symbolic or magical actions. When Xerxes set out to invade Greece in 480, one of several propaganda initiatives undertaken by his Greek advisers portrayed the invasion as the justified vengeance of Trojans on Greeks. The Greeks played the game better, however: when Agesilaus set out against the Persians in 396, he sailed from Aulis on the east coast of Boeotia, because this in legend was where the Greeks had embarked for their voyage to Troy; there was even considerable turmoil surrounding his pre-voyage sacrifice –

though at least it was due to his having slighted the Thebans, not because, like Agamemnon, he had been trying to sacrifice his daughter. And when Alexander the Great marched east, his advisers got him to begin with actions that explicitly reversed those of Xerxes: it was payback time.

Toying with Homer's meaning was one thing, but panhellenism began to mature in 472 with the staging in Athens of Aeschylus's play *The Persians*, 'the first unmistakable file in the archives of Orientalism'. Greek tragedians invariably took a mythical or legendary episode and developed it for their own purposes; this play by Aeschylus was experimental, one of only a very few such tragedies known to us, in that its background was formed by a historical event – one, in fact, in which the playwright himself had taken part just eight years previously. Aeschylus's theme was the effect on the Persian royal family of the news of their disastrous defeat in the battle of Salamis. Though he was sympathetic to his characters' anguish, he gave them many of the features that later authors and orators came to see as peculiarly Persian.

The deep structure of the play came ready made: the old, unwritten law that excess leads to downfall. The Persian king, mired in hubris, is a godlike master of slaves who live in fear and total submission. The Greeks, by contrast, are well aware of the boundaries ordained between gods and men, enjoy freedom of speech, and are equal and willing participants in their politics. Aeschylus hints that this has military benefits: slaves driven into battle by fear will perform less well than those fighting for freedom. In the long run, the Persians are bound to fail, while the Greek way will prosper. Greece is rugged and masculine, while Persia is so soft and fertile and luxurious that it spoils its inhabitants and makes them over-emotional; Persians fight with cowardly bows, while the Greeks are 'spearmen'. Before the invasions Greeks thought of Persians as invincible, afterwards as feeble. Extraordinary shifts such as this are not unparalleled: before the emancipation of slaves in the British colonies, blacks were regularly portrayed as effeminate, afterwards as virile.

A torrent of dramas of every hue, from the lightest comedy to the darkest tragedy, as well as poems and histories, found an audience hungry for eastern tales, especially if they were couched within a framework of the Persian empire's rise and miraculous reversal at the hands of the Greeks. It was not just the Persians themselves who fascinated and amused Greek audiences, but the dozens of foreign races and hundreds of tribes contained by the Persian empire, many of which the Greeks had never before heard of. Their names tripped poorly off Greek tongues and some were spoken of in approximations or neologisms: the territory Suguda became Sogdia, more obscure tribes were just 'Black-cloak-wearers' or 'Dwellers in wooden towers'. With frightening insensitivity, all these various peoples were often lumped together as 'barbarians', to serve the contrast with Greeks. Just occasionally, specific but crude differences were recognized: Persians were luxurious, soft and emotional, Lydians addicted to sex, Phrygians cowardly, Egyptians deceitful, venal and superstitious, Thracians untrustworthy, savage and polygamous, Scythians uncultured.

But there were influential thinkers who avoided superficial and supremacist prejudices. In his *Histories*, published (or first read out) in the 430s, Herodotus agreed with Aeschylus that the subjects of kings are feebler because they are not fighting for themselves, but for the wealth and aggrandizement of their masters, and he agreed that Persian kings have a propensity for hubris. But he was no supremacist; he was a cultural relativist, for whom Greek customs were not inherently better than others. 'Custom is king of all': Herodotus's near-contemporary Pindar, the most famous lyric poet of the ancient Greek world, coined the saying, and Herodotus quoted it with approval. In any case, for Herodotus the dividing line between Greek and barbarian was uncertain: in his account, the distant forefathers of many, if not most, mainland Greek states turned out to be easterners themselves. Xenophon was very familiar with Herodotus's work.

Nevertheless, Herodotus had agreed with Aeschylus that life under an absolute monarch contributes to servility, and this view continued to condition Greek perception of the east. A hundred years later, for instance, when Aristotle infamously described some people as 'natural slaves', he was thinking above all of easterners. Two features of Persian society were seized upon by Greeks to carry the burden of their contempt. The first was that, in battle, Persian soldiers had to be whipped into action. The second was the alleged obligation all men had to prostrate themselves on the floor in front of the Persian king. To many Greeks, this was the perfect symbol of eastern lack of independence. And so, in a famous story, Spartan envoys simply refused to kowtow to the king; in another, a Theban ambassador somehow thought he could preserve his sense of integrity by surreptitiously dropping his ring and letting the king believe that he was doing obeisance, when all he was doing was picking it up.

In fact, though, a large element of Greek prejudice was involved in both cases. The use of the whip to deter battlefield desertion and to encourage the reluctant was only marginally more humiliating than methods employed even by Greeks for the same ends. And the homage due to the king involved prostration only in extreme cases of supplication from low-born individuals; otherwise one greeted him respectfully with a slight bow (or at the most a bent knee and lowered head) and with a kiss passed from the mouth towards him with a hand gesture. The Greeks genuflected before their gods, and they assimilated Persian obeisance to the most subservient form they knew from their own experience – especially since they liked to imagine that the Persians treated their kings as gods, rather than just as the gods' chosen instruments. The prejudice that easterners were servile was fed by the fact that most of the easterners they had genuine contact with were their own slaves, for whom obsequiousness was a survival mechanism.

Prejudice can affect science as well as rumour, and the Greeks came up with a 'scientific' justification for their supremacist views. The anonymous author of *Airs, Waters, Places* (a fascinating but plainly written fifth-century medical treatise) developed the idea that the location and climate of a place are largely responsible not just for the kinds of bodies and therefore the kinds of diseases to which the inhabitants are liable, but also for their temperament:

As for the lack of spirit and manliness of the people, the main reason why the Asian character is less warlike, more placid, is that the seasons there hardly change in terms of getting hotter or colder; the temperature remains fairly constant. This means that people there do not experience the kind of mental shocks nor their bodies the kind of powerful changes that are likely to steel the temper and make it reckless and passionate rather than uniform. For in all cases it is changes that stir the human spirit and prevent its stagnation. In my opinion, this is the main reason why Asiatics are feeble.

Environmental determinism became, along with absolute monarchy, the chief plank in Greek denigration of Persians.

As the fifth century progressed, panhellenist and supremacist attitudes became so thoroughly accepted that they could be merely hinted at in more or less subtle ways. 'Barbarian' became a term of abuse that

Since the Persian (bending over, in typical exotic clothing) is identified as
'Eurymedon', the message is plain: the dominant Greeks humiliated the Persians
at the battle on the Eurymedon river in the early 460s. The vase was painted in
Athens ten or so years later.

could be used of Greeks, if they committed horrendous enough crimes.
There is a famous Athenian vase of a Greek advancing, erect penis in
hand, towards a Persian who is bending over – the message of course
being, 'We buggered the Persians.' The victim is identified in an
inscription on the vase as 'Eurymedon', which was the name of the
river where Cimon won his famous battle against the Persians.
Athenians regarded being penetrated as effeminate, and so the image
of Persians as effeminate had already taken hold by around 460, when
the vase was made.

Barbarians made brief appearances in many fifth-century dramas.
They were emotional (especially when grieving), stupid (or, on the
contrary, cunning), cruel, subservient, cowardly (or falsely boastful
about their prowess), lacking in self-restraint, soft, lustful (especially
for innocent Greek maidens), overly fond of pomp, and generally
exotic. Even in tragedies, they were often used to provide a little light
relief. None of their behaviour on stage displayed moderation. We can
easily imagine the extravagant gestures the actors were directed to display, and the dances of barbarian choruses in Greek plays.

When painters and sculptors chose a popular theme such as the Trojan War, or the battle of the human Lapiths against the semi-human Centaurs, or the conflict between Greeks and Amazons, in all cases the non-Greek, uncivilized side was meant to resonate with accepted ideas about the Persians. There was a saying that was considered so smart that it was attributed to more than one sage: 'I thank Fortune for three blessings: first, that I was born a human being, not an animal; second, that I was born a man, not a woman; third, that I was born a Greek, not a barbarian.' It was easy for these attitudes to take root: Greeks were traditionally xenophobic, with a long aversion to granting citizenship even to those from other Greek states, and, in any case, the uninformed assumption of people conditioned by their own culture is always that their own society is the only one that makes sense.

The situation was ripe for exploitation, and politicians began to pay lip service to panhellenism, usually as a front for promoting their own interests. Ethnicity is not a given, something essential, but a construct – and all constructs can be manipulated for political ends. When, for instance, the great Athenian statesman Pericles, some time in the 440s, suggested a panhellenic conference at which the Greek states would debate anti-Persian strategy, the underlying agendas were Athens's need for international permission to continue to extract tribute from her 'allies' and Pericles's need to overcome internal opposition to his foreign policy by appearing to favour co-operation with Sparta.

But panhellenism had its gentler ramifications. One was the attempt to see what it was that was common to all Greeks everywhere. Herodotus had an Athenian respond as follows to Spartan fears that Athens would come to terms with the Persians and desert the Greek alliance:

> You should have known that there is not enough gold on earth, or any land of such outstanding beauty and fertility that we would accept it in return for collaborating with the enemy and enslaving Greece. Even if we were inclined to do so, there are many important obstacles in the way. First and foremost, there is the burning and destruction of the statues and homes of our gods; rather than entering into a treaty with the perpetrator of these deeds, we are duty-bound to do our utmost to avenge them. Then again, there is the fact that we are all Greeks – one race speaking one language,

with temples to the gods and religious rites in common, and with a common way of life. It would not be good for Athens to betray all this shared heritage.

Leaving aside the poignant undertones of a passage written when war rather than co-operation between Sparta and Athens was imminent, Herodotus chose to define Greek ethnicity by its culture – by shared language, religious practices and, vaguely, 'a common way of life' (he was thinking perhaps of things like hoplite warfare, a love of competition, similar clothing and domestic habits). He could have added a collective name, because they were all 'Hellenes', whether they came from Trapezus, Athens or Massalia (Marseilles); he could have added myths of common descent, but he could not ignore, as later drumbeaters could, the lack of shared history. The Trojan War was legend, and only a tiny percentage of the Greek states had stood up to the Persian invasions. The only history the Greeks shared was one of competition with one another, and it was a rare voice that described war between Greeks as 'civil war'. The Greeks were also geographically scattered, which was why they had to struggle in the first place to search for cultural markers to justify a vague feeling of kinship.

And it was more of a struggle than Herodotus's simple words imply. He claimed that you could recognize a Greek chiefly by his language and his religious customs, but neither claim is unqualifiedly true. Before the invention, over a century after the historian was writing, of Koine (the 'common tongue') to serve as the lingua franca of the vast Macedonian empire, Greeks spoke different dialects of a common language that existed only in theory, based on the fact that they could generally understand one another. The same rather woolly idea of unity held for religious practices. There were great panhellenic festivals, such as the Olympic games; there were common religious sanctuaries, such as Delos and Delphi; there were similarities in what and how the Greeks sacrificed; and they pictured their major deities in similar ways; but there were marked differences in cult practices, even of superficially similar deities, around the Greek world. In every aspect of their culture, there were divisions as well as causes for unity. In the fifth and early fourth centuries, panhellenism had to be squeezed out of the facts; it was a rhetorical trope, not a reality.

Panhellenism in the Fourth Century

About a century of rhetoric, then, preceded the use fourth-century panhellenists made of Xenophon's expedition, or of the stories that circulated about it. One side of the coin stressed the unity of all Greeks, while the other made easterners out to be their polar opposites. All the usual generalizations and projections about easterners continued to be rehearsed in the fourth century. They had become firmly lodged in nearly every Greek's mind, making it easy for orators to stir emotion by reference to them.

Politicians were increasingly calling for Greek unity and asking what it would take to engender it, or at least put an end to strife. A few philosophers were asserting the kinship of all human beings, but such a rarefied notion was unlikely to galvanize action or deter warfare. More hoped that a common enemy would stop Greek bickering, and they knew just where to look for that common enemy. Gorgias of Leontini in Sicily, one of the most popular orators of the time and the equivalent of an A-list celebrity today, told the panhellenic audience at Olympia in 392, 'Trophies erected over fallen barbarians call for hymns of praise, while those erected over fallen fellow Greeks call for lamentation.' Lysias of Athens (the son of an immigrant from Syracuse in Sicily) spoke in a similar vein at the games of 388. Orators began to belittle Persian military resources by pointing to how often Persians relied on Greek mercenaries – and also by citing the expedition of the Ten Thousand.

The most vociferous of these nationalistic orators was Isocrates, who tried to persuade his fellow Athenians that it was their historical right and destiny to lead the Greeks once more against Persia. He ranted about 'revenge' against the common enemy, when the Persian Wars were over a century old. His speeches returned time and again to the usual Greek generalizations about Persians as barbarians and, for all that he was deeply suspicious of raggle-taggle mobs such as the Cyreans, he used the expedition as evidence of Persian weakness. He also suggested that the solution to Greek poverty was to be found in the conquest of the east; he wanted to resettle the undesirable poor far away, to leave Greece stable and in the hands of the old land-owning elite, men like himself. In desperation, after decades of trying and failing to get Athens to lead the Greeks against Persia, he finally appealed to Philip of Macedon to take up the cause. But in truth this represented a climb-down from panhellenism: the Macedonians were commonly regarded themselves as more barbarian than Greek.

So fourth-century politicians with panhellenist agendas were pre-pared to use the expedition as evidence of Persian weakness. Did Xenophon agree with them? *The Expedition of Cyrus* does at first sight seem to offer support. The Greeks marched all the way to Babylonia unopposed; they were victorious in battle (according to Xenophon, any-way); they refused to surrender their weapons and they fought their way back to the sea: 'For all our small numbers ... we made the king a laugh-ing stock.' At one point, the Greeks jokingly tell some Paphlagonian vis-itors to the camp that the Persians could have been defeated by the women in the army's train. At another, Xenophon reflects, probably mistakenly: 'It was obvious to anyone who thought about it that although its size and the huge size of its population gave the king's empire strength, the length of the journeys involved and the fact that its forces were scattered made it weak and vulnerable to a sudden offen-sive.' In Isocratean mode, he suggests in one of the speeches he delivers to the men that carving out some Greek space within the Persian empire could solve the perennial problem of Greece, that of too many mouths consuming too little produce: 'Our main efforts should be put towards getting back to Greece and our families, so that we can prove to the Greeks that their poverty is self-inflicted. They could bring here those who are now living a hard life there and watch them prosper.'

The edge is taken off this panhellenist propaganda, however, by the bleaker, more pessimistic facets of the book. The Greeks may have successfully invaded the Persian empire, but they were not alone and unaided; they endured horrific hardship and lost almost half their force; they quarrelled among themselves and demonstrated their thug-gery and greed to all the Greek settlers of the southern Black Sea; Xenophon himself became disillusioned and wanted to leave. At one point Xenophon has Cyrus, a Persian, lament Persian servitude and praise Greek freedom and the courage it affords the mercenaries; but these panhellenic sentiments are marred by what immediately follows, as one by one the Greek officers approach Cyrus to extract promises from him about how much they will be paid. Their freedom is tainted by greed, their courage is for sale. If the scene on Mount Theches, with Greeks of all ranks and all states embracing, is meant to be a panhel-lenic moment, our impression of the scene is also meant to be coloured by the disintegration of the army over the next few weeks.

Xenophon himself, then, muddied the superficially clear waters of his panhellenism with a strong undercurrent of pessimism. His was a tale of disillusionment and suffering, not one of the glorious conquest of an over-ripe empire. Any chauvinist assumptions he inherited from his upbringing were tempered by the fact that his men had not behaved like representatives of a superior culture, and by first-hand experience of noble Persians, such as Cyrus and Pharnabazus. He not only expressed admiration for many of their customs and laws, but also chose to present a utopian vision of early Achaemenid society under Cyrus the Great. But politicians practise economy with the truth. They needed a concrete example in which to root their fantasies, and it would take only a little tweaking to get the expedition of Cyrus to fit the bill. Over the course of the fourth century, the rhetorical momentum built up until it became a cliché. The result was that once the Greek city-states had achieved a large measure of unity (even if it was imposed on them by their Macedonian conquerors), the Persian empire was the natural next target.

We have the works of no contemporary historians of Alexander's eastern campaigns, but there can be no doubt that they would have told us what later historians do. In the second century BCE, the thoughtful historian Polybius identified as the most important cause of Alexander's invasion of Asia 'the retreat of the Greeks under Xenophon from the inland satrapies, during the course of which no barbarian dared to stay and face them, even though they crossed all of Asia, a hostile land'. Three hundred years later, Arrian (Flavius Arrianus of Bithynia), who wrote several works in imitation or revision of his hero and was pleased to call himself 'the new Xenophon', penned a history of Alexander's eastern campaigns, which, in homage to Xenophon, he entitled the *Anabasis* (the Greek title of *The Expedition of Cyrus*); in the course of the book he twice compared Alexander's achievements with those of Xenophon. And who can deny that to a certain extent these historians, and the orators who preceded them, were right? There had been countless palace intrigues surrounding successive successions to the Persian throne, but Cyrus's was the first true invasion. The next had Alexander at its head and ineradicable changes to the world in its train.

Alexander the Great

In the first half of the fourth century, Persian energy was largely absorbed by containment. This consisted of a prolonged struggle against Egypt, which had been in a constant state of rebellion since around 404, and various attempts to stabilize their western possessions against any knock-on effects of the Egyptian rebellion. By 386, they had resolved their century-long dispute with the Greeks to their perfect satisfaction.

After Artaxerxes II died of natural causes in 359, his son came to the throne as Artaxerxes III. He was as harsh towards anyone he considered a threat to his throne as any other Persian king, but after a rocky start he stabilized an empire that had been plagued by a succession of satrapal rebellions in the 360s. He was also a ruthless and experienced field commander: he savagely crushed a Phoenician revolt in 345 and, in a war pitting Greek mercenaries against their fellows on the other side, regained Egypt in 343. History might have been very different had he not been murdered along with the rest of his family in 338. One son was spared, to become the puppet king Artaxerxes IV, until he had served his purpose and was done away with and replaced by a cousin, who took the throne as Darius III. Darius was a competent strategist, but it would have taken more than mere competence to match Alexander the Great, and he has gone down in history as the man who lost the Persian empire to the Macedonians.

Philip II came to the Macedonian throne in 359. By 355, by a combination of diplomacy, assassination and military force, he had warded off external threats and united the country under his autocratic rule. He developed the army and superseded Greek hoplite tactics until he had a stupendous fighting force at his personal command. He could call on an army of 2,000 cavalry and 30,000 soldiers trained to high professional standards, equipped with superior weaponry (especially lighter shields, and an enormously long, sturdy, two-handed pike, which impeded the approach of the enemy line), accustomed to longer periods of warfare than the short Greek campaigning season, and accompanied by fewer camp followers to allow for greater speed of movement. Even apart from their lack of professionalism, many Greek states would have to unite in order to field an army of comparable size. Their failure to do so meant that Philip could pick them off one by one, or league by league.

Athens became the focus of what little resistance there was to Macedon, but it was the last gasp of traditional Greek city-state autonomy. War, financed in part by Persia, was waged in a ragged fashion by Athens and its allies against Philip, until in 338 he marched south. Alongside Boeotian troops, Athenians faced the Macedonians at Chaeronea in Boeotia. Although the armies were numerically more or less equal, and although the Athenians and Boeotians had a good defensive position, the trained and experienced Macedonian infantrymen and cavalry cut the Greeks to shreds. Athens and the rest of southern Greece lay open.

Almost the first action Philip took as ruler of southern Greece was to form the conquered states into a league. Among the provisions of the 'common peace' he imposed on them were that the Greek states should respect one another's freedom, autonomy and territorial integrity; that they should not make war on one another unless a treaty had been violated; that they should not interfere with another state's shipping; and that they should not help politically disaffected men from another state. In effect, he forced the old panhellenic ideals upon them. He next got the league to appoint him supreme commander for the long-promised 'Greek' war against Persia. But Philip was murdered by a disgruntled fellow Macedonian at a wedding party on the eve of his journey east, and both the Macedonian throne and the eastern expedition devolved on to his son, Alexander, soon to be known as 'the Great'. Alexander inherited his father's panhellenic mantle and in 334 crossed the Hellespont into Asia. In a series of amazing and closely fought battles, which were nowhere near as easy as the orators had promised, he crushed the Persians and took control of the empire.

The battle at Granicus river in 334 took care of the Persian armies of Asia Minor, and four satraps, the Greek commander of the Persians' mercenaries and three members of the king's family lay dead on the battlefield. The remnants of the king's western army were ordered to fall back to Babylonia, where a fresh army was mustering. While Alexander marched south into Phoenicia, Darius marched north into Cilicia. Alexander turned back, and annihilated the Persians near Issus in 333. It was a notable victory: not only were Persian losses serious, but the king's 8,000 remaining mercenaries deserted in despair after the battle and Alexander swelled his war chest with the capture of the king's treasury at Damascus.

Alexander returned to Phoenicia and protected his rear by conquering Egypt in 332. By the time he returned from Egypt and marched to Thapsacus, Darius had had almost two years in which to gather another army. Battle was joined at the village of Gaugamela close to the Tigris. As usual, both luck and superior strategy were on

Alexander's side, and despite its vastly superior numbers the Persian army was routed. It was the end of the empire: the king fled to Ecbatana, and Alexander proclaimed himself King of Asia. Babylon and Susa opened their gates without a fight, and the rest of the empire lay open to his unstoppable energy. Hill-tribes were defeated or spared as the whim took him – whatever it took to ensure his security. A minor defeat near Persepolis hardly delayed his taking the city. In the summer of 330 he marched on Ecbatana. Darius fled before him with a scorched-earth strategy – but Darius was killed by some of his eastern satraps and courtiers.

This was, perhaps, not so much an assassination as an assisted suicide: the king had no intention of letting himself fall alive into Alexander's hands and be paraded in triumph before his former subjects. No king of Persia had ever been taken alive and Darius had enough guts and sense of history to make sure that he was not the first. The conspirators fought on, in a bloody and ultimately futile war. By 326 Alexander had extended the empire through Pakistan to northern India, but his troops had had enough and he was forced to turn back. A reign of terror ensued, with satraps and senior officers deposed or executed, in a bid to secure the former Persian empire for the future. By the time of his premature death on 10 June 323 – of a fever exacerbated by wounds, hard drinking, even harder campaigning, and grief over lost friends and at least one lover – Alexander's empire stretched from the Danube to the Nile to the Indus.

Alexander's world-changing victories are a true legacy of the expedition of Cyrus and Xenophon. Alexander himself is said to have recalled the Cyreans' 'success' in the exhortation he delivered to his troops before the battle of Issus. Eunapius of Sardis, the historian of the fourth century CE, was not exaggerating too much when he coined the memorable saying that 'Alexander the Great would never have become "Great" without Xenophon'. The Macedonians and the Persians would have come to blows anyway, as neighbouring imperialists must. But Xenophon's expedition and its panhellenist promoters helped to make the conflict possible by giving Greeks, or in this case Macedonians, the belief that they could conquer the east. And Xenophon himself, at a superficial reading, could be taken to be a propagandist for the conquest. As well as incidental details of the route and of some of the enemy's tactics, he gave Alexander's army both propaganda and confidence, two critical factors in any campaign.

The conflict that Xenophon recorded helped to trigger a huge shift in the balance of power in the ancient world – a shift that in the short term ushered in the Hellenistic world, and in the long term has affected the destinies of whole civilizations. It is not just that much of the world as we know it today is the product of the territorial entities bloodily carved out by Alexander's Successors in their interminable wars against one another. Nor is it even that the cultural ripples of Alexander's and his Successors' export of Hellenic culture as far east as India never end. It is not too far-fetched to believe that Alexander himself may have entertained dreams of uniting west and east in a common, hybrid culture, even though the dreams were bound to fail, since the Macedonians came as conquerors.

As a conqueror, Alexander perpetuated the panhellenic division between west and east and helped to fix a geopolitical dynamic that has always encouraged major clashes between the two zones: Parthians and Romans (once the Romans had taken over the remains of Alexander's eastern empire), Sassanids and Byzantines, Moslems and European Franks, Ottomans and the European superpowers, and now Moslems against the US alliance. And so the legacy of Cunaxa has proved not to be limited to ancient Persia, or even to ancient Greece. The expedition of Cyrus, and *The Expedition of Cyrus*, may be no more than tributaries, but their waters are still present in the stormy sea on which the world is tossed today.

Timeline

c. 1200	Trojan War
1050–950	first period of colonization from mainland Greece
776	traditional date of first Olympic Games
750–550	second period of colonization from mainland Greece
c. 700	Homer and Hesiod composing their epic poems
700–600	diffusion of hoplite tactics and weaponry in Greece
687	foundation of kingdom of Lydia
630	Spartan control of southern Peloponnese complete
585–550	reign of Astyages of Media
560–546	reign of Croesus of Lydia
559–330	Achaemenid dynasty rules Persia
559–530	reign of Cyrus the Great of Persia
c. 550	Persian revolt and conquest of Medes
c. 550	first great temple of Artemis at Ephesus
547–546	Cyrus annexes Lydia
546–510	Pisistratid tyranny in Athens
539	Cyrus gains Babylonia
530–522	reign of Cambyses II of Persia
527–510	tyranny of Hippias in Athens
c. 525	Persian conquest of Egypt
522	reign of Smerdis of Persia
521–486	reign of Darius I of Persia
520–490	reign of Cleomenes I of Sparta
513–510	Persian campaigns in Scythia and Thrace
508	Cleisthenes introduces democracy to Athens
499–494	Ionian Revolt
492	first Persian invasion of Greece wrecked off Athos
490	second Persian invasion; battle of Marathon
486–465	reign of Xerxes I of Persia
480	third Persian invasion of Greece; battles of Thermopylae, Artemisium and Salamis
479	battles of Plataea and Mycale end Persian invasion
477	Delian league formed, later to become the Athenian empire
472	Aeschylus's *The Persians*
469	birth of Socrates
c. 468	Cimon's victory at Eurymedon
465–424	reign of Artaxerxes I of Persia
459–446	open hostility between Athens and Sparta

450s	Athenian support for Egyptian rebellion against Persia
c. 448	Peace of Callias ends overt hostilities between Athens and Persia
c. 435	Herodotus publishes his *Histories*
431–404	Peloponnesian War
430–427, 410	plague in Athens
c. 428	birth of Xenophon
424	reign of Xerxes II of Persia
424–404	reign of Darius II of Persia
424	renewal of Peace of Callias between Athens and Persia
423	birth of Cyrus the Younger
415–413	Athenian expedition to Sicily
415	Athenian support for rebellion of Pissuthnes and Amorges of Sparda
415	Tissaphernes becomes satrap of Sparda
414	Pharnabazus II becomes satrap of Phrygia
412–404	Alcibiades of Athens active in Asia Minor
407–404	Lysander of Sparta active in Asia Minor
407	Cyrus the Younger becomes viceroy of Asia Minor
404–359	reign of Artaxerxes II of Persia
404–371	Spartan hegemony in the Aegean
404–403	rule of the Thirty Tyrants in Athens
404–343	Egyptian rebellion against Persia
401	battle of Cunaxa and death of Cyrus the Younger
401–400	Xenophon's retreat
400–360	reign of Agesilaus of Sparta
400–399	Xenophon and Cyreans employed in Thrace
399	trial and execution of Socrates
399–394	Xenophon serves under Spartans in Asia Minor
399 or 394	banishment of Xenophon from Athens
395–386	Corinthian War
395–347	Plato active in Athens
395	death of Tissaphernes
c. 392–370	Xenophon in Scillus; main writing period
387–338	Isocrates active in Athens
386	Peace of Antalcidas (King's Peace)
384–322	Aristotle
371–362	Theban hegemony in Greece
c. 368	Xenophon's banishment repealed
362	death of Xenophon's son Gryllus
359–338	reign of Artaxerxes III of Persia
359–336	reign of Philip II of Macedon
c. 354	death of Xenophon, perhaps in Corinth
338–336	reign of Artaxerxes IV of Persia
338	battle of Chaeronea gives Philip control of southern Greece
336–330	reign of Darius III of Persia
336–323	reign of Alexander III of Macedon, the Great
334–330	Alexander conquers Persian empire

Maps

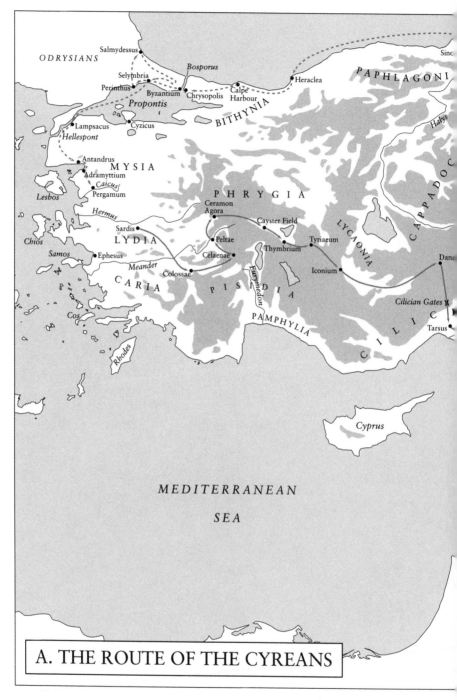

ODRYSIANS

Salmydessus

Sinc

PAPHLAGONI

Bosporus

Selymbria

Heraclea

Perinthus

Byzantium   Chrysopolis   Calpe
Harbour

Propontis

BITHYNIA

Lampsacus   Cyzicus

Hellespont

Halys

Antandrus

MYSIA

Adramyttium

Caicus

Lesbos   Pergamum

PHRYGIA

CAPPADOC

Hermus

Ceramon
Agora

Sardis

Cayster Field

LYCAONIA

Dana

Chios   LYDIA

Peltae

Tyriaeum

Samos   Ephesus

Celaenae   Thymbrium

Meander

Colossae

Iconium

CILIC

Cilician Gates

Tarsus

Cos

CARIA

PISIDIA

Eurymedon

PAMPHYLIA

Rhodes

Cyprus

MEDITERRANEAN

SEA

A. THE ROUTE OF THE CYREANS

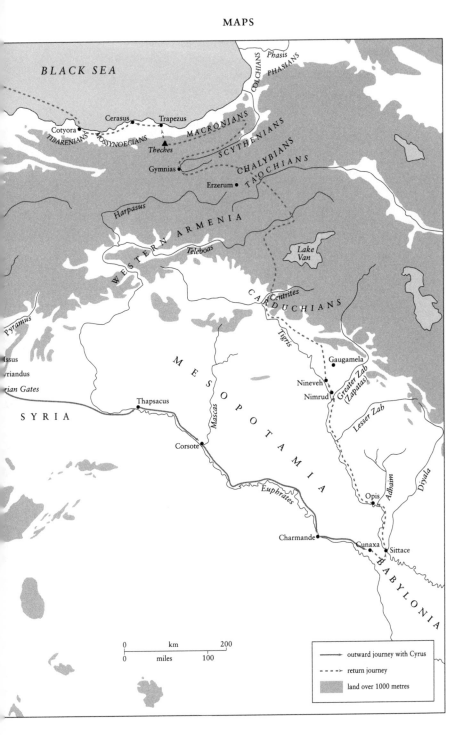

outward journey with Cyrus

- - - - return journey

land over 1000 metres

MACEDON

THESSALY

Artemisium

Thermopylae

Coronea

Delphi • • Coronea

BOEOTIA • Thebes
• Plataea

A C H A E A

E L I S

Piraeus • • At

Corinth •
• Nemea   *Salamis*   Pha

Olympia •   ARCADIA
• Scillus   Mantinea • • Argos

*THE
PELOPONNESE*

I O N I A N

S E A

Sparta •
LACONIA

• Gytheum

Cythera

B. GREECE AND THE AEGEAN

0   km   100
0   miles   60

THRACE

Bosporus

Byzantium

Propontis

CHERSONESE

Hellespont

Dascyleum

Graniucus

MYSIA

TROAD

Lesbos

Cyme

LYDIA

Castolus
Plain

Sardis

Chios

AEGEAN

I
O
N
Z
I
A

SEA

Ephesus

Meander

Samos

Mycale

Miletus

Delos

Halicarnassus

Cnidus

Rhodes

Crete

land over 1000 metres

C. THE PERSIAN EMPIRE

Weights and Measures

Values varied somewhat from place to place within the ancient Greek world; what follows is just one system, the one that Xenophon used.

MEASURING DISTANCE
16 fingers (breadth) = 4 palms = 1 foot
12 fingers = ½ cubit = 1 span (the distance between the tip of the thumb and the little finger when the hand is fully spread)
1¼ feet = 1 pygon (the distance from the elbow to the bottom joint of the little finger)
1½ feet = 1 cubit (the distance from the elbow to the tip of the middle finger)
6 feet = 1 fathom (the distance from the fingertips of the left hand to those of the right hand when the arms are stretched out horizontally)
100 feet = 1 plethron
600 feet = 1 stade
30 stades = 1 parasang*
1 foot on the Attic scale has been estimated to be 29.6 cm (11.65 in.). Therefore:
1 finger = 1.85 cm (0.73 inch)
1 palm = 7.4 cm (2.91 inches)
1 span = 22.2.cm (8.74 inches)
1 pygon = 37 cm (14.57 inches)
1 cubit = 44.4 cm (17.5 inches)
1 fathom = 1.776 m (1.94 yards)

* Scholars have sometimes been confused by the facts that (a) other ancient authors took a parasang to be as much as 60 stades, and (b) the later Persian farsang could be used as a measure of a distance that could be covered in an hour, rather than as a determinate unit – much as until recent times in rural Greece distances were occasionally measured by how many cigarettes could be smoked during the journey. But ancient Greeks clearly regarded the parasang as a fixed unit of length (though they differed as to its length), and indeed it is possible that there were parasang markers along many of the main roads of the Persian empire.

1 plethron = 29.6 m (32.38 yards)
1 stade = 177.6 m (194.29 yards)
1 parasang = 5.328 km (3.33 miles)

MONEY, OR MEASURING WEIGHT

Greek coinage was not on the whole fiduciary, but was worth its weight. Hence measures of weight are at the same time monetary measures.

1 talent = 60 mnas = 6,000 drachmas = 36,000 obols
1 obol = 722 mg (0.025 oz)
1 drachma = 4.332 g (0.15 oz)
1 mna = 433.2 g (15.16 oz)
1 talent = 25.992 kg (57.31 lb)

MEASURING CAPACITY

Liquid measures: 1 amphora ('jar') = 12 choes ('pitchers') = 144 cotylae ('cups') = 864 cyathi ('spoons'). Since 1 amphora = about 39 litres (68.64 pints, 8.58 gallons), then 1 chous = 3.25 litres (5.72 pints), 1 cotyle = 270 ml (0.48 pint), and 1 cyathus = 45 ml (0.079 pint, 1.58 fl. oz).

Dry measures: 1 medimnus = 48 choenixes = 192 cotylae. Since 1 cotyle = 270 ml. (0.48 pint), then 1 choenix = 1.08 litres (1.90 pints), and 1 medimnus = 51.84 litres (91.24 pints, 11.40 gallons).

References

CHAPTER I

1 *ancient estimates*: 400,000 in Ctesias of Cnidus, fragment 22 Jacoby; 900,000 according to Xenophon, *The Expedition of Cyrus* 1.7.12.
8 *'With head already white ... body stripped of armour'*: Tyrtaeus 10.23–7 West.
10 *Laches*: Plato, *Laches* 190e.
10 *'He never held a shield ...'*: Euripides, *Heracles* 159–64.
11 *'only at cocktail parties or tennis tournaments'*: John Keegan, *The Face of Battle: A Study of Agincourt, Waterloo and the Somme* (London: Jonathan Cape, 1976), pp. 168–9 (Penguin edition).
12 *'With the fighting over ...'*: Xenophon, *Agesilaus* 2.14, on the battle of Coronea.
12 *'Greek hoplite warfare ...those rules'*: J.E. Lendon, *Soldiers and Ghosts*, p. 83.
17 *'Here I am ...'*: Plutarch, *Artaxerxes* 8.2.
19 *celebrated in later Greek literature*: e.g. Aelian, *Varied History* 12.1.

CHAPTER 2

21 *'Greeks improve ...'*: Philip of Opus, *Epinomis* 987d; this work was in ancient times wrongly attributed to Plato.
22 *'If you make war on the Persians ...'*: Herodotus, *Histories* 1.53.
23 *Cyrus Cylinder*: British Museum, ANE (Ancient Near East) 90920.
26 *according to Herodotus*: *Histories* 3.95.
26 *'The king,' they said, ...'*: Xenophon, *The Education of Cyrus the Great* 8.2.12.
27 *'Whatever the conditions ...'*: Herodotus, *Histories* 8.98.
29 *In his eulogistic biography of the Spartan king Agesilaus*: Xenophon, *Agesilaus* 9.1.
32 *'the beginning of misfortune ...'*: Herodotus, *Histories* 5.97.
32 *'Meanwhile, news ...'*: Herodotus, *Histories* 5.105.
34 *Mill famously quipped*: in *Discussions and Dissertations*, 11 (1859), p. 283.

CHAPTER 3

39 *'If there's no need for me to be in Athens ...'*: Xenophon, *On the Management of an Estate* 11.15–18.

41 'People had fewer inhibitions ...': Thucydides, The Peloponnesian War 2.53.

42 'Before all else ...': Xenophon, On Cavalry Command 1.1–2.

43 At one point towards the end of the retreat: Xenophon, The Expedition of Cyrus 6.4.12–20. With Xenophon's three-day delay here, compare the Spartan Dercyllidas's four-day delay at Hellenica 3.1.17–18, which again ended badly for those who ignored the omens.

43 'Xenophon was as agitated ...': Xenophon, The Expedition of Cyrus 3.1.11–14.

45 'Follow me, and find out': Diogenes Laertius, Lives of Eminent Philosophers 2.48.

45 'In those days everyone ...': Aristophanes, Birds 1281–2.

46 the orator Aeschines: Aeschines, Against Timarchus 173.

46 'My trial ...': Plato, Gorgias 521e.

48 'Socrates thought that friendship ...': Xenophon, The Expedition of Cyrus 3.1.5–8.

49 As he himself says: Xenophon, The Expedition of Cyrus 5.8.19.

50 'The contrast between aristocracy and democracy ...': Pseudo-Xenophon, Constitution of Athens 1.5. The anonymous author is familiarly known as the 'Old Oligarch'.

51 'partners in prejudice': Robin Lane Fox, 'Introduction', p. 12, in id. (ed.), The Long March.

51 'Meanwhile, Xenophon ...': Xenophon, The Expedition of Cyrus 7.7.57.

52 admiration of Theramenes: Xenophon, Hellenica 2.3.56, with a constant portait of him throughout the book as the voice of reason.

53 A relatively neglected piece of evidence: Xenophon, The Expedition of Cyrus 5.3.5.

54 We know that Agesilaus: Plutarch, Life of Agesilaus 19.

CHAPTER 4

57 'All the territory ...': Thucydides, The Peloponnesian War 8.18.

58 'our usual bad habit ...': Andocides, On the Peace with Sparta 28, echoing Thucydides, The Peloponnesian War 6.13.2.

63 This story: Plutarch, Artaxerxes 3. The story may originate with Ctesias. The story about Parysatis's murder of Stateira comes from Artaxerxes 19, again probably via Ctesias.

65 Xenophon twice mentions: The Expedition of Cyrus, 1.4.9, 2.4.27.

66 by our sources: especially Plutarch, Life of Alcibiades 39; Diodorus of Sicily, Library of History 14.11.

68 Xenophon tamely agreed: The Education of Cyrus the Great 8.8.12. For Xenophon's personal opinion of Cyrus, see The Expedition of Cyrus 1.9 and On the Management of an Estate 4.18–19.

68 Xenophon was impressed with this: On the Management of an Estate 4.20–5.

71 'bronze men': Herodotus, Histories 2.152.

71 Alcaeus: fragment 350 Lobel-Page.

CHAPTER 5

73 *a thumbnail sketch*: Xenophon, *The Expedition of Cyrus* 2.6.1–15.
73 *Lawrence Tritle*: in his book *From Melos to My Lai*, and also in his essay in the collection *Xenophon and His World*, edited by Christopher Tuplin.
74 *the Cyreans certainly did*: Xenophon, *The Expedition of Cyrus* 3.4.5.
74 *'It will never be said of me …'*: Xenophon, *The Expedition of Cyrus* 1.3.5.
75 *an obituary from Xenophon*: *The Expedition of Cyrus* 2.6.21–9.
76 *Xenophon says bluntly*: *The Expedition of Cyrus* 2.2.6.
77 *In his portrait of Cyrus*: Xenophon, *The Expedition of Cyrus* 1.9.
81 *vagabonds, deserters and criminals*: Isocrates, *On the Peace* 44–6; see also Plato, *Laws* 630b.
81 *Xenophon idealistically thought*: *On Cavalry Command* 9.3–4.
81 *Hybrias*: poem 909 in D.L. Page, *Poetae Melici Graeci* (Oxford University Press, 1962), pp. 478–9.
84 *'This enabled them to capture …'*: Xenophon, *The Expedition of Cyrus* 6.6.38.
85 *Herodotus delights in a story*: Herodotus, *Histories* 8.105–6.
86 *'There was in the army a man called Xenophon …'*: Xenophon, *The Expedition of Cyrus* 3.1.4.
87 *'The eagle is a magnificent bird …'*: Xenophon, *The Expedition of Cyrus* 6.1.23.

CHAPTER 6

93 *'If not … slaughtermen'*: William Shakespeare, *Henry V* 3.3.116–24.
93 *When the number of accomplices …*: Machiavelli, *Discorsi* 3.6.
96 *Two companies from Meno's force*: Xenophon, *The Expedition of Cyrus* 1.2.25. Scholars need to know that I read the brilliant emendation suggested by M.W. Mather and J.W. Hewitt (eds), *Xenophon's Anabasis Books I–IV* (Norman: University of Oklahoma Press, 1969), ad loc.
98 *'These gates consist of two forts…'*: Xenophon, *The Expedition of Cyrus* 1.4.4–5.
101 *as flat as the sea*: Xenophon, *The Expedition of Cyrus* 1.5.1.
103 *'they needed … for all those people'*: Xenophon, *The Expedition of Cyrus* 4.1.13.
104 *'Was it that I had asked you…?'*: Xenophon, *The Expedition of Cyrus* 5.8.4.
105 *top of his list of grievances*: Xenophon, *The Expedition of Cyrus* 5.1.2.
108 *'We can formulate a general principle …'*: Donald Engels, *Alexander the Great and the Logistics of the Macedonian Army*, p. 22.
111 *Xenophon's considered opinion*: *On Cavalry Command* 7.6–7.

CHAPTER 7

112 *'that he would give horses …'*: Plutarch, *Artaxerxes* 6.2.
112 *'If you are men …'*: Xenophon, *The Expedition of Cyrus* 1.7.4.
115 *If we are to believe Ctesias*: fragment 26 Jacoby, preserved by Plutarch, *Artaxerxes* 14–17.

116 *from a reading of Herodotus: Histories* 1.136, confirmed by Persian inscriptions such as that quoted in Amélie Kuhrt, *The Ancient Near East*, vol. 2, p. 681.

118 '*Only the king* ...': Xenophon, *The Expedition of Cyrus* 2.5.23.

119 '*A short while later* ...': Xenophon, *The Expedition of Cyrus* 2.5.32–4.

121 '*In peacetime* ...': Xenophon, *The Expedition of Cyrus* 3.1.37.

123 *There is said to be an Amazonian tribe*: see Petru Popescu, *Amazon Beaming* (New York: Viking, 1991).

126 *Plato's memorable image*: Plato, *Phaedo* 109b.

127 *Xenophon attempted to address: The Expedition of Cyrus* 3.2.23–6; for settling in Persian heartland, see 2.4.21–2.

127 '*Meanwhile ... Black Sea coast*': Xenophon, *The Expedition of Cyrus* 5.6.15–16.

128 *Xenophon describes Byzantium: The Expedition of Cyrus* 7.1.29.

129 *accounts of similar treks*: see Tim Rood in my translation, *Xenophon: The Expedition of Cyrus* (Oxford: Oxford University Press, 2005), pp. xi–xii.

129 '*I believe ... teems with uncertainties*': Xenophon, *The Expedition of Cyrus* 2.5.8–9.

130 *beautiful women and luxurious living*: Xenophon, *The Expedition of Cyrus* 3.2.25.

CHAPTER 8

133 *Xenophon believed* ...: *On Cavalry Command* 4.16; at *The Expedition of Cyrus* 4.4.15, he says of Democrates of Temnos, the army's chief scout, 'If he said that something was the case, it was the case, and if he said it was not, it was not.' At 7.3.41, he draws attention to Seuthes, their paymaster at the time, doing some personal scouting.

134 '*They lost no time ... could manage*': Xenophon, *The Expedition of Cyrus* 4.1.23–4.

135 *Xenophon ... proudly informs us: The Expedition of Cyrus* 4.3.10.

136 *When everything was in place ... a few of them too were wounded*: Xenophon, *The Expedition of Cyrus* 4.3.16–34.

141 '*the straps sank ... on to their feet*': Xenophon, *The Expedition of Cyrus* 4.5.14.

141 '*low hovels, mere holes in the hillside*': Austen Layard, *Discoveries in the Ruins of Nineveh and Babylon, with Travels in Armenia, Kurdistan and the Desert* (London: John Murray, 1853), p. 14.

142 '*The climate here is so severe ... tops of the houses*': John Macdonald Kinneir, *Journey*, pp. 346–7.

144 *paid tribute to the Ten Thousand*: Plutarch, *Life of Antony* 45.

144 '*pretentiously simple*': T.E. Lawrence, quoted in J.M. Wilson, 'T.E. Lawrence and the Translating of the *Odyssey*', *Journal of the T.E. Lawrence Society*, 3.2 (1994), p. 37.

145 *Xenophon saw the essential ingredient* ...: Xenophon's thoughts on leadership are scattered throughout his works, especially *The Expedition of*

Cyrus, The Education of Cyrus the Great, On Cavalry Command and
Hiero 8–11. Two summary passages are *Recollections of Socrates* 3.1.6 and
On the Management of an Estate 21.4–8. The sentence quoted is from
Recollections of Socrates 3.9.10.

146 *This threefold division had a long history*: in what follows I refer, in order,
to the following authors and passages: Polybius, *Universal History* 6.3–10;
Diogenes Laertius, *Lives of Eminent Philosophers* 7.131 = J. von Arnim,
Stoicorum Veterum Fragmenta 3.700; Pindar, *Pythian Odes* 2.85;
Herodotus, *Histories* 3.80–3; Plato, *Statesman* 291c–303c; Aristotle,
Politics 3 (with a specific reference shortly to 1265b). Reflections of the
threefold division in the fourth century may be found in, for insance,
Isocrates, *Nicocles* 15 and *Panathenaicus* 132. The Xenophontic passages
are scattered liberally throughout *The Expedition of Cyrus* and are too
many to mention.

149 *a breakaway company commander ... a demagogue*: Xenophon, *The
Expedition of Cyrus* 5.7.27–32, 7.6.4.

CHAPTER 9

151 *one of the most famous passages in Western literature*: Xenophon, *The
Expedition of Cyrus* 4.7.21–5.

152 *'crusted with parasangs'*: Louis MacNiece, 'Round the Corner', *Collected
Poems*, 2nd edn (London: Faber & Faber, 1979), p. 583.

154 *There were a lot ... treated with medicine*: Xenophon, *The Expedition of
Cyrus* 4.8.20–1.

155 *the local tribes ... are said*: Strabo, *Geography* 12.3.18.

156 *'snow lacuna'*: Robin Lane Fox, 'Introduction', p. 45, in id. (ed.), *The Long
March*.

158 *'I'm fed up ... like Odysseus'*: Xenophon, *The Expedition of Cyrus* 5.1.2.

159 *'These were the men left alive ...'*: Xenophon, *The Expedition of Cyrus*
5.3.3.

161 *his speeches began to be coloured*: Xenophon, *The Expedition of Cyrus*
6.1.27–8 and 7.1.26–7; the purification of the army is mentioned at
5.7.35.

163 *'They show the marks of his descent ...'*: Xenophon, *The Expedition of
Cyrus* 6.2.2. 'Jason's Point' is mentioned a couple of sentences earlier.
There are several places on the south coast of the Black Sea with 'Jason' as
part of their name, but they were named by the Greeks as a result of mis-
understanding the West Iranian term for a holy site: *ayazana* would have
sounded to a Greek like 'Iasonia', and was suitably on the route supposedly
taken by Jason and the Argonauts.

163 *John Freely*: *The Black Sea Coast of Turkey* (Istanbul: Redhouse Press,
1996), p. 113 (on much the same region): 'Here a road leads inland to
Kusköy, or Bird Village ... Kusköy is aptly named, since the villagers are
renowned for their ability to communicate across intervening valleys with
their shrill "whistle talk", which is believed to be an ancient language
indigenous to remote regions such as the Pontic Mountains.'

163 *'The people of the friendly towns ...'*: Xenophon, *The Expedition of Cyrus* 5.4.32–4.

168 *Calpe Harbour is situated ...*: Xenophon, *The Expedition of Cyrus* 6.4.3–6.

CHAPTER 10

176 *'the man who had been in charge of the Cyreans'*: Xenophon, *Hellenica* 3.2.7.

177 *'the Dercyllideans'*: 'The Oxyrhynchus Historian', *Hellenica Oxyrhynchia* 16.2.

178 *'Alas for Greece! ...'*: Xenophon, *Agesilaus* 7.5.

180 *'the most remarkable battle of modern times'*: Xenophon, *Agesilaus* 2.9 = *Hellenica* 4.3.16.

180 *thirty pieces of silver*: the comparison is made, for instance, by Andreas Panagopoulos, 'Ξενοφῶν Ἀθηναῖος', *Ἱστορικά* 205 (2 October 2003), p. 7.

181 *'After Xenophon became an exile ...'*: Xenophon, *The Expedition of Cyrus* 5.3.7–13.

186 *watching an old documentary on television*: Italo Calvino, *Why Read the Classics?*, p. 19.

187 *'a pioneer experimenter in biographical forms'*: Arnaldo Momigliano, *The Development of Greek Biography* (Cambridge, MA: Harvard University Press, 1971), p. 47.

190 *a comic-book superhero*: Italo Calvino, *Why Read the Classics?*, p. 20.

190 *Themistogenes of Syracuse*: Xenophon, *Hellenica* 3.1.2.

191 *Nimrud and Nineveh*: on Nimrud (which Xenophon calls 'Larisa') and Nineveh ('Mespila'), see Xenophon, *The Expedition of Cyrus* 3.4.7 and 10.

191 *the end of* The Education of Cyrus the Great: 8.8. It is only fair to add that some scholars do not believe that this final chapter was written by Xenophon himself. I agree that it is a later appendix, but I suspect it is authentic. Plato seems to summarize and correct Xenophon's views at *Laws* 694a–695e.

191 *the end of* Spartan Society: the final chapter 15 in Talbert's translation (see bibliography); a penultimate and interruptive chapter 14 in the manuscript tradition.

192 *some harsh words*: Xenophon, *Hellenica* 5.3.16 and 5.4.1 are famous passages, but otherwise his occasional hostility manifests as much in what he does *not* say as in what he says, which makes references tricky. On the whole topic, see especially John Dillery, *Xenophon and the History of His Times*, pp. 195–237.

192 *'soaring expectations'*: Diodorus of Sicily, *Library of History* 14.21.6.

194 *and Aristotle ... gods*: *Politics* 1253a; see also *Politics* 1256b–1258a for Aristotle's conservative disgust at changing business practices.

194 *two references to it*: Xenophon, *The Expedition of Cyrus* 5.3.7, 7.7.57.

195 *'We are told that Xenophon...'*: Diogenes Laertius, *Lives of Eminent Philosophers* 2.54.

196 *guides ... used to show visitors a tomb*: Pausanias, *Guide to Greece* 5.6.6.

CHAPTER 11

197 *or so Xenophon tells us*: Hellenica 3.4.2; for Jason of Pherae's take on the expedition, see *Hellenica* 6.1.12.

198 *as described by Edward Said*: in his book *Orientalism*, originally published in 1978.

200 *'the first unmistakable file in the archives of Orientalism'*: Edith Hall, *Inventing the Barbarian*, p. 99.

201 *'Custom is king of all'*: Pindar, fragment 169 Bergk, quoted with approval by Herodotus at 3.38.

201 *'natural slaves'*: Aristotle, *Politics* 1254b.

201 *had to be whipped into action*: e.g. Herodotus, *Histories* 7.103 (in the course of an instructive series of contrasts between Greek and Persian societies), 7.223 (at Thermopylae); Xenophon, *The Expedition of Cyrus* 3.4.26.

201 *in a famous story*: Herodotus, *Histories* 7.136; the next story is told by Aelian, *Varied History* 1.31.

202 *'As for the lack of spirit ... Asiatics are feeble'*: pseudo-Hippocrates, *Airs, Waters, Places* 16.

202 *Environmental determinism*: see also Aeschylus, *Suppliant Women* 497–8; Herodotus, *Histories* 9.122; Xenophon, *The Expedition of Cyrus* 3.2.25; Aristotle, *Politics* 1327b.

204 *'I thank Fortune for three blessings'*: Diogenes Laertius, *Lives of Eminent Philosophers* 1.33, attributing the saying to both Thales of Miletus and Socrates of Athens.

204 *'You should have known ... shared heritage'*: Herodotus, *Histories* 8.144.

205 *a rare voice*: Theognis, *Elegies* 781; Herodotus, *Histories* 8.3; Plato, *Republic* 469b–471c.

206 *A few philosophers*: Antiphon of Athens, fragment 44 Diels/Kranz; Hippias of Elis as reflected in Plato's *Protagoras* 337c–d.

206 *'Trophies erected over fallen barbarians ...'*: Gorgias of Leontini, fragment 5b Diels/Kranz (speech delivered in 392 BCE). A couple of other contemporaneous speeches on the need for Greek unity against the barbarians: Lysias of Athens 2 and 33.

206 *He ranted about 'revenge'*: Isocrates, *Panegyricus* 185; then in the rest of the paragraph, I refer to *Panegyricus* 50, 145, and 173–4, and *Panathenaicus* 76–96. To *Philip* 90–92 is another example of Isocrates's use of the expedition of Cyrus.

207 *'For all our small numbers ... we made the king a laughing stock'*: Xenophon, *The Expedition of Cyrus* 2.4.4. Then, for the rest of this paragraph: 6.1.13; 1.5.9; 3.2.26.

207 *At one point, Xenophon has Cyrus ...*: The Expedition of Cyrus 1.7.3–4.

208 *such as ... Pharnabazus*: Xenophon, Hellenica 4.1.30–9, a delightful vignette.

208 *admiration for many of their customs and laws*: see especially Xenophon, *The Education of Cyrus the Great*, but also *On the Management of an Estate* 4 and 14.

208 *Polybius identified*: *Universal History* 3.6.10–12.

208 *Arrian ...twice compared*: *Anabasis* 1.12.3–4, 2.7.8–9.

211 *Alexander himself is said to have recalled ...'*: Arrian, *Anabasis* 2.7.8–9.

211 *'Alexander the Great would never have become "Great" without Xenophon'*: Eunapius, Introduction to *Lives of the Philosophers and Sophists*.

Bibliography

The reconstruction of many ancient events is uncertain, and insights into the lives and works of ancient authors vary, but in order to make the stories told in this book accessible to as wide a readership as possible, I have omitted most of the caveats scholars normally include. In order to offset any false impressions created by this strategy, I have included in this bibliography many more scholarly works than is usual in a popular history book, so that anyone wishing to pursue the controversies I have glossed over, and to see how different reconstructions are occasionally possible, has sufficient material to begin with. Even so, this is not by any means a complete list – either of the available material, or of the works I have read in preparing this book. It includes, however, all those works that I consider reliable and entertaining enough to recommend to an audience that might extend from history enthusiasts, via university students, to professional historians.

ANCIENT GREEK SOURCES

Very little of this book is mere paraphrase, but its foundation is given by Xenophon's *Anabasis*. This is available in several English versions, of which I would of course recommend my own, published by Oxford University Press in their World's Classics series as *The Expedition of Cyrus*. It is the most recent translation (published in 2005), and the introduction and notes by Tim Rood are more complete and wide-ranging than in comparable volumes. Xenophon's eyewitness account of Cyrus's campaign against his brother, and its aftermath, is by far the most important source, but it can occasionally be supplemented by Plutarch's *Life of Artaxerxes* (available in the Loeb series of texts and translations, published by Harvard University Press): though written 500 years after the events, the Life drew on earlier sources. Not the least of these was Ctesias of Cnidus, who actually spent time in Artaxerxes's court and was present at the battle of Cunaxa, but whose *Persian Tales* now exists only in fragments or summaries; these have been splendidly edited by Dominique Lenfant (*Ctésias de Cnide: La Perse, L'Inde, Autres fragments* (Paris: Les Belles Lettres, 2004)). Diodorus of Sicily's account of the expedition, in the fourteenth book of his *Universal History* (chapters 19–31), adds little, despite the fact that he drew on sources other than Xenophon; and the few relevant fragments of other works, such as Deinon of Colophon's and

Heraclides of Cyme's histories of Persia (both written in the second half of the fourth century BCE), have hardly helped this book.

Other works of Xenophon are available as follows: *Conversations of Socrates* (Penguin, 1990; translated, introduced and annotated by Robin Waterfield and Hugh Tredennick; this volume contains *Socrates' Defence, Recollections of Socrates, Symposium* and *On the Management of an Estate*); *Hiero the Tyrant and Other Treatises* (Penguin, 1997; translated by Robin Waterfield, with introductions and notes by Paul Cartledge; this volume contains *Hiero, Agesilaus, On Cavalry Command, On Horsemanship, On Hunting* and *Ways and Means*); *Hellenica*, under the title *A History of My Times* (Penguin, 1979; translated by Rex Warner, with an introduction by George Cawkwell); *The Education of Cyrus the Great* (London: J. M. Dent, 1992; translated by H. G. Dakyns, with introduction and notes by Richard Stoneman); *Spartan Society*, in *Plutarch on Sparta*, translated by Richard Talbert (new edn, London: Penguin, 2005).

REFERENCE BOOKS

The only atlas of the ancient world worth recommending is Richard Talbert (ed.), *Barrington Atlas of the Greek and Roman World* (Princeton: Princeton University Press, 2000). *The Oxford Classical Dictionary* (3rd edn, Oxford: Oxford University Press, 1996), edited by Simon Hornblower and Antony Spawforth, is a mine of information on every aspect of the ancient world. Xenophon can be placed in his literary context by reading Oliver Taplin (ed.), *Literature in the Greek World* (Oxford: Oxford University Press, 2000), and in his philosophical context with the help of Christopher Taylor (ed.), *The Routledge History of Philosophy*, vol. 1: *From the Beginning to Plato* (London: Routledge, 1998). The best introduction to Greek religion is Louise Bruit Zaidman and Pauline Schmitt Pantel, *Religion in the Ancient Greek City*, trans. by Paul Cartledge (Cambridge: Cambridge University Press, 1992; later reprints have enlarged bibliographies).

COLLECTIONS OF ESSAYS

Three recently published collections of essays must be singled out. Two of them are dedicated to *The Expedition of Cyrus*, and though the third does not have this exclusive focus, it touches on many relevant issues. Between them, they bear witness to a welcome revival of scholarly interest in Xenophon, and almost all the contributions they contain are of such a high standard that in order to save space and avoid repetition I have not listed individual essays in any of the sections below. They are: Pierre Briant (ed.), *Dans les Pas des Dix-Mille* (Toulouse: Presses Universitaires du Mirail, 1995), Robin Lane Fox (ed.), *The Long March: Xenophon and the Ten Thousand* (New Haven: Yale University Press, 2004), and Christopher Tuplin (ed.), *Xenophon and His World* (Stuttgart: Steiner, 2004; = *Historia* Einzelschriften 172). Scholars are also referred to an important review of Briant's volume: Christopher Tuplin, 'On the Track of the Ten Thousand', *Revue des études anciennes* 101 (1999), 331–66.

BIBLIOGRAPHY

XENOPHON

The best survey of what little can be known about Xenophon's life, and of his military and literary activities, is J. K. Anderson, *Xenophon* (London: Duckworth, 1974). More detailed and superbly insightful accounts of his writing, especially his history-writing, are John Dillery, *Xenophon and the History of His Times* (London: Routledge, 1995) and Vivienne Gray, *The Character of Xenophon's Hellenica* (London: Duckworth, 1989). Other useful studies include: Vivienne Gray, 'Xenophon and Isocrates', in Christopher Rowe and Malcolm Schofield (eds), *The Cambridge History of Greek and Roman Political Thought* (Cambridge: Cambridge University Press, 2000), 142–54; Peter Green, 'Text and Context in the Matter of Xenophon's Exile', in Ian Worthington (ed.), *Ventures into Greek History* (Oxford: Oxford University Press, 1994), 215–27 (repr. in Peter Green, *From Ikaria to the Stars: Classical Mythification, Ancient and Modern* (Austin: University of Texas Press, 2004), 133–43); William Higgins, *Xenophon the Athenian* (Albany: State University of New York Press, 1977); Clifford Hindley, 'Eros and Military Command in Xenophon', *Classical Quarterly* 44 (1994), 347–66; Steven Hirsch, *The Friendship of the Barbarians: Xenophon and the Persian Empire* (Hanover: Tufts University Press/University Press of New England, 1985); Noreen Humble, 'Xenophon's Sons at Sparta? Perspectives on *Xenoi* in the Spartan Upbringing', in Thomas Figueira (ed.), *Spartan Society* (Swansea: Classical Press of Wales, 2004), 231–50; Godfrey Hutchinson, *Xenophon and the Art of Command* (London: Greenhill Books, 2000); Steven Johnstone, 'Virtuous Toil, Vicious Work: Xenophon on Aristocratic Style', *Classical Philology* 89 (1994), 219–40; John Kane, 'Greek Values in Xenophon's *Hellenica*', in Andros Loizou and Harry Lesser (eds), *Polis and Politics: Essays in Greek Moral and Political Philosophy* (Aldershot: Avebury, 1990), 1–11; Rusudan Rzchiladze, 'L'Orient dans les oeuvres de Xénophon', *Klio* 62 (1980), 311–16; Robin Seager, 'Xenophon and Athenian Democratic Ideology', *Classical Quarterly* 51 (2001), 385–97; Christopher Tuplin, 'Xenophon's Exile Again', in Michael Whitby *et al.* (eds), *Homo Viator: Classical Essays for John Bramble* (Bristol: Bristol Classical Press, 1987), 59–68, and 'Xenophon, Artemis and Scillus', in Thomas Figueira (ed.), *Spartan Society* (Swansea: Classical Press of Wales, 2004), 251–81; Neal Wood, 'Xenophon's Theory of Leadership', *Classica et Mediaevalia* 25 (1964), 33–66.

THE EXPEDITION OF CYRUS

Plenty of works in other sections cover aspects of the expedition. The academic world is eagerly awaiting the long-promised commentary on *The Expedition of Cyrus* by Christopher Tuplin, but in the meantime there is an adequate German commentary by Otto Lendle: *Kommentar zu Xenophons Anabasis* (Darmstadt: Wissenschaftliche Buchgesellschaft, 1995).

My account of the battle of Cunaxa chiefly follows those of Graham Wylie ('Cunaxa and Xenophon', *L'antiquité classique* 61 (1992), 119–34) and Sherylee Bassett ('The Death of Cyrus the Younger', *Classical Quarterly* 49 (1999), 473–83), but also worth reading is J. M. Bigwood, 'The Ancient Accounts of the Battle of Cunaxa', *American Journal of Philology* 104 (1983), 340–57.

Apart from the battle itself, there is much to be gleaned from the following: Sherylee Bassett, 'The Enigma of Clearchus the Spartan', *Ancient History Bulletin* 15 (2000), 1–13, and 'Innocent Victims or Perjurers Betrayed? The Arrest of the Generals in Xenophon's *Anabasis*', *Classical Quarterly* 52 (2002), 447–61; T. S. Brown, 'Menon of Thessaly', *Historia* 35 (1986), 387–404; Italo Calvino, 'Xenophon's *Anabasis*', in id., *Why Read the Classics?*, trans. by Martin McLaughlin (London: Jonathan Cape, 1999), 19–23 (the essay was written in 1978); Andrew Dalby, 'Greeks Abroad: Social Organization and Food among the Ten Thousand', *Journal of Hellenic Studies* 112 (1992), 16–30; Krzysztof Głombiowski, 'The Campaign of Cyrus the Younger and the Retreat of the Ten Thousand: The Chronology', *Pomoerium* 1 (1994), 37–44; Gerald Nussbaum, *The Ten Thousand: A Study in Social Organisation and Action in Xenophon's Anabasis* (Leiden: Brill, 1967); Shalom Perlman, 'The Ten Thousand: A Chapter in the Military, Social and Economic History of the Fourth Century', *Rivista storica dell' antichità* 6–7 (1976–7), 241–84; Joseph Roisman, 'Klearchos in Xenophon's *Anabasis*', *Scripta Classica Israelica* 8–9 (1985–8), 30–52, and 'Anaxibios and Xenophon's *Anabasis*', *Ancient History Bulletin* 2 (1988), 80–7; James Roy, 'The Mercenaries of Cyrus', *Historia* 16 (1967), 287–323, 'Xenophon's Evidence for the *Anabasis*', *Athenaeum* 46 (1968), 37–46, and 'Arcadian Nationality as Seen in Xenophon's *Anabasis*', *Mnemosyne* 25 (1972), 129–36; Peter van Soesbergen, 'Colonisation as a Solution to Social-economic Problems: A Confrontation of Isocrates with Xenophon', *Ancient Society* 13–14 (1982–3), 131–45; Jan Stronk, *The Ten Thousand in Thrace* (Amsterdam: J. C. Gieben, 1995); Christopher Tuplin, 'Heroes in Xenophon's *Anabasis*', in Alberto Barzanò *et al.* (eds), *Modelli eroici dell'antichità alla cultura europea* (Rome: 'L'Erma' di Bretschneider, 2003), 115–56; H. D. Westlake, 'Diodorus and the Expedition of Cyrus', *Phoenix* 41 (1987), 241–54 (repr. in id., *Studies in Thucydides and Greek Historiography* (Bristol: Bristol Classical Press, 1989), 260–73).

The afterlife of Xenophon's book – or at least of its most famous episode – has been explored with wit and erudition by Tim Rood in *The Sea! The Sea! The Shout of the Ten Thousand in the Modern Imagination* (London: Duckworth Overlook, 2004).

XENOPHON'S JOURNEY

Trying to trace Xenophon's route in detail will drive you crazy. His sense of distances is not always accurate and is sometimes downright schematic; he does not provide enough details of places or topography or directions to allow certainty for many stretches of the journey; rivers have changed course or dried up and coastlines have receded or advanced; towns, let alone villages, have vanished without trace. Xenophon's perspective was always military, with an eye on his own and possibly on future expeditions. Rather than the precise location of rivers or their surroundings, for instance, we hear about their depth and width, because these factors made it more or less easy for the army to cross them; villages are mentioned chiefly when they helped to supply the army. These 'deficits' are at least partly explained by the fact that Xenophon's geographic framework was, like those of nearly all pre-map people, 'odological' rather than 'cartographic'. That is, rather than thinking spatially of extended areas of territory, he thought in linear terms of routes, and their borders and obstacles, such as rivers, coastlines and mountain ranges.

Several of the works listed elsewhere touch on aspects of Xenophon's route and the identification of ancient places. The standard, invaluable work is Valerio Manfredi's *La Strada dei Diecimila: Topografia e geografia dell' Oriente di Senofonte* (Milan: Jaca, 1986), but it is still fun to read some of the older travellers' accounts, such as John Macdonald Kinneir's *Journey through Asia Minor, Armenia and Koordistan in the Years 1813 and 1814* (London: John Murray, 1818; repr. Elibron Classics, 2003) or W. F. Ainsworth's *Travels in the Tracks of the Ten Thousand Greeks* (London: John W. Parker, 1844). Other books, old and new, of travels in the relevant regions, will give some idea of the topography and subsequent history of the places visited by the Cyreans.

Detailed studies tend to be buried away in academic journals: R. D. Barnett, 'Xenophon and the Wall of Media', *Journal of Hellenic Studies* 83 (1963), 1–26; Anthony Comfort and Rifat Ergeç, 'Following the Euphrates in Antiquity: North–South Routes around Zeugma', *Anatolian Studies* 51 (2001), 19–50; Fred Donner, 'Xenophon's Arabia', *Iraq* 48 (1986), 1–14; W. J. Farrell, 'A Revised Itinerary of the Route Followed by Cyrus the Younger through Syria', *Journal of Hellenic Studies* 81 (1961), 153–5; David French, 'The Site of Barata and Routes in the Konya Plain', *Epigraphica Anatolica* 27 (1996), 93–114, and 'Pre- and Early-Roman Roads of Asia Minor: The Persian Road', *Iran* 36 (1998), 15–43; Michal Gawilowski, 'Thapsacus and Zeugma: The Crossing of the Euphrates in Antiquity', *Iraq* 58 (1996), 123–33; David Graf, 'The Persian Royal Road System', *Achaemenid History* 8 (1994), 167–89; Nicholas Hammond, 'One or Two Passes at the Cilicia–Syria Border?', *Ancient World* 25 (1994), 15–26; Robert Hewsen, 'Introduction to Armenian Historical Geography II: The Boundaries of Achaemenid Armina', *Revue des études arméniennes* 17 (1983), 123–43; Tim Mitford, 'Thalatta, Thalatta: Xenophon's View of the Black Sea', *Anatolian Studies* 50 (2000), 127–31 (see also Norman Hammond in *The Times* (London), 30 November 1996, 16); Jan Retsö, 'Xenophon in Arabia', in Sven-Tage Teodorsson (ed.), *Greek and Latin Studies in Memory of Caius Fabricius* (Göteborg: University of Göteborg Press, 1990), 122–31; David Thompson, 'The Passage of the Ten Thousand through Cilicia', *La Parola del Passato* 19 (1964), 22–5; Christopher Tuplin, 'Modern and Ancient Travellers in the Achaemenid Empire: Byron's *Road to Oxiana* and Xenophon's *Anabasis*', *Achaemenid History* 7 (1991), 37–57, 'Achaemenid Arithmetic', *Topoi* suppl. vol. 1 (1997), 365–421, and 'Xenophon in Media', in Giovanni Lanfranchi *et al.* (eds), *Continuity of Empire (?): Assyria, Media, Persia* (Padova: Sargon, 2003), 351–448; Frank Williams, 'Xenophon's Dana and the Passage of Cyrus' Army over the Taurus Mountains', *Historia* 45 (1996), 284–314.

ANCIENT GREEK WARFARE

The bibliography here is understandably enormous. What follows is a very cur-
tailed list, concentrating as usual on accessible books rather than articles. First,
there are five startlingly good works, affording eye-opening insights into the
nature of ancient Greek warfare (and often disagreeing with one another): Victor
Davis Hanson, *The Western Way of War: Infantry Battle in Classical Greece* (2nd
edn, Berkeley: University of California Press, 2000); J. E. Lendon, *Soldiers and
Ghosts: A History of Battle in Classical Antiquity* (New Haven: Yale University
Press, 2005); W. Kendrick Pritchett, *The Greek State at War*, 5 vols (Berkeley:
University of California Press, 1971–91; first volume originally published as
Ancient Greek Military Practices, Part I (Berkeley: University of California Press,
1971)); Harry Sidebottom, *Ancient Warfare: A Very Short Introduction* (Oxford:
Oxford University Press, 2004); and Hans van Wees, *Greek Warfare: Myths and
Realities* (London: Duckworth, 2004).

Then see also: J. K. Anderson, *Military Theory and Practice in the Age of
Xenophon* (Berkeley: University of California Press, 1970); Donald Engels,
Alexander the Great and the Logistics of the Macedonian Army (Berkeley:
University of California Press, 1978); Victor Davis Hanson, *The Wars of the
Ancient Greeks* (London: Cassell, 1999), and (ed.), *Hoplites: The Classical Greek
Battle Experience* (London: Routledge, 1991); John Lazenby, 'Logistics in
Classical Greek Warfare', *War in History* 1 (1994), 3–18; Alan Lloyd (ed.), *Battle
in Antiquity* (London/Swansea: Duckworth/Classical Press of Wales, 1996);
Josiah Ober, 'The Rules of War in Classical Greece', in Michael Howard *et al.*
(eds), *The Laws of War: Constraints on Warfare in the Western World* (New
Haven: Yale University Press, 1994), 12–26, 227–30 (repr. in Josiah Ober, *The
Athenian Revolution* (Princeton: Princeton University Press, 1996), 53–71); John
Rich and Graham Shipley (eds), *War and Society in the Greek World* (London:
Routledge, 1993); Frank Russell, *Information Gathering in Classical Greece* (Ann
Arbor: University of Michigan Press, 1999); Michael Sage, *Warfare in Ancient
Greece: A Sourcebook* (London: Routledge, 1996); Christine Salazar, *The
Treatment of War Wounds in Graeco-Roman Antiquity* (Leiden: Brill, 2000);
Anthony Snodgrass, *Arms and Armour of the Greeks* (London: Thames and
Hudson, 1967); I. G. Spence, *The Cavalry of Classical Greece* (Oxford: Oxford
University Press, 1993); Lawrence Tritle, *From Melos to My Lai: War and
Survival* (London: Routledge, 2000); Hans van Wees (ed.), *War and Violence in
Ancient Greece* (London: Duckworth, 2000).

GREEK MERCENARIES

Several of the works in the previous section naturally have something to say about
Greeks serving as mercenaries, but there are also a number of useful specialized
studies: G. T. Griffith, *The Mercenaries of the Hellenistic World* (Cambridge:
Cambridge University Press, 1935; repr. Chicago: Ares Press, 1984); Jens
Krasilnikoff, 'Aegean Mercenaries in the Fourth to Second Centuries BC. A Study
in Payment, Plunder and Logistics of Ancient Greek Armies', *Classica et
Mediaevalia* 43 (1992), 23–36, and 'The Regular Payment of Aegean Mercenaries

in the Classical Period', *Classica et Mediaevalia* 44 (1993), 77–95; Ludmila Marinovich, *Le Mercenariat grec et la crise de la polis* (Paris: Les Belles Lettres, 1988); Paul McKechnie, 'Greek Mercenary Troops and Their Equipment', *Historia* 43 (1994), 297–305; Harvey Miller, 'The Practical and Economic Background to the Greek Mercenary Explosion', *Greece and Rome* 31 (1984), 153–60; H. W. Parke, *Greek Mercenary Soldiers from the Earliest Times to the Battle of Ipsus* (London: Oxford University Press, 1933; repr. Chicago: Ares Press, 1981); Alexandre Tourraix, 'Les mercenaires grecs au service des Achéménides', in Patrice Brun (ed.), *Guerres et sociétés dans les mondes grecs (490–322)* (Paris: Editions du Temps, 1999), 201–16; Matthew Trundle, *Greek Mercenaries from the Late Archaic Period to Alexander* (London: Routledge, 2004); David Whitehead, 'Who Equipped Mercenary Troops in Classical Greece?', *Historia* 40 (1991), 105–13.

GREEKS AND PERSIANS

A good discussion of the Greeks' cultural debts to their eastern neighbours in general is Walter Burkert, *Babylon, Memphis, Persepolis: Eastern Contexts of Greek Culture* (Cambridge, MA: Harvard University Press, 2004). There is a prosopography of named Greeks known to have been in Persia in Josef Hofstetter, *Die Griechen in Persien* (Berlin: Reimer, 1978), but by far the best discussion of cultural contacts between Greece and Persia is Margaret Miller, *Athens and Persia in the Fifth Century: A Study in Cultural Receptivity* (Cambridge: Cambridge University Press, 1997). Although she focuses on the fifth century, and on Athens rather than Greece as a whole, she mentions a great deal of non-Athenian contacts, and in any case our evidence here as elsewhere is largely Athenocentric.

For military history, there is a brief account in John Sharwood Smith, *Greece and the Persians* (Bristol: Bristol Classical Press, 1990), and longer accounts in A. Robin Burn, *Persia and the Greeks* (2nd edn, London: Duckworth, 1985), George Cawkwell, *The Greek Wars: The Failure of Persia* (Oxford: Oxford University Press, 2005), and John Lazenby, *The Defence of Greece* (Warminster: Aris & Phillips, 1993).

Then see also: Jack Balcer, 'The Greeks and the Persians: The Processes of Acculturation', *Historia* 32 (1983), 257–67, and 'The East Greeks under Persian Rule: A Reassessment', *Achaemenid History* 6 (1991), 57–65; J. M. Cook, *The Greeks in Persia and the East* (London: Thames and Hudson, 1962); Robert Drews, *The Greek Accounts of Eastern History* (Washington: Center for Hellenic Studies, 1973); Samuel Eddy, 'The Cold War between Athens and Persia *ca.* 448–412 B.C.', *Classical Philology* 68 (1973), 241–58; David Graf, 'Greek Tyrants and Achaemenid Politics', in John Eadie and Josiah Ober (eds), *The Craft of the Ancient Historian: Essays in Honor of Chester G. Starr* (Lanham, MD: University Press of America, 1985), 79–123; David Lewis, *Sparta and Persia* (Leiden: Brill, 1977); Chester Starr, 'Greeks and Persians in the Fourth Century BC: A Study in Cultural Contacts before Alexander', *Iranica Antiqua* 11 (1975), 39–99 and 12 (1977), 49–115.

ACHAEMENID HISTORY

Xenophon is not the only important Greek source for the history of Persia under the Achaemenid dynasty (though he is the only surviving Greek author who had close contact with Persians). There is also Herodotus; again, I prefer my own translation of his *Histories* (Oxford: Oxford University Press, 1998), with a brilliant commentary by Carolyn Dewald. Our knowledge of Persian history is still increasing year by year, so it is very much a matter of finding works that are both recent and reliable. The starting point is Pierre Briant's monumental *From Cyrus to Alexander: A History of the Persian Empire*, trans. by Peter Daniels (Winona Lake: Eisenbrauns, 2002). Two excellent short accounts are to be found in Amélie Kuhrt, *The Ancient Near East c.3000–330 BC*, 2 vols (London: Routledge, 1995; the Persian empire concludes the second volume) and in Josef Wiesehöfer, *Ancient Persia from 550 BC to 650 AD*, trans. by Azizeh Azodi (London: I. B. Tauris, 1996), whose focus is more on cultural history and everyday life than political and military exploits. Other good histories: J. M. Cook, *The Persian Empire* (New York: Dent, 1983); Ilya Gershevitch (ed.), *The Cambridge History of Iran*, vol. 2: *The Median and Achaemenian Periods* (Cambridge: Cambridge University Press, 1985). Then more specialist relevant works include: Jack Balcer, 'The Ancient Persian Satrapies and Satraps in Western Anatolia', *Archäologische Mitteilungen aus Iran* 26 (1993), 81–90; Mary Boyce, *A History of Zoroastrianism*, 3 vols (Leiden: Brill, 1975–91); Maria Brosius, *Women in Ancient Persia, 559–331 BC* (Oxford: Oxford University Press, 1996); Elspeth Dusinberre, *Aspects of Empire in Achaemenid Sardis* (Cambridge: Cambridge University Press, 2003); Amélie Kuhrt, 'Earth and Water', *Achaemenid History* 3 (1988), 87–99; Donald Lateiner, 'Tissaphernes and the Phoenician Fleet', *Transactions of the American Philological Association* 106 (1976), 267–90; Alexander Nefiodkin, 'On the Origin of the Scythed Chariot', *Historia* 53 (2004), 369–78; Stephen Ruzicka, 'Cyrus and Tissaphernes, 407–401 BC', *Classical Journal* 80 (1984–5), 204–11; Heleen Sancisi-Weerdenburg, 'Gifts in the Persian Empire', in Pierre Briant and Clarisse Herrenschmidt (eds), *Tribut dans l'empire perse* (Paris: Peeters, 1989), 129–46; Nicholas Sekunda, *The Persian Army* (Oxford: Osprey, 1992); Christopher Tuplin, 'The Administration of the Achaemenid Empire', in Ian Carradice (ed.), *Coinage and Administration in the Athenian and Persian Empires* (British Archaeological Reports 334, 1987), 109–66, 'Xenophon and the Garrisons of the Persian Empire', *Archäologische Mitteilungen aus Iran* 20 (1987), 167–245, and *Achaemenid Studies* (Stuttgart: Steiner, 1996; = *Historia* Einzelschriften 99).

OTHER RELEVANT HISTORICAL ACCOUNTS

This section is almost indefinitely expandable, but the following are the most important: Antony Andrewes, 'Two Notes on Lysander', *Phoenix* 25 (1971), 206–26, and 'Spartan Imperialism?', in Peter Garnsey and C. R. Whittaker (eds), *Imperialism in the Ancient World* (Cambridge: Cambridge University Press, 1978), 91–102; Zofia Archibald, *The Odrysian Kingdom of Thrace: Orpheus Unmasked* (Oxford: Oxford University Press, 1998); John Boardman, *The Greeks*

Overseas: Their Early Colonies and Trade (4th edn, London: Thames and Hudson, 1999); John Boardman *et al.* (eds), *The Cambridge Ancient History*, vol. 4: *Persia, Greece and the Western Mediterranean c. 525–479 BC* (2nd edn, Cambridge: Cambridge University Press, 1988); A. Brian Bosworth, *Conquest and Empire: The Reign of Alexander the Great* (Cambridge: Cambridge University Press, 1988); John Buckler, *Aegean Greece in the Fourth Century BC* (Leiden: Brill, 2003); Paul Cartledge, *Agesilaos and the Crisis of Sparta* (London: Duckworth, 1987), 'The Effects of the Peloponnesian (Athenian) War on Athenian and Spartan Societies', in David McCann and Barry Strauss (eds), *War and Democracy: A Comparative Study of the Korean War and the Peloponnesian War* (New York: Armonk, 2001), 104–23, and *Alexander the Great: The Hunt for a New Past* (London: Macmillan, 2004); John Davies, *Democracy and Classical Greece* (2nd edn, London: Fontana, 1993); Nicholas Fisher, *Slavery in Classical Greece* (2nd edn, London: Bristol Classical Press, 2001); Gabriel Herman, *Ritualised Friendship and the Greek City* (Cambridge: Cambridge University Press, 1987); Simon Hornblower, *The Greek World 479–323 BC* (3rd edn, London: Routledge, 2002); Sally Humphreys, 'Economy and Society in Classical Athens', *Annali* 39 (1970), 1–26 (repr. in id., *Anthropology and the Greeks* (London: Routledge & Kegan Paul, 1978), 136–58); A. H. M. Jones, 'The Athenian Democracy and Its Critics', *Cambridge Historical Journal* 11 (1953), 1–26 (reprinted in id., *Athenian Democracy* (Oxford: Basil Blackwell, 1957), 41–72); Robin Lane Fox, *Alexander the Great* (London: Allen Lane, 1973); David Lewis *et al.* (eds), *The Cambridge Ancient History*, vol. 5: *The Fifth Century BC* (2nd edn, Cambridge: Cambridge University Press, 1992) and *The Cambridge Ancient History*, vol. 6: *The Fourth Century BC* (2nd edn, Cambridge: Cambridge University Press, 1994); Paul McKechnie, *Outsiders in the Greek Cities in the Fourth Century BC* (London: Routledge, 1989); Robin Osborne (ed.), *Classical Greece, 500–323 BC* (Oxford: Oxford University Press, 2000); Paul Rahe, 'The Military Situation in Western Asia on the Eve of Cunaxa', *American Journal of Philology* 101 (1980), 79–96; Barry Strauss, *Athens after the Peloponnesian War: Class, Faction and Policy 403–386 BC* (London: Croom Helm, 1986); Christopher Tuplin, 'The Treaty of Boiotios', *Achaemenid History* 2 (1987), 133–53; Frank Walbank, *The Hellenistic World* (2nd edn, London: Fontana, 1992); H. D. Westlake, 'Decline and Fall of Tissaphernes', *Historia* 30 (1981), 257–79.

THE GREEKS ON THEMSELVES AND OTHERS

The starting point here must be Paul Cartledge's *The Greeks: A Portrait of Self and Others* (2nd edn, Oxford: Oxford University Press, 2002), a superbly informative and eminently readable study of how the Greeks defined themselves by a series of us-and-them oppositions. Then there is a superlative collection of essays, focusing on the contrasts between Greeks and non-Greeks: Thomas Harrison (ed.), *Greeks and Barbarians* (Edinburgh: Edinburgh University Press, 2002). After these two books, the following are also good and relevant: John Coleman and Clark Walz (eds), *Greeks and Barbarians: Essays on the Interactions between Greeks and*

Non-Greeks in Antiquity and the Consequences for Eurocentrism (Bethesda, MD: CDL Press, 1997); Pericles Georges, *Barbarian Asia and the Greek Experience* (Baltimore: Johns Hopkins University Press, 1994); Edith Hall, *Inventing the Barbarian: Greek Self-definition through Tragedy* (Oxford: Oxford University Press, 1989); Jonathan Hall, *Hellenicity: Between Ethnicity and Culture* (Chicago: University of Chicago Press, 2002); François Hartog, *The Mirror of Herodotus: The Representation of the Other in the Writing of History*, trans. by Janet Lloyd (Berkeley: University of California Press, 1988) and *Memories of Odysseus: Frontier Tales from Ancient Greece*, trans. by Janet Lloyd (Edinburgh: Edinburgh University Press, 2001); Benjamin Isaac, *The Invention of Racism in Classical Antiquity* (Princeton: Princeton University Press, 2004); Ippokratis Kantzios, 'The Politics of Fear in Aeschylus' *Persians*', *Classical World* 98 (2004), 3–19; Timothy Long, *Barbarians in Greek Comedy* (Carbondale: Southern Illinois University Press, 1986); Irad Malkin (ed.), *Ancient Perceptions of Greek Ethnicity* (Washington: Center for Hellenic Studies, 2001); Shalom Perlman, 'Panhellenism, the Polis and Imperialism', *Historia* 25 (1976), 1–30; Edward Said, *Orientalism* (new edn, London: Penguin, 1995); Pierre Vidal-Naquet, 'The Place and Status of Foreigners in Greek Tragedy', in Christopher Pelling (ed.), *Greek Tragedy and the Historian* (Oxford: Oxford University Press, 1997), 109–19.

Index